PEACE HANDBOOKS

SR Scholarly Resources Inc.
Wilmington, Delaware

SCHOLARLY RESOURCES, INC.
1508 Pennsylvania Avenue
Wilmington, Delaware 19806

Reprint edition published by Scholarly Resources in 1973
First published in 1920 by H. M. Stationery Office,
   London

Library of Congress Catalog Card Number: 73-82619
ISBN: 0-8420-1704-6 (Complete 25 Volume Set)

Manufactured in the United States of America

PEACE HANDBOOKS

Issued by the Historical Section
of the Foreign Office

VOL. XXV

INDEMNITIES,

PLEBISCITES, &c.

LONDON:
H.M. STATIONERY OFFICE.

1920

Editorial Note.

IN the spring of 1917 the Foreign Office, in connection with the preparation which they were making for the work of the Peace Conference, established a special section whose duty it should be to provide the British Delegates to the Peace Conference with information in the most convenient form—geographical, economic, historical, social, religious and political—respecting the different countries, districts, islands, &c., with which they might have to deal. In addition, volumes were prepared on certain general subjects, mostly of an historical nature, concerning which it appeared that a special study would be useful.

The historical information was compiled by trained writers on historical subjects, who (in most cases) gave their services without any remuneration. For the geographical sections valuable assistance was given by the Intelligence Division (Naval Staff) of the Admiralty; and for the economic sections, by the War Trade Intelligence Department, which had been established by the Foreign Office. Of the maps accompanying the series, some were prepared by the above-mentioned department of the Admiralty, but the bulk of them were the work of the Geographical Section of the General Staff (Military Intelligence Division) of the War Office.

Now that the Conference has nearly completed its task, the Foreign Office, in response to numerous enquiries and requests, has decided to issue the books for public use, believing that they will be useful to students of history, politics, economics and foreign affairs, to publicists generally and to business men and travellers. It is hardly necessary to say that some of the subjects dealt with in the series have not in fact come under discussion at the Peace Conference; but, as the books treating of them contain valuable information, it has been thought advisable to include them.

It must be understood that, although the series of volumes was prepared under the authority, and is now issued with the sanction, of the Foreign Office, that Office is not to be regarded as guaranteeing the accuracy of every statement which they contain or as identifying itself with all the opinions expressed in the several volumes; the books were not prepared in the Foreign Office itself, but are in the nature of infomration provided for the Foreign Office and the British Delegation.

The books are now published, with a few exceptions, substantially as they were issued for the use of the Delegates. No attempt has been made to bring them up to date, for, in the first place, such a process would have entailed a great loss of time and a prohibitive expense; and, in the second, the political and other conditions of a great part of Europe and of the Nearer and Middle East are still unsettled and in such a state of flux that any attempt to describe them would have been incorrect or misleading. The books are therefore to be taken as describing, in general, *ante-bellum* conditions, though in a few cases, where it seemed specially desirable, the account has been brought down to a later date.

G. W. PROTHERO,
*General Editor and formerly
Director of the Historical Section.*

January 1920.

HANDBOOKS PREPARED UNDER THE DIRECTION OF THE
HISTORICAL SECTION OF THE FOREIGN OFFICE.—No. 158

INDEMNITIES OF WAR:
SUBSIDIES AND LOANS

LONDON:
PUBLISHED BY H. M. STATIONERY OFFICE.

1920

I
INDEMNITIES OF WAR

TABLE OF CONTENTS

[1] This survey is not intended to extend beyond 1914.

A 2

Wt. 9157/860. 1000. 6/20. O.U.P

I. INDEMNITIES IMPOSED SINCE 1814

I. INTRODUCTORY

IN accordance with international practice, as well as with the views of jurists and with public opinion, a victorious State is justified in demanding an indemnity from its defeated adversary. Practice and opinion agree also that such indemnity should take the form not of a punitive exaction, but of a compensation or reimbursement for the actual losses and expenditure brought about by the prosecution of hostilities.

In many cases no indemnity has been demanded. This was sometimes due either to considerations of prudence or moderation that weighed with the victorious party, or to the fact that the vanquished Power was, and seemed likely to remain for a long time, in such financial difficulties, that it appeared to be futile to make a pecuniary demand upon it. In such circumstances as the latter, however, a substitute for pecuniary compensation has occasionally been stipulated, e. g. territorial cession. Sometimes, too, the whole or a portion of the indemnity has been waived in consideration of commercial concessions. In other cases, territorial aggrandizement has been deliberately preferred to a pecuniary indemnity, the war having been undertaken for this purpose, or having produced results which made such gain of territory possible. In a few cases—notably that of the Franco-German War (1870-71)—both territorial cessions and pecuniary indemnity have been demanded and obtained. The territorial changes made in 1814-15 at the expense of France were not cessions of land properly belonging to the defeated State, but retro-cessions of territory previously conquered. It should be added that this was the justification alleged for the cession of Alsace-Lorraine in 1871.

In earlier instances, notably in the Napoleonic wars, we find the pecuniary indemnity replaced or supple-mented, as the case may be, by valuable objects—provisions, horses, and other things.

During the last hundred years, the first important instance of the imposition of a war indemnity was that in the Treaty of Paris, November 20, 1815 ; the last occurred in the Treaty of Constantinople, 1897. The most remarkable case of all—mainly because of the magnitude of the indemnity—was that of the Franco-German War. Prussia had also exacted indemnities from all the States opposed to her in the war of 1866. It has been calculated that the total exacted by Prussia in her wars of 1866 and 1870 was about three times as large as the entire sum demanded by all the victorious States in all the other wars between 1795 and 1871.

As to guarantees, in some instances no special provision was made ; in others financial guarantees—e. g. by the deposit of specified securities—were stipulated ; and in others, again, territorial guarantees in the form of military occupation were insisted on, either alone or in conjunction with the former mode.

The customary manner of paying the indemnity has been by instalments spread over a number of years. In some cases the payment of interest was stipulated in the event of failure to pay an instalment at or before the specified date ; in others interest was pay-able irrespectively of punctual discharge. In one or two instances discount was deducted on payments made before the stipulated time.

ii. ILLUSTRATIONS

TREATY OF PARIS, Nov. 20, 1815 [1]

(GREAT BRITAIN, AUSTRIA, PRUSSIA, RUSSIA—FRANCE)

Amount of Indemnity.—The Allied Powers imposed on France a pecuniary indemnity of 700,000,000 francs (£27,737,500) (Art. IV).

Mode of payment, time of payment, guarantees.—The mode and the time of payment, as well as the guarantees, were prescribed by the Annexed Convention of the same date : [2]

1. The sum of 700 million francs shall be discharged, day by day, in equal portions, in the space of 5 years, by means of *bons au porteur* on the Royal Treasury of France, in the following manner.

2. The Treasury shall deliver immediately to the Allied Powers 15 engagements for 46⅔ millions each : the first payable March 31, 1816, the second July 31, 1816, and so on in every fourth month during the five successive years.

3. These engagements shall not be negotiable, but they shall be periodically exchanged against negotiable *bons au porteur* drawn in the form used in the ordinary service of the Royal Treasury.

4. In the month preceding the four months, in the course of which an engagement is to be paid, that engagement shall be divided by the Treasury of France into *bons au porteur* payable in Paris, in equal portions, from the first to the last day of the four months.

Thus the engagement of 46⅔ millions falling due March 31, 1816, shall be exchanged in November 1815, against *bons au porteur* payable in equal portions from December 1, 1815, to March 31, 1816.

The engagement of 46⅔ millions which will fall due July 31, 1816, shall be exchanged in March 1816, against *bons au porteur* payable in equal portions from April 1, 1816, to July 31, 1816, and so in every four months.

---

[1] *British and Foreign State Papers*, vol. iii, pp. 280 et seq.

[2] Ibid., vol. iii, pp. 293 et seq.

5. No single *bon au porteur* shall be delivered for the sum due each day, but the sum so due shall be divided into several bills (*coupures*) of 1,000, 2,000, 5,000, 10,000 and 20,000 francs, which sums added together will amount to the sum total of the payment due for each day.

6. There shall never be in circulation *bons* for more than 50 millions at a time.

7. No *interest* shall be paid for the delay of five years.

8. As a *guarantee* for the regularity of payments, France shall make over to the Allied Powers on January 1, 1816, a fund of interest, inscribed in the ' Grand Livre ' of the public debt of France, of 7 million francs, on a capital of 140 millions. This fund of interest shall be used to make good, if necessary, the deficiencies in the ' acceptances ' of the French Government, and to render the payments equal, at the end of every six months, to the *bons au porteur* which shall have fallen due, as hereafter detailed.

9. This fund of interest shall be inscribed in the name of such persons as the Allied Powers shall point out ; but these persons cannot be the holders of the inscriptions, except in the case provided for in Art. 11.

The Allied Powers further reserve to themselves the right to transfer the inscriptions to other names, as often as they shall judge necessary.

10. The *deposit* of these inscriptions shall be confined to one treasurer named by the Allied Powers, and to another named by the French Government.

11. There shall be a *mixed commission*, composed of an equal number of members on both sides, who shall examine every six months the state of the payments, and shall regulate the balance.

The *bons* of the Treasury paid shall constitute the payments ; those which shall not yet have been presented to the Treasury of France shall enter into the account of the subsequent balance ; those also which shall have fallen due, been presented and not paid, shall constitute the arrear, and the sum of inscriptions to be applied, at the market price of the day, to cover the deficit.

As soon as that operation shall have taken place, the *bons* unpaid shall be given up to the French commissioners, and the mixed commission shall order the treasurers to pay over the sum so determined upon, and the treasurers shall be authorized and obliged to pay it over to the commissioners of the Allied Powers, who shall dispose of it as they think proper.

12. France engages to replace immediately in the hands of the treasurers an amount of inscriptions equal to that which may have been made use of, according to the foregoing Article, in order that the fund stipulated in Art. 8 may be always kept at its full amount.

13. France shall pay an interest of 5 per cent. per annum, from the date of the *bons au porteur* falling due, upon all such *bons* the payment of which may have been delayed by the act of France.

14. When the first 600 millions shall have been paid, the Allies, in order to accelerate the entire liberation of France, will accept, should it be agreeable to the French Government, the fund mentioned in Art. 8, at the market price of that day, to such an amount as will be equal to the remainder due. France will have to furnish only the difference, should any exist.

15. Should this plan not be convenient to France, the 100 million francs which would remain due may be discharged in the manner pointed out in Arts. 2, 3, 4, and 5 ; and after the complete payment of the 700 millions, the inscriptions stipulated for in Art. 8 shall be returned to France.

On February 2, 1819, a definitive arrangement [1] was made for regulating the mode and time of payment of the last 100 millions of the pecuniary indemnity.

In addition to this war indemnity, there were other special claims (e. g. of the Allied subjects, of the Bank of Hamburg, of the Duchy of Warsaw), which were settled by separate Conventions. [2]

Occupation of French territory by an Allied army.— By Art. V of the principal treaty, supplemented by an Additional Convention [3] of the same date, provision was made for the occupation of certain military

---

[1] *British and Foreign State Papers*, vol. vi, p. 20.
[2] Ibid., vol. iii, pp. 315, 341, 342, 559 ; vol. v, pp. 179, 192.
[3] Ibid., vol. iii, pp. 298 et seq.

positions along the frontiers of France by an Allied
army. This occupation was intended to be a measure
of precaution and temporary guarantee for ensuring
a tranquil settlement in France and preventing a
revolutionary recrudescence. The maximum period of
occupation was restricted to five years ; but evacuation might be effected after a lapse of three years, if
the Allied Powers agreed that the situation and their
reciprocal interests warranted a withdrawal before the
expiration of the maximum period. The occupying
army was to be maintained by France ; and various
regulations as to lodging, fuel, lighting, provisions,
forage, rations, &c. were drawn up. To meet the expenses due to pay, equipment, clothing, &c., France
was to contribute 50 million francs per year, payable
monthly. Certain neutral zones were marked out in
several departments. France might maintain limited
garrisons in a number of towns situated in the
occupied territory. The Commander-in-Chief of the
Allied troops was to exercise military command in the
occupied departments, excepting places in which France
held garrisons and within a radius of 1,000 *toises* round
each of them. The civil and judicial administration,
the collection of taxes, customs duties, &c., and the
service of the gendarmerie in the occupied territory
were to continue as before. Finally, the places occupied
were to be restored, on evacuation, in the condition
in which they were at the commencement of the
occupation, subject to ' damages . . . caused by time '.

It is to be noted that this military occupation was
entered into, not with a view to ensure the payment
of the indemnity, but independently thereof. It is
true that the period of payment, under the treaty,
coincided with the maximum period of occupation.
But the occupation might be terminated before the
indemnity had been paid off ; and payment in full

before the expiration of the prescribed period did not
necessarily entail evacuation. Nevertheless, the occupation amounted, in fact, to an additional guarantee
for the due payment of the indemnity or the greater
part of it.

Under Article I of the Treaty of Aix-la-Chapelle,
October 9, 1818, the evacuation of French territory
was completed by November 30, 1818.[1]

TREATY OF ADRIANOPLE, SEPT. 14, 1829 [2]

(RUSSIA—TURKEY)

Amount of indemnity.—Besides agreeing to pay
compensation to Russian subjects for losses and
injuries—1,500,000 Dutch ducats (£737,250) within 18
months [3]—Turkey agreed to pay 10 million ducats
(£4,915,000), and also to cede certain territory in Asia,
by way of a war indemnity. The sum was later [4]
reduced to 8 million ducats, then to 6 millions.

Form of payment.—Instead of payment in specie,
Russia consented to receive compensation in kind and
in articles agreed upon—e. g. building-wood, copper,
and silk.[5] Moreover, instead of Dutch ducats, which
Turkey found it difficult to procure, Russia afterwards
agreed to accept bills of exchange calculated in Turkish
piastres.[6]

Time of payment.—At first 8 annual payments of
1 million ducats each were stipulated, beginning May

[1] *British and Foreign State Papers*, vol. vi, p. 6.

[2] French text in *British and Foreign State Papers*, vol. xvi, p. 647 ;
English text in Hertslet, *Map of Europe by Treaty*, vol. ii, p. 813.

[3] Separate convention annexed to the principal treaty, *British
and Foreign State Papers*, vol. xvi, p. 657 ; Hertslet, *Map of Europe*,
vol. ii, p. 828.

[4] Convention of St. Petersburg, April 25, 1830 : *Treaties, &c.,
between Turkey and Foreign Powers* (London, 1855), p. 770.

[5] Ibid., Article 6.   [6] Ibid., Article 7.

1831 and ending May 1838. But four years later, by the Treaty of St. Petersburg, Jan. 29, 1834,[1] it was agreed that a sum of half a million per annum should be paid, and not necessarily in May, but by degrees. The sum having been twice reduced, a third reduction was made under the Treaty of Constantinople, March 27, 1836,[2] leaving 160,000 purses (a total of 80 million Turkish piastres) payable in specie, within 5 months of the date of signing the treaty, thus : in 15 days from that date, 50,000 purses; 15 days later, 17,000 purses ; at the end of two months from the said date, 33,000 ; the balance (60,000) by degrees in the course of the three following months. If full payment were made before the end of the 5 months, evacuation would take place earlier.

Guarantee.—Occupation of Silistria by Russian troops till payment of the last instalment. If, however, Turkey should reach an understanding with reputable bankers in Europe who were prepared to offer Russia sufficient guarantees for payment, Silistria would be immediately restored.[3]

Treaty of Nankin, Aug. 29, 1842 [4]

(Great Britain—China)

Amount of indemnity.—China was required to pay Great Britain the sum of 21 million dollars (approximately, £2,100,000) ; of which, however, 6 millions represented the value of opium delivered up in 1839

---

[1] *British and Foreign State Papers*, vol. xxvi, p. 1245 ; Hertslet, *Map of Europe*, vol. ii, p. 936.

[2] *British and Foreign State Papers*, vol. xxiv, p. 1078; Hertslet, vol. ii, p. 961.

[3] Convention of St. Petersburg, April 25, 1830; *Treaties, &c., between Turkey and Foreign Powers*, Articles 5, 9.

[4] Hertslet, *Collection of Treaties and Conventions*, vol. vi, p. 221.

at Canton for the lives of the British superintendent
and certain British subjects, and 3 million dollars
represented debts due to British subjects from Chinese
merchants. Thus the remaining sum of 12 million
dollars represented the amount of expenditure incurred
in the dispatch of the expedition to China.

Time of payment.—As follows : 6 millions immediately ; 6 millions in 1843—one-half by June 30, the
other half by Dec. 31 ; 5 millions in 1844—one-half
by June 30, the other half by Dec. 31 ; 4 millions
in 1845—one-half by June 30, the other half by
Dec. 31.

Interest at rate of 5 per cent. per annum to be paid on
any portion not punctually discharged at the periods
fixed.

Guarantee (Occupation).—On receipt of the first
instalment, the British forces were to retire from
Nankin and the Grand Canal, as well as from Chinhai
But the islands of Koolangsoo and Chusan were to
continue to be held by the British forces until the
completion of the money payments.

TREATY OF MILAN, AUG. 6, 1849 [1]

(AUSTRIA—SARDINIA)

Amount of indemnity.—Sardinia to pay Austria
75 million francs (£2,971,875), as indemnity for war
expenses, for damages suffered by the Austrian Government and its subjects, towns, and corporations, and
for claims (due to the same cause) of the Archduke,
Duke of Modena, and Duke of Parma.

Mode and time of payment.—15 millions, by order
(*mandat*) payable in Paris, at the end of the following
October, without interest ; 60 millions, in six suc-

[1] G. F. von Martens, *Nouveau Recueil de Traités*, 2 vols.,
Gottingen, 1843–75, vol. i, p. 181.

cessive payments, one every two months, beginning at the end of the following December, with 5 per cent. interest on the amount to be paid.

Guarantee.—Sardinia to hand over to Austria, at the exchange of ratifications, 60 inscriptions of a million francs each. These inscriptions to be restored in proportion to the payments made in Vienna, in bills of exchange on Paris (as above). Failing payment, Austria to realize on the inscriptions; and the deficit to be made good by Sardinia, by means of bills of exchange on Paris.

Treaty of Pekin, Oct. 24, 1860 [1]

(Great Britain—China)

Amount.—China to pay Great Britain 8 million taels (approximately, £1,200,000)—of which 2 millions represented the losses suffered by the British mercantile community at Canton, and 6 millions the war expenses.

Time and mode of payment.—As follows: at Tientsin, on or before Nov. 30, 1860, 500,000 taels; at Canton, on or before Dec. 31, 1860, 333,333 taels (less a certain sum advanced by the Canton authorities); the remainder at ports open to foreign trade, in quarterly payments consisting of one-fifth of the gross customs revenue there collected, the first being due on Dec. 31, 1860, for the quarter ending on that day. The money to be paid to an officer appointed by the British representative, and the accuracy of the amounts to be ascertained before payment by specially appointed British and Chinese officers.

Guarantee (Occupation).—Option for Great Britain to retain a force at certain places till the full payment of the indemnity.

[1] L. Hertslet, *Collection of Treaties*, vol. xi (1864), p. 112.

A similar treaty was concluded, Oct. 25, 1860, between China and France,[1] which had taken part along with Great Britain in the expeditions of 1858 and 1860.

TREATY OF TETUAN, APRIL 26, 1860 [2]

(SPAIN—MOROCCO)

Amount.—Morocco to pay Spain 20 million piastres (approximately, £170,000), as an indemnity for war expenses.

Time and mode of payment.—Four equal instalments to be paid respectively on July 1, Aug. 29, Oct. 29, and Dec. 28, 1860, to the person designated by the King of Spain, in the port designated by the King of Morocco.

Guarantee (Occupation). A Spanish army to remain in occupation of Tetuan and territory till full payment. If payment made earlier, evacuation to take place earlier.

TREATY OF SAIGON, JUNE 5, 1862 [3]

(FRANCE, SPAIN—ANNAM)

Amount.—Annam to pay France and Spain 4 million dollars (approximately, £400,000), as indemnity for war expenses.

Mode and time of payment.—To be paid within 10 years. Each year a sum of 400,000 dollars to be handed to the French representative at Saigon— a dollar being equivalent to 72/100 of a tael.

[1] De Clercq, *Recueil des traités de la France*, vol. viii, p. 136.
[2] von Martens, *Nouveau Recueil*, vol iii, pt. 2, p. 590.
[3] De Clercq, *Recueil*, vol. viii, p. 416.

Treaty of Miramar, April 10, 1864 [1]

(France—Mexico)

Amount.—In addition to an indemnity to French subjects for losses suffered (the amount of which to be determined by a mixed commission), Mexico to pay France 270 million francs for the cost of the expedition. Interest payable at 3 per cent. per annum.

Mode and time of payment.—Mexico to hand over 54 million francs (£2,137,500), plus 12 millions on account of the indemnity to French subjects, immediately, in loan securities at the rate of issue; and the balance to be paid in specie by annual instalments of 25 million francs. These provisions were, however, abrogated by the Convention of Mexico, July 30, 1866, under which the Mexican Government assigned to France half of the customs-duties, which were to be collected, till the indemnity was paid off, by special agents stationed at Vera Cruz and Tampico under the protection of the French flag.[2] Difficulties in regard to the rights of the contracting parties having arisen, the execution of this Convention was suspended by an arrangement concluded at Mexico, February 22, 1867; but in the meantime the Mexican Government was to pay to a special French agent, or to a French Consul at Vera Cruz, a sum of 250,000 francs at the end of each month.

Guarantee (Occupation).—Continued occupation of Mexican territory by French troops, whose cost was to be discharged by Mexico at the rate of 1,000 francs per man per year.

[1] De Clercq, *Recueil*, vol. ix, p. 18; *British and Foreign State Papers*, vol. liv, p. 944.
[2] De Clercq, *Recueil*, vol. ix, p. 605.

TREATY OF YOKOHAMA, OCT. 22, 1864 [1]

(GREAT BRITAIN, FRANCE, UNITED STATES, THE NETHERLANDS—JAPAN)

Amount.—Japan to pay the four Powers a sum of 3 million dollars (approximately, £300,000), to cover claims, indemnities, and expenses incurred in the operations of the allied squadrons.

Time of payment.—Payable quarterly in instalments of 500,000 dollars, to begin from the date of communicating to Japan the ratification.

Substitute for money payment.—' As the receipt of money has never been the object of the said Powers ', Japan was invited to offer, in lieu thereof, the opening of Shimonoseki or some other eligible port in the Inland Sea, the four Powers reserving the option to accept the same or insist on the payment. The alternative having been adopted (November 26, 1867), whereby Yedo, Niigata, and Ebisuminato were opened to foreign trade, April 1, 1868, the indemnity was not exacted.[2]

TREATY OF PRAG, AUG. 23, 1866 [3]

(PRUSSIA—AUSTRIA)

Amount.—Austria to pay Prussia 40 million Prussian thalers (£5,928,000), 'to cover part of the expenses which Prussia has been put to by the war '. (From this sum were deducted 15 million Prussian thalers due to Austria under the Treaty of Vienna, 1864, and 5 millions representing the cost of maintaining the Prussian army in Austrian territories occupied till the conclusion of peace.)

[1] Hertslet, *Collection of Treaties, &c.*, vol. xii, p. 597.
[2] Ibid., p. 1153.
[3] *British and Foreign State Papers*, vol lvi, p. 1050.

Time of payment.—One-half to be paid on the ratification of the treaty, the second half three weeks later at Oppeln.

Guarantee (Occupation).—Evacuation to be completed within three weeks after the exchange of the ratifications.

TREATY OF BERLIN, AUG. 13, 1866 [1]

(PRUSSIA—WÜRTTEMBERG)

Amount.—Württemberg to pay Prussia 8 million florins (£677,500).

Time of payment.—Within two months. Discount at 5 per cent. per annum to be deducted on payments made before the stipulated time.

Guarantee (Occupation).—Württemberg to deposit $3\frac{1}{2}$ per cent. and 4 per cent. Württemberg State Bonds to the amount of the indemnity. These securities to be reckoned at the exchange of the day, and the amount of the guarantee to be raised 10 per cent. On payment of the indemnity or provision of a guarantee, Prussian troops to be withdrawn. Their provisioning during the withdrawal to be made in accordance with the existing Federal regulations.

TREATY OF BERLIN, AUG. 17, 1866 [2]

(PRUSSIA—BADEN)

Amount.—Baden to pay Prussia 6 million florins (£508,100).

Time of payment and guarantee.—(As in Treaty of Berlin, Aug. 13, 1866, above.)

---

[1] Hertslet, *Map of Europe*, vol. iii, p. 1703.
[2] Ibid., p. 1707.

TREATY OF BERLIN, AUG. 22, 1866 [1]

(PRUSSIA—BAVARIA)

Amount. — Bavaria to pay Prussia 30 million florins (£2,540,600).

Mode and time of payment.—Payable in silver thalers or silver bars (a pound of fine silver reckoned at 29 thalers 25 silver groschen).

10 millions to be paid at exchange of ratifications, with allowance of discount on 2 months at 5 per cent. per annum; 10 millions within 3 months; and 10 millions within 6 months after the ratification—the last two instalments bearing interest at 5 per cent. from beginning of the third month after ratification.

Guarantee (Occupation).—(As in Treaty of Berlin, Aug. 13, 1866, above.)

TREATY OF BERLIN, SEPT. 3, 1866 [2]

(PRUSSIA—HESSE-DARMSTADT)

Amount.—Hesse-Darmstadt to pay Prussia 3 million florins (£254,100).

Time of payment and guarantee.—(As in Treaty of Berlin, Aug. 13, 1866, above.)

TREATY OF BERLIN, OCT. 21, 1866 [3]

(PRUSSIA—SAXONY)

Amount.—Saxony to pay Prussia 10 million thalers (£1,482,000).

Time of payment.—Payable in three equal instalments: the first on Dec. 31, 1866, the second on Feb. 28, 1867, and the third on April 30, 1867. Discount

---

[1] *British and Foreign State Papers*, vol. lvi, p. 1044.
[2] Ibid., p. 1058.   [3] Ibid., p. 1086.

at 5 per cent. per annum to be deducted on payments made before the stipulated time.

Guarantee.—Deposit of bills and bonds (as in Treaty of Berlin, Aug. 13, 1866, above).

PRELIMINARIES OF VERSAILLES, FEB. 26, 1871,[1]

AND TREATY OF FRANKFORT, MAY 10, 1871[2]

(GERMANY—FRANCE)

Amount.—5,000 million francs (£198,125,000).

At the conference of Feb. 21, Bismarck had demanded 6,000 millions, but at the instance of the British Government the sum was reduced to the above amount (Feb. 24). In the course of the negotiations M. Thiers and M. Favre urged that the war should not be regarded by Prussia as a kind of financial speculation, and that no more than the actual war expenditure should be claimed. Bismarck accepted this view, and conformably thereto justified the sum insisted on by specifying its composition and destined appropriation :

(1) 2,000 millions—for the war expenditure itself.

(2) 3,000 millions—for (i) the restoration of material, (ii) indemnities to German subjects expelled from France, (iii) compensation to ship-owners and crews of captured vessels, (iv) maintenance of French prisoners (who were much more numerous than the German prisoners), (v) indemnities to German wounded and to the widows and orphans of the fallen.[3]

This calculation was questioned by the French

---

[1] *British and Foreign State Papers*, vol. lxii, p. 59 ; Hertslet, *Map of Europe*, vol. iii, p. 1912.

[2] *British and Foreign State Papers*, vol. lxii, p. 77 ; Hertslet, *Map of Europe*, vol. iii, p. 1954 (English trans.).

[3] Bill before the Reichstag, May 25, 1872 ; Villefort, *Recueil des traités, conventions, lois, décrets et autres actes relatifs à la paix avec l'Allemagne* (5 vols., Paris, 1872–9), vol. ii, pp. 548–50.

negotiators, but in vain. In the report[1] on the Preliminaries laid before the National Assembly, March 1,
1871, it was stated that Europe was astonished at the
enormous sum demanded, and that Germany was
desirous of enriching herself with the spoils extorted
from France, believing she would indirectly disarm
the vanquished country by reducing it to financial
impotence.

Mode and time of payment.—
    500 millions within 30 days after the re-estab-
        lishment of the authority. of the French
        Government in the City of Paris.
    1,000 millions in the course of the year 1871.
    500 millions on May 1, 1872.
    3,000 millions within 3 years of the ratification
        of the Preliminaries (i. e. by March 2, 1874).

Interest.—From March 2, 1871, interest at 5 per cent.
per annum payable each year on March 3 on the
3,000 millions last mentioned, provided that 'all sums
paid in advance on the last 3,000 millions shall cease
to bear interest from the day on which the payment is
made'.[2]

Payment to be made in the principal German commercial towns ; in metal (gold or silver), in Prussian
bank-notes, in Netherlands or Belgian bank-notes, in
first-class negotiable bills to order or letters of exchange
payable at sight (a Prussian thaler = 3 f. 75 c.). The
German Government to be informed 3 months in advance of all payments intended to be made into the
German Treasury. French bank-notes were thus
excluded. But, when the first instalment fell due,
the French Government—which was burdened also
with the payment of $1\frac{1}{4}$ million francs each day for

[1] De Clercq, vol. x, p. 440.
[2] Hertslet, *Map of Europe*, vol. iii, p. 1958.

the German army of occupation—requested Germany to accept for once only payment in French bank-notes. As Germany had liabilities to meet in the occupied departments and in Alsace–Lorraine, she consented on condition that 125 millions were paid by June 15.

When 2,000 millions had been paid off, a convention [1] was arrived at for *extending the period of payment* for the remainder:

> 500 millions within two months after exchange of ratifications.
> 500 millions on Feb. 1, 1873.
> 1,000 millions on March 1, 1874.
> 1,000 millions on March 1, 1875.

Guarantee (Occupation).—The Preliminaries of Versailles had declared (Art. III) the willingness of Germany to substitute a financial guarantee for the territorial; but this declaration was subsequently disregarded, on the ground that the condition of the internal affairs of France and the danger of French military reorganization made earlier evacuation inexpedient. Thus, the departments between the right bank of the Seine and the eastern frontier remained in German military occupation by way of guarantee.

Evacuation took place in proportion to the payments made, the details being regulated by a considerable number of special conventions. The army of occupation was maintained at the expense of France. Till the conclusion of peace there were 500,000 men and 150,000 horses. After the payment of the first instalment of 500 millions there were 150,000 men and 50,000 horses. On Nov. 10, 1871, arrangement was made for a further reduction to 120,000 men and 40,000 horses; this was soon followed by another reduction, leaving 80,000

[1] De Clercq, vol. x, p. 596; *British and Foreign State Papers*, vol. lxii, p. 983.

men and 30,000 horses. From Jan. 1, 1872, after the payment of 2,000 millions, till the entire evacuation there were 50,000 men and 18,000 horses. The whole sum due was paid off by March 1, 1875, that is, exactly four years after the ratification of the Preliminaries of Versailles.

(For the year 1871 alone the cost to France of the army of occupation amounted to 248,625,000 francs, nearly £10,000,000.)

PRELIMINARIES OF SAN STEFANO, MARCH 3, 1878,[1] AND TREATY OF CONSTANTINOPLE, FEB. 8, 1879[2]

(RUSSIA—TURKEY)

Amount.—The Preliminaries required Turkey to pay Russia 1,410 million roubles (approximately, £152,750,000), being 900 millions for war expenses, and the rest for damage and injuries to commerce, industries, railways, to Russian subjects in Turkey, &c. But Russia consented to accept certain territorial cessions as a substitute for 1,100 millions of the said indemnity. The terms of the Preliminaries were, however, modified by the Congress of Berlin, 1878 ; and the modifications were embodied in the definitive Treaty of Constantinople, 1879. The latter stipulated that, after deducting the value of the territories ceded by Turkey under the Treaty of Berlin, the war indemnity should be 802,500,000 francs (£32,100,000). The claims of Russian subjects and establishments in Turkey for losses during the war were not to exceed 26,750,000 francs (£1,070,000), and were to be settled by a joint commission *ad hoc.*

---

[1] *British and Foreign State Papers*, vol. lxix, p. 732 ; Hertslet, *Map of Europe*, vol. iv, p. 2672.

[2] *British and Foreign State Papers*, vol. lxx, p. 551 ; Hertslet, *Map of Europe*, vol. iv, p. 2845.

A special joint commission was to be appointed for drawing up accounts of the cost of maintaining prisoners of war; and, after deducting the cost incurred by Turkey from the cost incurred by Russia, the balance was to be paid by Turkey in 21 equal instalments within the space of 7 years.

Occupation; but not by way of guarantee.—A Russian army occupied Bulgarian territory merely for the purpose of giving armed assistance to the commissioner, pending the establishment of a native militia able to preserve order, security, and tranquillity.

Subsequent dispute settled by Arbitration.—A dispute arose later in regard to the delay of Turkey in settling the claims of Russian subjects and establishments, as determined and prescribed. by the stipulated commission. The Russian Government claimed that the Ottoman Government was responsible to the Russian claimants for damages due to the delay, while the Ottoman Government denied such liability. As the parties failed to reach an understanding by diplomatic methods, they agreed, under the Treaty of Constantinople, July 22/August 4, 1910, to submit the difference to arbitration in accordance with the Hague Convention of Oct. 18, 1907.

TREATY OF SHIMONOSEKI, APRIL 17, 1895 [1]

(JAPAN—CHINA)

Amount.—China to pay Japan as a war indemnity 200 million Kuping taels (approximately, £30,000,000).

Time of payment.—8 instalments. The first (50 million taels) to be paid within 6 months of the exchange of ratifications; the second (50 millions) within 12 months thereof. The remainder to be paid in 6 equal annual instalments: the first within 2 years,

---

[1] *British and Foreign State Papers*, vol. lxxxvii, p. 800.

the second within 3 years, the third within 4 years, the fourth within 5 years, the fifth within 6 years, and the sixth within 7 years after the exchange of ratifications.

Interest at 5 per cent. per annum to run on all unpaid portions of the indemnity from the date at which the first instalment falls due. If the whole indemnity were paid within 3 years after the exchange of ratifications, all interest to be waived ; and the interest for $2\frac{1}{2}$ years, or for any less period if then already paid, to be included as part of the principal amount of the indemnity.

Guarantee (Occupation).—Japanese forces to occupy Wei-hai-wei. After the payment of the first two instalments, evacuation was to take place, provided China pledged, under suitable and sufficient arrangements, her customs revenue as security for payment of the rest. Failing such arrangements, evacuation to take place on the payment of the final instalment. (There was an additional condition relating to the conclusion of a commercial treaty.)

Separate regulations were made in regard to the army of occupation.[1]

PRELIMINARIES OF CONSTANTINOPLE, SEPT. 18, 1897,[2]

AND TREATY OF CONSTANTINOPLE, DEC. 4, 1897 [3]

(TURKEY—GREECE)

Amount.—When peace negotiations were begun, Turkey demanded 230 million francs (£9,113,750). But the Powers intervened ; they pointed out that this sum was in excess of Turkey's war expenditure, and was beyond the capacity of Greece to pay. A special commission, appointed by the six Powers, estimated the sum at 100 millions (£3,962,500), which was afterwards agreed to. An additional sum of £T100,000

---

[1] Ibid., p. 804.   [2] Ibid., vol. xc, p. 546.   [3] Ibid., p. 422.

iii. INDEMNITIES PAID TO DEFEATED COUNTRIES

Cases in which an indemnity, or rather compensation, has been paid, not *by*, but *to*, a defeated country, hardly come into consideration here, but the following may be mentioned.

1. During the war of Greek independence, it was arranged, in the protocol of the conference between representatives of Great Britain and Russia, Dec. 12, 1828, Art. XI, that an indemnity should be paid by the Greeks to the dispossessed Mussulman proprietors of lands, &c. In the definitive treaty between Great Britain, France, Russia, and Turkey, July 21, 1832, Art. II stipulates as follows: ' With respect to the indemnity, it remains fixed at the sum of 40 millions of Turkish piastres (approximately, £240,000),' &c.[1]

2. In two instances victorious States have paid large pecuniary compensations for ceded territory which they might have claimed by right of conquest.

(*a*) By the Convention between Great Britain and the Netherlands (Aug. 13, 1814), the Dutch colonies of the Cape of Good Hope, Demerara, Essequibo and Berbice became British possessions, Great Britain paying to the Netherlands therefor the sum of £6,000,000.

(*b*) By the Treaty of Paris between Spain and the United States (Dec. 10, 1898), Spain ceded the Philippine Islands to the United States, for which the latter paid $20,000,000 (£4,000,000) by way of compensation. It should, however, be stated that Spain had to take over the public debt on the Islands.

indemnity, but subject to a *plébiscite* at the end of ten years in the case of two districts (Tacna and Arica), which has never been held.

[1] Hertslet, vol. ii, pp. 802, 905.

II. ECONOMIC EFFECTS OF AN INDEMNITY ON THE NATION RECEIVING IT

§ i. THE only indemnity in history which at all resembles, either in size or in the conditions of collection and payment, the indemnities demanded at the end of the late war is that of £198,125,000 (or £212,500,000, including interest, &c.), paid by France to Germany in and after 1871. In 1873 Germany went through a serious financial crisis. In consequence of this it was argued at the time, especially in France, and was argued just before the late war, especially in England, that the reception of an indemnity is bound to do more harm than good. This view is not accepted by any economist of repute in any country, though it is freely admitted that the receiving of an indemnity, or rather the injudicious use of an indemnity, *may* bring evils upon the victorious country. That the financial crisis of 1873 was not due primarily to the indemnity is sufficiently proved by the fact that it began in Vienna, not in Berlin ; and that there were also financial disturbances (failures, &c.) on a large scale at the same time in New York.

§ ii. To understand the effects of the indemnity of 1871, the following facts as to the way in which it was raised, paid over, and used should be borne in mind. It was raised in two loans—the first of two milliards, the second of three milliards (1871 and 1872). The first was almost entirely subscribed by Frenchmen ; about a third of the second was taken by foreigners, but this third was very soon bought back by French investors. France was allowed to pay £13,000,000 in the form of the privately-owned railways of Alsace-Lorraine, the French Government having subsequently to compensate the shareholders ; £29,500,000 were paid in cash of various sorts ; and £170,000,000 were paid in bills. If France had been able to export actual goods to this amount, in excess of what she imported, either by consuming less or producing more, the whole payment would have resembled that small portion which was represented by the Alsatian railways, in other words, it would have been an immediate transference of ' things ' from Frenchmen to Germans. In some cases Frenchmen sold property in the annexed territory (e. g. mines in Lorraine), and put the money into the indemnity loan, a transaction closely resembling the transfer of the railways ; the individual German paid for his mines, but the German State got back their value. It was a kind of free export to Germany. But France was not able to do this sort of thing generally. What she did was to make use of her very large holdings of foreign investments. Frenchmen sold these and bought the indemnity loans, or they put the interest into the indemnity loans instead of using it.

What was involved was simply the transference to Germany of already existing French claims on the world's production (or taxation), and the diversion to Germany of the right to receive (for particular years or in perpetuity) the income already being paid. This income might be, and no doubt largely was, received in the form of the commodities which the debtor countries had been in the habit of exporting, not in the form of specially large exports from France.

§ iii. Thanks to the indemnity, Germany was able (1) to tax her people less than she would otherwise have had to do ; (2) to re-equip her army and fortify her new frontiers at the expense of France ; (3) to establish a gold currency, which she had not had before. The reception of a large amount of French gold was a great assistance here. Germany also put away £6,000,000 as a war reserve at Spandau ; but the experience of 1914–18 has shown again what Adam Smith pointed out,[1] that such hoards do not materially assist the financing of a great war.

§ iv. The financial crisis of 1873 only slightly interrupted the progress of Germany in trade and wealth ; but it did harm her, and the harm was to some extent connected with the indemnity. Firstly, the German Government, by a mistaken arrangement, received payments only at definite intervals. In the meantime the agents of France were accumulating in the German banks funds from which these payments were to be made. The bankers were tempted to lend these funds on short loans until they were wanted. There were thus alternations of ' cheap money ' (in the money-market sense) and stringency—the first before, and the second just after, the fixed dates of payment. This was an inconvenience, and had bad results ; but obviously it is not an inevitable outcome of an indemnity. Secondly, there is some reason to think that the German Government put too much of the actual cash which it got from France into circulation, and so drove up prices in an unhealthy fashion. This, however, is not certain. Supposing it true, the detrimental consequences might have been avoided by holding up some of the cash until business had developed sufficiently to make good use of it all without undue inflation of the currency. Thirdly, the German Government used part of the indemnity to pay back the debts of its predecessor—the North German Confederation—and of the larger German States. So far as the investors, who

---

[1] He mentioned that the King of Prussia was the only monarch in Europe who kept such a hoard. England financed Prussia without one.

were thus forced to find new uses for their capital, merely bought foreign securities which the French sold, no harm was done ; but some of the capital found its way into new investments in Germany, many of which were of a dubious character. It was enterprises of this type that collapsed in the crisis of 1873. Also the managers of various permanent funds which were created out of the indemnity (wounded soldiers' fund, &c.) put their capital into high-class German securities, thus setting free further capital for the more risky enterprises. In these ways the injudicious use of the indemnity did hasten and intensify the financial crash which, in any case, would almost certainly have occurred in 1873.

§ v. It was pointed out by Professor Wagner, of Berlin, in 1874 that these incidental evils connected with the reception of the indemnity might to some extent have been avoided (1) by spreading the payment over a longer period; (2) by investing the proceeds to a greater extent in foreign securities ; (3) by enforcing payment to a greater degree in actual useful things (e. g. the Alsatian railways) rather than in money. Following out this line of thought, various German writers, in discussing the indemnities which they hoped to be able to extract from the Allies after the late war, laid stress on the desirability of gradual payment and of payment in ' things '. They talked of 'concessions, mines, railways, and ships', or of ' the whole yield of the South African gold mines for ten years '. Such forms of indemnity are certainly free from some of the difficulties attendant upon the methods adopted in 1871.

II

SUBSIDIES AND LOANS

TABLE OF CONTENTS

Wt 9157/860 1005 7/20 F.O.P. [3828]

SUBSIDIES AND LOANS (BRITISH)

THE number of occasions on which this country has made or guaranteed a loan to an ally in time of war during the 125 years before 1914 is remarkably small. The complete list is as follows :—

(1 and 2) 1795 and 1797.—Two loans were raised in London for the Emperor of Austria, the first of £4,600,000 and the second of £1,620,000. They took the form of Imperial 3 per cent. annuities and of a small terminable annuity (£230,000). The latter expired in 1819. Interest on the first loan was guaranteed by 35 Geo. III, c. 93; and interest and sinking fund were guaranteed on the second by 37 Geo. III, c. 59.

(3) 1809.—By 49 Geo. III, c. 71, Portugal was allowed to raise in London a loan of £600,000. She undertook to meet all charges, including a sinking fund, but was subsequently relieved of this liability by the British Government. (See below.)

(4) 1813.—A small loan (£200,000) was made to Holland by the British Government direct.

(5) 1814.—A similar loan (£200,000) was made to France.

(6) 1815.—As part of the adjustment at the Congress of Vienna and by 55 Geo. III, c. 115, Great Britain undertook to pay 6 per cent.

per annum, including a sinking fund, on a
sum of £2,000,000 raised many years before
by Russia in Holland.

(7) 1855.—Advances by way of loan amounting to
£2,000,000, under Acts 18 and 19 Vict., c. 17,
and 19 and 20 Vict., c. 39, were made in aid
of the expenses incurred by Sardinia in the
Crimean War.

(8) 1855.—During the same war Great Britain and
France, the former by Act 18 and 19 Vict.,
c. 99, guaranteed jointly and severally 4 per
cent. per annum on a sum of £5,000,000
raised for Turkey.[1]

Subsidies.—The greater part of the payments
made to Allies during the Revolutionary and
Napoleonic Wars, the total amount of which during
the years 1793-1816 was upwards of £57,000,000, was
by way of subsidy, not of loan. From 1816 to 1914 no
subsidies were paid to Allies in time of war; but in
1818-1820 £1,530,000 was advanced to Holland to be
spent on fortifications.

(1 and 2) *Austrian Loans* (1795 *and* 1797).—
According to Lord Liverpool, in 1816, a main reason for
adopting the subsidy policy was the unfortunate history
of the Austrian loans of 1795 and 1797 (1 and
2). "He believed it became a maxim with every
Administration, after the experience of the Austrian
Loan, not to engage in any transaction of that kind."[2]
The experience was as follows. Owing to diplomatic
and military considerations, Austria was never pressed

---

[1] This list is based on two Parliamentary papers: (a) No. 466 of
1854—Account of all sums of money paid or advanced by way of
loan subsidy or otherwise to any foreign State from 1792; and (b)
No. 180 of 1900—Return (1) of advances by way of loan; (2) of
payments by way of subsidy to foreign States; and (3) of loans
raised by foreign States of which the interest or capital has been
guaranteed by Parliament since 1792.

[2] Hansard, Parliamentary History, vol. XXXII, p. 1031.

for any interest, although, when the loan was raised, securities were taken and the Imperial creditors were empowered to sue the Emperor in his own Courts. Part of the interest on the first loan was paid out of the second; and within a few years the whole had become a charge on the Consolidated Fund.

The ultimate result was the creation of 3 per cent. stock to the nominal value of £7,502,633, besides the terminable annuity of £230,000 per annum.[1] Between 1799 and 1816 the old German Empire and its successor, the Austrian Empire, received subsidies of nearly £6,000,000, besides the numerous payments made to individual German princes.

In 1816 it was evidently not anticipated by Government that anything would be recovered on the Austrian Loans. But by a Convention of November 7, 1823, the Emperor undertook to pay £2,500,000 " in satisfaction of the whole of the British claims upon His Imperial Majesty " through Messrs. Baring and Messrs. Rothschild. Payment was spread over the years 1823-7. The "original Letters of Octroi . . . . and Imperial Bonds " were returned to the Austrian Government; and the balance of the loan was added to the 3 per cent. Consols (Act 5 Geo. IV, c. 9).

(3) *The Portuguese Loan of* 1809.—Portugal met the charges on this loan, including the sinking fund, down to 1815. Under a treaty of January 22, 1815, all the charges were taken over by the British Government. Exclusive of this loan, nearly £9,000,000 had been advanced to Portugal, between 1798 and 1815, by way of subsidy, including special payments amounting to £100,000 to " Portuguese sufferers " in 1811-12. Practically, therefore, down to 1815, Portugal met the charges on the loan out of subsidies.

(4 and 5) *Dutch Loan* (1813) *and French Loan* (1814).—The two small loans to Holland and France,

---

[1] Report on Public Income and Expenditure, 1799; Hansard, Parliamentary History, vol. XXXIV, p. 1146.

each of £200,000, were repaid.[1] No special measures appear to have been necessary for their recovery.[2]

(6) *The Russian-Dutch Loan of* 1815.—Great Britain formally undertook the burden of this loan in connection with the establishment, largely by British diplomacy, of the new Kingdom of the Netherlands in 1815. Great Britain was to pay the interest for Russia so long as the Low Countries (Belgium) remained united to Holland. This proviso was intended to bind Russia to the new settlement;[3] it was not, however, insisted upon when the Kingdom of Belgium was created. The first payment of interest on the loan was one of £122,000, made in 1816. Owing to the operation of the sinking fund, the amount of interest payable annually had fallen by 1853 to £88,577.[4] Payments continued in spite of the Crimean War. By 1891 the amount of capital outstanding was reduced to £520,000. This sum was paid off, under Act 54 and 55 Vict., c. 26, by means of a terminable annuity expiring in the year 1906.[5]

(7) *The Sardinian Loan of* 1855.—This sum lent (£2,000,000), like the small loans to Holland and France, 1813-14, was an advance direct from the British Government, not a loan raised in London and guaranteed by the British Government. The Sardinian Government undertook to pay 4 per cent. per annum, of which 1 per cent. was to be for a sinking fund. The

[1] The dates of repayment do not appear to be discoverable. There is no trace of the loans in the Financial Reports of 1813-20. In the Parliamentary Paper (1854) referred to above, these loans are entered as " repaid," without date.

[2] Enquiries have been made both from Messrs. Baring and Messrs. Rothschild with the object of eliciting information as to the manner in which the loans and subsidies of the period 1792-1815 were financed, but no information was forthcoming, the records for that period having apparently been destroyed.

[3] Lord Liverpool in the House of Lords, March 1, 1816; Hansard, vol. XXXII, p. 1032.

[4] Parliamentary Paper No. 466 of 1854.

[5] Parliamentary Paper No. 180 of 1900.

payment was regularly made; and the debt, which was subsequently taken over by the Italian Government, was steadily reduced. On February 22, 1903, a final account was presented to the House of Commons, showing that three repayments on capital account had closed the transaction.

(8) *The Turkish Loan* of 1855.—By the Convention, under which Great Britain and France guaranteed the interest on a loan of £5,000,000 to be raised by Turkey, the rate of interest was fixed at 4 per cent., plus 1 per cent. for sinking fund. Interest and sinking fund were to form a charge on the whole Ottoman revenue, and especially on the tribute of Egypt and the Customs of Smyrna and Syria. The amount outstanding in 1875 was £3,815,200. The further history of the loan is part of the general history of the Ottoman Debt, which it seems unnecessary to follow out here.

HANDBOOKS PREPARED UNDER THE DIRECTION OF THE HISTORICAL SECTION OF THE FOREIGN OFFICE, No. 159

PLEBISCITE
AND
REFERENDUM

LONDON :
PUBLISHED BY H.M. STATIONERY OFFICE

1920

NOTE.

—

The portion of this Treatise dealing with the French plebiscites is by Mr. R. S. Rait (Professor of Scottish History in the University of Glasgow and Historiographer Royal of Scotland) and Miss Beatrice A. Lees (Lecturer in History, University of Manchester). That on the Italian plebiscites is by Miss Rachel Reid (Lecturer in History, University College, London), with additions by Prof. Rait. Capt. G. M. Gathorne-Hardy contributed the account of the plebiscites in Norway ; Major Basil Williams, that of the referendum in Natal ; Major Frank Fox the note on the referendum in Australia. Miss Lees supplied the notes on that institution in the United States, and Prof. Rait those on the referendum in Switzerland, and the promised plebiscite in North Schleswig.

TABLE OF CONTENTS.

CHRONOLOGICAL SUMMARY.

1792 Plebiscites in Savoy and Nice on annexation to France.

1793 Plebiscites in Mainz and Belgium on annexation to France.

1793 Plebiscite on the French Constitution of 1793.

1795 Plebiscite on the French Constitution of 1795.

1800 Plebiscite on the French Constitution of 1799.

1802 Plebiscite on the First Consulate for life.

1804 Plebiscite on the first Imperial title.

1848 Plebiscites in North Italy.

1848 Plebiscite on Revision of the Swiss Constitution authorised.

1848 Plebiscite on the Presidency of the French Republic.

1851 Plebiscite on Louis Napoleon's *Coup d'Etat.*

1852 Plebiscite on the proclamation of the Second Empire.

1860 Plebiscites in Savoy and Nice, Central Italy, Naples, and Sicily.

1866 Plebiscite in Venetia.

1870 Plebiscite on the Liberal Empire in France.

1870 Plebiscite in Rome.

1877 Plebiscite in St. Barthélemy.

1898-99 Referendum on the Federal Constitution in Australia.

1905 Plebiscites in Norway.

1909 Referendum in Natal.

1911, 1913, 1916 Referenda in Australia.

I.—INTRODUCTION.

(i) *Plebiscite and Referendum.*—The political
terms plebiscite and referendum in their modern
acceptation are of comparatively recent origin,
but the idea behind them—the ultimate right
of the sovereign people to exercise direct legislative
power—is of great antiquity. The Roman *plebiscitum* was, at least after the enactment of the
Lex Hortensia of 287 B.C., a decree passed by the
Plebians in their *concilium plebis*, under their own
magistrates, the tribunes, and by their own forms
of procedure, in virtue of the power delegated to
them by the sovereign people, the " populus."
The " plebs " thus gained a right to legislate for
the nation. " The assembly of the plebs became
the delegated alter ego of the sovereign *populus
Romanus.*"[1] Hence, as the decree of the plebs
constituted a law, the term " lex " came to be
loosely used for plebiscitum, and the term
" populus " for " plebs."

In mediæval Latin and in Old French the words
plebiscitum, plébiscite, plebiscite, retained their
classical sense of a popular law (*statutum, estatut,
establissement*), but were also, by an extension of
meaning, applied to the popular assembly (*con-
ventus plebis*) in which such laws were passed,

---

[1] *English Historical Review*, vol. I, 1886, April, p. 209 *et
seq.* ; J. L. Strachan-Davidson, *The Growth of Plebeian
Privilege at Rome*, vol. V, 1890, July, p. 462 *et seq.* ; *Ibid.*,
The Decrees of the Roman Plebs.

while the constituent members of the assembly could even be described as *plebisciti*.[1]

In pre-Revolutionary France, Montesquieu and Rousseau used " plébiscite " as equivalent to the Latin " plebiscitum," a law made by the Plebians alone, without the Patricians or the Senate.[2] To Voltaire, on the contrary, influenced probably by his knowledge of the Swiss referendum in its early form, the word " plébiscite " seems to have suggested the popular legislative assembly, the *concilium plebis*, rather than the law made in that assembly.[3]

> " Dans l'ancienne Rome," he wrote in 1776, " et même encore à Genève et à Bâle, et dans les petits cantons, ce sont les plébiscites qui font les lois."[4]

In Voltaire's time, indeed, the final legislative power in many of the Swiss cantons actually rested with the people in their local assemblies, and not with the general assembly.[4]

---

[1] Du Cange, *Glossarium mediæ et infimæ Latinitatis* ed. 1845, *sub voce*. Godefroy, *Dictionnaire de l'ancienne Langue Française*: Paris, 1902, *sub voce*. La Curne de Sainte-Palaye., *Dictionnaire Historique de l'ancien Langage François*: Paris, 1880, *sub voce*.—" Plebiscite estoit apelé aucun establissement que le menu peuple fesoit en sa cour par ses tribuns et par ses ediles et par ses majestraz." Murray, *New Eng. Dict.*, 1909: *sub voce*.—The earliest instance given of the use of the word plebiscite in English is in 1637, in the sense of a popular decree or maxim.

[2] Montesquieu, *De l'Esprit des Lois*, chap. XVI. Rousseau, J. J., *Du Contrat Social, livre* III, chap. XV.

[3] *Œuvres Complètes*, 1785, vol. 63. *Correspondance Générale*, pp. 214-215. *Lettre* CXIX, *à M. Le Comte d'Argental*, 30 de mars, 1776. Murray, *New Eng. Dict.*, thinks that Voltaire here is using the word in the modern sense, for the popular vote. From the connection with Rome and Switzerland it seems more probable that he, in common with some mediæval writers, understood by it the popular assembly.

[4] *Eng. Hist. Rev.*, vol. VI, 1891, Oct., p. 674 *et seq* W. A. B. Coolidge, *The Early History of the Referendum*. A. Lawrence Lowell, *Governments and Parties in Continental Europe*, vol. II, chap. XII, p. 238 *et seq.*: London, 1904.

In modern politics the term " plébiscite " or
" plebiscite," both in French and English, has come
to mean " a direct vote of the whole of the electors
of a State to decide a question of public importance "[1]—the machinery whereby the sovereign
people gives expression to its will, not, as in
Roman days, the embodiment of that will in the
form of a law or decree. Although votes of this
kind were taken in France several times between
1792 and 1804, they do not seem to have been
called *plébiscites*. The word apparently only
became familiar during the Second French Empire,
when Napoleon III used the direct vote to
strengthen and popularize his arbitrary seizure of
power. From this association the term plebiscite
acquired a somewhat disparaging connotation,
since it was held to imply the abdication of
popular sovereignty, and the delegation of the
supreme power of the community to one man.[2]
Thus M. Aulard, the historian of the French
Revolution, describes the period of the Consulate
(1799-1804) as " la république plébiscitaire,"
because the people, by a plebiscite, had abdicated
their rights in favour of one man, Napoleon
Bonaparte.[3]

If the experiences of the Second Empire discredited the plebiscite as a means of testing
public opinion on constitutional questions, the
Italian plebiscites of 1860 to 1870 showed the
defects of the direct popular vote as a method
of deciding questions of annexation, or of the
cession of territory by one State to another. Yet
it is chiefly in this sense that the plebiscite, as
the expression of the principle of self-determination, had found favour in modern Liberal and

---

[1] Murray, *New Eng. Dict., sub voce.*
[2] Bodley, J. E. C., *France,* vol. II, bk. III, §IV, p. 161
note 1 : London, 1898.
[3] Aulard, A., *Histoire Politique de la Révolution Française.
Avertissement*, pp. v., vi. Paris, 1901.

Socialist circles, though with the proviso, that it must be an " honest plebiscite."[1] The Central Organization for a Durable Peace includes a clause in its Minimum Programme which provides that—

> " No annexation or transfer of territory shall be made contrary to the interests and wishes of the population concerned. Where possible their consent shall be obtained by plebiscite or otherwise."[2]

It is also one of the " four cardinal points " of the policy of the Union of Democratic Control that—

> " No Province shall be transferred fi om one Government to another without the consent, by plebiscite or otherwise, of the population of such province."

In accordance with these views the Berne International Labour and Socialist Conference of February, 1919, received a unanimous report from the Commission on territorial problems in favour of the self-determination of nationalities and plebiscites under the control of the League of Nations. Two days later, however, the German Majority representatives found themselves compelled to withdraw their proposal demanding a plebiscite for Alsace-Lorraine.[3]

Strictly speaking, the term " plebiscite " connotes the actual vote given by the whole body of electors ; and the " referendum," the practice or principle of submitting questions to that body.[4] The referendum implies the appeal to the people, the act of reference ; the plebiscite, the process and result of that appeal. Referendum and plebiscite may be described as complementary parts of one legislative action. In practice, however, the two terms are often used almost interchangeably, and the fine shades of distinction

---

[1] Brailsford, H. N., *Publications of the Union of Democratic Control*, No. 4, p. 19.

[2] *The Framework of a Lasting Peace*, ed. L. S. Woolf, II, p. 63. London, 1917.

[3] *Manchester Guardian*, Feb. 8, Feb. 10, 1919.

[4] Murray, *New English Dictionary*. s.v. Referendum.

in their meanings are disregarded. Thus Mr.
Lowell describes the referendum, not the plebiscite,
as "the popular voting upon laws,"[1] while
Professor Dicey, more accurately, identifies it
with the " appeal to the people," and the " national
veto."[2] Mr. Bodley, who narrows down the
plebiscite to the delegation of supreme power, by
the majority of voices, to one man, sees in the
referendum "the approval or disapproval by
that majority of a definite act or policy of the
Government," and cites French advocates of the
referendum for the opinion that it represents
" the permanent power to exercise the national
sovereignty."[3]

(ii) *The Referendum.*—The substantive use of
the word " referendum "[4] seems to have passed
into modern political terminology from Switzerland, where the delegates to the Diet of the early
Confederation were commissioned *ad audiendum
et referendum*—to hear what was proposed, and to
report, or refer back to their governments—before
matters of importance were settled.[5] But this
ancient form of the referendum arose from the
nature of the federal tie,[6] and was different in
character from the modern Swiss referendum,
which only came into existence in the nineteenth
century, by the Federal Constitution of 1848,

---

[1] Lowell, A. Lawrence, *Governments and Parties in
Continental Europe*, vol. II, chap. XII, p. 238 : London, 1904.
[2] *Quarterly Review*, April, 1910.   Dicey, A. V.   *The
Referendum and its critics*, p. 538, *seq.*
[3] Bodley, J. E. C., *op. cit.*, vol. II, p. 161 and *note* 1.
[4] It is used as a verb by Vulpius, who died in 1706, in his
Historia Rhætica. " The chief men decree what seems to
them good, but everything is done *ad referendum.*" (*Eng.
Hist. Rev.*, vol. VI, 1891, p. 681.)
[5] *Eng. Hist. Review*, vol. VI, 1891, p. 674 *et seq.*   Lowell,
A. Lawrence, *op. cit., Quarterly Review*, April, 1911.   *The
Referendum in Operation*, p. 509.
[6] Lowell, A. Lawrence, *op. cit.*, vol. II, p. 238.

and its amendments in 1874 and 1891.[1] The earliest use of the word in English given in the New English Dictionary is in 1882[2] ; and in 1885 Sir Henry Maine could write of the Swiss referendum in his " Popular Government " as the " most recent of democratic inventions."[3] Historically, however, the referendum is only a Swiss invention in the limited sense of its application to ordinary laws. As a method of appealing to the people on important constitutional changes, it was practised in the eighteenth and nineteenth centuries, both in the United States of America and in France ; while the annexation plebiscite, which involves the reference of a definite issue to the people, was used in France in the Revolutionary Period.

(iii) *The Popular Initiative.*—The Swiss Popular Initiative, whereby a definite number of the people has the right to propose legislative measures to the whole body, and to require a popular vote on such proposals, is " a complement of the referendum," which goes beyond it in the direction of popular legislation. In its various modern forms the Initiative is a device of the nineteenth century, but it goes back to a primitive right in the smaller cantons, where any qualified voter might, after observing certain formalities, bring proposals before the *Landesgemeinde*, or local assembly. This, as Mr. Lowell has pointed out, " is a case where every man is a member of the legislature, rather than one where the people can make laws directly without the help of any assembly at all."[4]   Voltaire, however, was

---

[1] *Encyclop. Brit.*, ed. 1911.   Articles : *Referendum, Switzerland.* Lowell, A. Lawrence, *op. cit. Quarterly Review,* April, 1910, p. 538, *et seq.* ; April, 1911, p. 509 *seq.*

[2] Murray, *New Eng. Dict., sub voce.* " A referendum or appeal to the people." *Daily News,* Feb. 7, 1882.

[3] *Quarterly Review*, April, 1910, *ut supra.*

[4] Lowell, A. Lawrence, *op. cit.*, vol. II, p. 280 *et seq. Quarterly Review,* April, 1911, p. 512 *et seq. See below :* VII. *The Referendum in Switzerland.*

undoubtedly justified in comparing the machinery of popular legislation in the small Swiss cantons with that of ancient Rome, for both the *concilium plebis* and the *Landesgemeinde* could originate laws, whereas in the plebiscite or referendum proper the people as a whole can accept, reject, or confirm, but has no power of initiation.

(iv) *Forms of Plebiscite or Referendum.*—The various forms of plebiscite or referendum may be conveniently classified, according to the purposes for which the appeal to the people is employed, as (1) the Plebiscite or Referendum in Ordinary Legislation ; (2) the Constitutional Plebiscite or Referendum, and (3) the Annexation Plebiscite.[1]

The plebiscite, as an instrument of ordinary legislation, is really a Swiss invention, though a provision for a popular vote on laws was inserted in the abortive French Constitution of 1793. In the United States it has been to some extent copied from Swiss institutions ; and instances of its use are found in Australia. The Constitutional Plebiscite or Referendum, the appeal to the people to sanction a new constitution, or to accept fundamental constitutional changes, has been freely used in France, in the United States, and in Australia. Italy, France, and a few other countries afford instances of the Annexation Plebiscite.

(v) *Theoretical Basis of the Plebiscite.*—All these forms of popular legislation rest ultimately on those theories of the Rights of Man, Liberty and Equality, the General Will, and the Sovereignty of the People, which, vitalized by the genius of Rousseau, exercised an incalculable influence on the political thought of the later eighteenth century. The doctrine of the Sovereignty of

---

[1] On the veto as a form of direct popular voting, *see* Lowell, A. Lawrence, *op. cit.*, vol. II, p. 248 *et seq.*

the People, in particular, became one of the
fundamental principles of the French Revolution,
a Revolution whereby, as André Chénier wrote :—
" les peuples rentrent dans leur souveraineté
usurpée."

To Rousseau[1] sovereignty, being simply the
exercise of the general will, was inalienable ;
and the sovereign people could only be represented
by itself. Executive power might be delegated,
but legislative power, the heart of the body
politic, by which the State lives, must remain
with the sovereign people.

> " Le souverain," he wrote in the *Contrat Social*,[2] " n'ayant
> d'autre force que la puissance législative, n'agit que par
> des lois ; et les lois n'étant que des actes authentiques de la
> volonté générale, le souverain ne saurait agir que quand le
> peuple est assemblé." And again, in another passage : " La
> souveraineté ne peut être représentée . . . elle consiste
> essentiellement dans la volonté générale, et la volonté ne
> se représente point."[3]

Rousseau himself saw no possibility of the
full realization of this ideal save in States so
small that a primary assembly of all the citizens
was possible. In practical politics he would only
admit the principle of representation if the
deputies were mere delegates or mandatories of
the sovereign people, acting under a *mandat im-
peratif*, and unable to conclude anything definitively
without first submitting it to their constituents.
According to him, " Toute loi que le peuple en
personne n'a pas ratifié est nulle ; ce n'est point
une loi."[4]

---

[1] Rousseau, J., *Du Contrat Social*, ed. C. E. Vaughan,
Manchester Univ. Press, 1918. See also Vaughan's ed. of
Rousseau's Political Works.

[2] *Contrat Social*, livre II, chaps. I, II ; livre III, chaps.
XI, XII, XIII, XIV, XV, XVI. Cf. Lowell, A. Lawrence,
op. cit., vol. III, pp. 243-244.

[3] *Contrat Social*, livre III, chap. XV. *See* Professor
Vaughan's notes on this chapter in his edition of the *Contrat
Social*, Manchester, 1918.

[4] *Ibid.*

The questions of " imperative mandates " and
of the royal veto on legislation were keenly debated
in the National Assembly in the autumn of 1789 ;
and the arguments used against the principle
of the direct popular ratification of laws strikingly
anticipate the chief modern objections to the
plebiscite or referendum. Thus Mounier, the
proposer of the Tennis Court Oath, a clear-sighted
and temperate politician, after declaring that
" imperative mandates " would result in " tumul-
tuous democracy," and that the submission to
the local assemblies of laws which the king had
suspended would mean " a sovereignty divided
into more than 40,000 fractions," went on to
urge that such division of sovereignty would
lead to troubles and factions, and to the exercise
of undue influence over simple voters :—" On
irait dans les districts gagner les suffrages, et il
serait facile de séduire une foule peu éclairée."[1] The
Abbé Siéyès also spoke strongly of the danger of
entrusting direct legislative power to " elementary
assemblies " : " Proposer que la loi n'ait force de
loi que lorsque chaque citoyen l'aura consentie
immédiatement, c'est dire que la France est un
Etat démocratique."[2]

Mounier and Siéyès were right in their forecast
of the logical consequences of direct popular
government, but the democracy which they feared
was welcome to such ardent disciples of Rousseau
as Robespierre and St. Just, and to the other
leaders of the growing democratic and republican

---

[1] *Moniteur Universel*, No. 52, Sept. 4, 1789, p. 213 *seq.*
But Mounier distinguishes between the appeal to the people
on questions of the organization of government and the fixing
of a constitution, and on questions of ordinary legislation
which arise after the government is organized. In the first
case, the deputies entrusted with constituent powers must
act as mandatories of the electors.

[2] *Ibid.*, No. 54, Sept. 7 and 8, 1789, p. 223.

parties.[1] Robespierre was laughed at when, in October, 1789, he proposed in the National Assembly that the formula at the head of all laws should run : " Louis, par la grâce de Dieu, et par la volonté de la Nation, roi des Français ; à tous les citoyens de l'Empire Français : Peuple, voici la loi que vos représentans ont faite, et à laquelle j'ai apposé le sceau royal."[2] But the idea of the right of the people to something more than a passive share in government deepened in intensity as the Third Estate proved its mettle and its power.[3]

---

[1] Aulard, *op. cit.*, Pt. I, chap. IV, puts the beginnings of the first republican party in December, 1790. Robespierre was not at first a member of it.

[2] *Moniteur*, No. 69, Oct. 8, 1789, p. 283.

[3] Aulard, *op. cit.*, Part I, chap. III, § III, p. 60, calls the taking of the Bastille and the subsequent events, " la prise de robe virile du peuple."

II.—PLEBISCITES IN FRANCE.

(I.) THE REVOLUTIONARY PERIOD.

(i) *The Constitution of* 1791.—The Constitution of 1791 provided for primary assemblies of towns and cantons, in which the electors of the new Legislative Assembly were to be chosen ; but it retained the indirect method of election (*le suffrage a deux degrés*) to the central legislature, and it imposed conditions, including the payment of direct taxes, on the " active citizens " who had the right to vote in the primary assemblies, while from the electors who voted directly for the members of the legislature a property qualification was demanded.[1] Already, however, it was beginning to be recognized that genuine popular government must rest on universal suffrage.[2] In the debate of October 20, 1789, on the conditions of "active " citizenship, universal suffrage was demanded by five deputies, of whom Robespierre was one ; and by 1791 Robespierre was definitely leading the campaign against a suffrage based on taxability and on property qualifications. In April, 1791, he published a " Discourse to the National Assembly," in which he proposed a decree for the establishment of universal suffrage ; and, somewhat later, there were demonstrations in the

---

[1] *Camb. Mod. Hist.*, vol. VIII, chap. VII. The Constitution of 1791 " was actually framed for the most part during the last half of 1789 and the early months of 1790." Vaughan, *Contrat Social*, Manchester, 1918, Note B., p. lxvi.

[2] Aulard, *op. cit.*, Part I, chap. I, § VI, p. 25, writes of universal suffrage as " Chose alors [just before the French Revolution] innommée, tant l'idée en était étrangère aux penseurs du XVIII⁰ siècle." He notes, however, that it was demanded, under this name, by English Radicals, from about 1770.

primary assemblies in favour of this principle.[1] So early as 1790, Loustallot, editor of the *Révolutions de Paris*, had suggested that constitutional laws should be ratified by the people in their primary assemblies. "He . . . demanded a democracy with universal suffrage, and he published a regular system of *referendum* . . . for the popular sanction of laws." In June, 1791, the Cordeliers adopted this system, remodelled by René de Girardin. It aimed at controlling the Chamber of Deputies from below rather than from above, by the people, not by an Upper Chamber. "The Senate, in this ideal democratic constitution, would have been the French people."[2] After the flight to Varennes, the advanced democratic Clubs and Societies persistently demanded a national sanction for the laws. The formula of the Club of the Cordeliers was "un gouvernement national, c'est à dire la sanction ou ratification universelle et annuelle." When, after the capture of the royal family, the question arose of what should be done with Louis XVI, 30,000 citizens petitioned the National Assembly to decide nothing concerning the king without consulting the departments ; and other petitions of the same kind followed. A definite attempt was thus made to apply the system of popular *referendum* to the question of the king's fate.[3]

It was not, however, till after the *journée* of

---

[1] Aulard, *op. cit.*, Part I, chap. III, § III, chap. IV, § VI.

[2] *Ibid.*, chap. IV, § I, chap. V, § VII : *Révolutions de Paris,* Nos. XVII, XXXI, XXXVIII. The above account is taken from Aulard's *Hist. Pol. de la Révolution Française,* a valuable authority for this subject, as special stress is laid on parliamentary forms in general, and on plebiscites in particular. M. Aulard points out (Pt. I, chap. IV, § II), that the *fédérés* at the Fête of the Federation on July 14, 1790, were elected by the National Guard, who were practically all "active" citizens, and that these elections were regarded as a kind of plebiscite in favour of the Constitution.

[3] *Ibid.*, Pt. I, chap. V, § VIII.

August 10, 1792, the meeting of the National
Convention on September 21, and the proclamation of the Republic on the following day, that
France really became a democratic State, provided
with adequate machinery for the exercise of
popular government. A decree of August 10
established universal manhood suffrage, with
the one exception of domestic servants, who
were still excluded from " active " citizenship.
Indirect election was retained, with the " two
degrees " of suffrage ; but the triumph of the
democratic party, if not complete, was striking,
and this triumph made it possible to translate
the principle of direct legislation by the people
into immediate political action.

(ii) *The National Convention, 1792.*—On September 22, 1792, the Legislative Assembly,
" bowing before the majesty of the people,"
resigned its authority in the hall of the Tuileries,
where the members of the National Convention
were gathered. This new legislative body,
elected by universal suffrage in the primary
assemblies, claimed to represent the whole nation,
and prepared to establish a constitution based on
liberty and equality. The Convention adjourned
to the Salle du Manège, and there, after some
discussion, issued its first decree : " There can
be no constitution but that which is accepted
by the people."[1]

This decree was itself an amendment to a
previous motion that " there can be no constitution without the ratification of the people
in person" ; and in the course of debate it was
clearly shown that the idea of direct popular
consent was indissolubly connected with the
principle of popular sovereignty. " You have,"
said one speaker, when the decree had been

---

[1] For these debates, *see Moniteur Universel*, Sept., 1792,
and Aulard, A., *Histoire Politique de la Révolution Française.*

accepted, "just consecrated the sovereignty of the people." It was argued that the Convention was not charged with giving the people a constitution, but simply with proposing one to the nation which had created it. Though a member who suggested that the Assembly should never deliberate save in the presence of the people was silenced as out of order, Danton urged that there could be no constitution but that which had been accepted by the majority of the primary assemblies ; while the deputy Lasource emphasized the distinction between constitutional and general laws and particular laws, and insisted that the former were too important to be put into execution until the will of the nation had been formally manifested.

This distinction between the constituent powers and the ordinary legislative functions of the Convention seems to have been recognized in practice. The principle of a direct appeal to the people for the confirmation of laws was accepted for constitutional legislation,[1] and also in cases of territorial annexation, but in the work of ordinary legislation it was not observed.

(iii) *Annexation Plebiscites* : (*a*) *Savoy.*—It was on a question of annexation that the first practical application of the plebiscite occurred. French troops invaded the territories of Savoy and Nice, which formed part of the Kingdom of Sardinia ; and in September, 1792, General Montesquiou, commanding the army of the South, entered Chambéry. "La marche de mon armée est un triomphe," he wrote. "Le peuple des campagnes et celui des villes accourent au-devant de

---

[1] There were early precedents for submitting State Constitutions to the people for ratification in America. Massachusetts rejected a "Frame of Government" in 1778 and adopted a Constitution by this method in 1780. New Hampshire rejected a Constitution by *referendum* in 1779 and ratified one in 1783. *Quarterly Review*, April, 1911, p. 251.

nous. La cocarde tricolore est arborée partout."[1]
The municipal officers met him at the gate of
the city in robes of ceremony, with words of
welcome. On October 14 each commune elected
a deputy, with full powers to decide the fate
of the country in the " National Assembly of
the Allobroges." This Assembly met on October 21
in the cathedral of Chambéry ; and on the following
day the votes of the communes on the question
of union with France were verified. Of the
655 communes comprised in the seven provinces
of Savoy, 580 voted for union ; 70 gave their
deputies unlimited powers ; one voted for an
independent republic ; three were unable to vote
because they were occupied by Sardinian troops,
but they expressed a wish for union ; one alone
appears not to have given an opinion.[2] The
declaration in favour of union with France was
entered in the register, and the Assembly proceeded to decree the abolition of monarchy,
the suppression of feudal rights, of the hated
gabelle, and of the practice of torture, the seizure
of church lands, and the reorganization of municipal bodies and tribunals. As a member of
the National Convention said, the Savoyards
did more in a week than the Constituent Assembly
had done in three years.

On October 29, 1792, four citizens were appointed
by the " Assembly of the Allobroges " as " inter-
preters of the will of the people of Savoy "

---

[1] *Moniteur*, No. 273, Sept. 29, 1792. Letter from
Montesquiou dated from Chambéry, Sept. 22. He is often
said to have entered on Sept. 24. Sorel, *L'Europe et la
Révolution française*, Partie III., chap. II., p. 114 *et seq.*
Heimweh, *Droit de Conquête et Plébiscite*, I. *Les Plébiscites de
la Révolution*, Paris, 1896.

[2] Sorel, *op. cit.*, and Heimweh, *op. cit.*, give 658 communes
and Heimweh omits from this total the three which were
occupied by the Sardinians ; but the above figures are taken
from the *Moniteur* and appear to be correct.

to the National Convention. On November 27, in
the final debate on the question of the union of
Savoy with France, the deputy Grégoire, speaking
in the name of the " Comités de Constitution et
de Diplomatique," raised the question of the right
of separate nations to unite in a single body
politic, only to answer it decisively in the affirmative. Each nation, he said, was sovereign. By
uniting, they did not alienate sovereignty ; they
only agreed to increase the number of individuals
who exercised it collectively. The demand for
union made in the name of the Savoyard nation
was the free and solemn expression of the desire
of nearly the whole of the communes. They
had declared, through the organ of their representatives, that no violence or foreign influence
had directed their opinion Thus the sovereign
had spoken. When Grégoire read the *projet de
décret* on the incorporation of Savoy, only one
member objected. The whole Assembly rose and
showed its opinion by acclamation. The question was put to the vote by rising or remaining
seated. A solitary member rose in opposition.
The President then pronounced the decree :
" The National Convention declares, in the name
of the French people, the union of the *ci-devant*
Savoy with the French Republic." After the
applause had ceased, a deputy proposed to add
to the decree a declaration that the union could
not be regarded as definitive and irrevocable
until it had been ratified by the French people
This amendment was supported by Danton, but
it was rejected on the ground that by a previous
declaration all constituent laws (*lois constitutives*)
of the Republic must of right be submitted to
the ratification of the people, though they might
be provisionally put into execution in cases of
urgency.

On November 29 the Convention formally
adopted articles of incorporation, whereby, in

accordance with the " free and universal wish
of the sovereign people of Savoy," expressed in
the communal assemblies, the proposed union
was accepted ; and Savoy thus became an integral
part of the French Republic, of which it provisionally formed the 84th department, that of Mont
Blanc. The new department was to send ten
deputies to the National Convention ; and
primary electoral assemblies were at once to be
formed, on the French model. On December
24 a letter from the French Commissaries who
had been sent to the " department of Mont
Blanc " was read in the National Convention. It
described in glowing colours the entry of the
Commissaries into Chambéry, with bells ringing,
and cannon firing 84 times in honour of the 84
departments of the Republic.

There seems no reason to doubt that this
enthusiasm was genuine, or that the results of
the plebiscite in Savoy represented the real wishes
of the people. From the first it had been "difficult
to say whether the province had not always been
French." The vote for annexation had been
anticipated in France from the early days of
the occupation. The streets of Chambéry
resounded to the strains of the *Marseillaise* ; and
General Montesquiou said that the people received
him as a brother and a liberator rather than as
an enemy and a conqueror.[1] The French commissary, Dubois-Crancé, who had been sent to
enquire into Montesquiou's conduct of the campaign, was also careful to point out that no sort
of external influence, civil or military, had been
brought to bear on the Savoyard voters. The
communes assembled on their own initiative,
without French instigation ; they expressed their

---

[1] On September 21 Montesquiou wrote : " Il me parait que
les esprits sont disposés à une révolution semblable à la nôtre.
J'ai déjà entendu parler de proposer à la France un 84me
département, ou au moins une république sous sa protection."

own wishes, and sent their own representatives
to Paris.[1]

(b) *Nice.*—The expansion of Revolutionary
France, which was the immediate result of the war
with Austria and Sardinia, led to a formulation
of the policy to be pursued by the Republican
armies towards conquered peoples and occupied
territories. The National Convention renounced
all claim to rights derived from conquest. It
fully recognised the right of self-determination,
though it refused to give military assistance to
nations which retained a monarchical form of
government. " The right of the sword was
replaced by the authority of the plébiscite."[2]
The French generals were allowed to " open the
eyes " of the inhabitants of the countries they
invaded. They might speak to them of liberty, of
the Rights of Man, and of the " eternal principle
of the sovereignty of the people." They might
invite them to break the yoke of the oppressor
and to give themselves laws which should be the
" sacred emanations of their supreme will." But
they might not impose laws on them, or even
suggest that they should adopt French laws, nor
might they in any way interfere with the free
popular choice, or propose any form of government to the people.

On all these points Montesquiou's conduct in
Savoy seems to have been without reproach,
but the behaviour of General Anselme, the com-
mander of the expedition to Nice, caused considerable dissatisfaction On September 29, 1792, he
crossed the river Var, and took the town of Nice
without striking a blow. He then overran the
surrounding country, while the Sardinian troops
retired to the mountains. Serious disorders,
however, followed his occupation. The people

---

[1] *Moniteur*, September to December, 1792, No. 266 *et seq.*
[2] Heimweh, *op. cit. Moniteur, passim.*

appear to have been lawless and turbulent, but
Anselme carried things with a high hand, and,
when he took possession of the County of Nice in
the name of the French nation, he municipalized
it, and gave it administrative tribunals. The
question came up before the National Convention ;
and a proposal was adopted forbidding generals
to take possession of territory, ordering them to
proclaim, on entering a country, that the French
nation declares it liberated from the yoke of its
tyrants, and free to give itself, under the protection of the armies of the Republic, any provisional organization and any form of government
that it pleases.[1] When, on November 4, two
deputies from the provisional administrative bodies
of the town and County of Nice appeared before
the National Convention to demand annexation
to the Republic, their request was refused because
the bodies which they represented had been
arbitrarily formed by General Anselme. " Before
deliberating on the union," said the President of
the Convention, Hérault de Séchelles, " let the
people pronounce, let the sovereign express its
wishes ; and the sovereign is in the primary
assemblies, and nowhere else."[1]

A National Assembly was now formed in Nice,
under the name of " Convention nationale des
Colons marseillais." After copying the Assembly
of the " Allobroges," by pronouncing the deposition
of the King of Sardinia, it convoked the primary
assemblies. They met on December 9 and 15 ;
and the great majority of communes voted for
union with the French Republic. The same
deputies who had asked for annexation in November reappeared before the National Convention on
January 4, 1793, to repeat the request, as the
representatives of the people in Nice. The absorption of the Convention in the trial of Louis XVI

---

[1] *Moniteur, passim* ; Sorel, *op. cit.* ; Heimweh, *op. cit.*

delayed the reply till the end of the month, but on January 31 it was declared unanimously that the Convention, in the name of the French people, accepted the wish expressed by the *ci-devant* County of Nice ; and that, in consequence, it should form an integral part of the territory of the Republic. Under the name of the department of the Alpes Maritimes, it became the 85th department of France ; and the news of the union was received with great joy by the people of Nice, who celebrated it by a solemn *Te Deum*, music and salvoes of artillery, bonfires and illuminations.

In Nice, as in Savoy, the rejoicings were probably sincere enough ; and the French Government showed an honest desire to respect the popular freedom of choice and to check any autocratic tendencies in its officials. On two other occasions, however, when an annexation plebiscite was taken, the Convention appears to have frankly overridden the wishes of a hostile or indifferent majority by means of an " enlightened" and enthusiastic minority.

(c) *Mainz.*—It was obviously to the interests of the Republic to annex the rich and populous districts on the north-eastern and northern frontiers of France, on the Rhine and in the Austrian Netherlands. But here they met with opposition from the inhabitants, and they did not hesitate, while outwardly observing their own principles of action, to interpret them rather in the letter than in the spirit.

In the autumn of 1792 the Republican Army of the Rhine held a long line from Basel to Landau. The small German States were neutral. The towns were largely revolutionary ; the only strong opposition to France was found in the ecclesiastical principalities of Köln, Trier and Mainz.[1] On

---

[1] *Camb. Mod. Hist.*, vol. VIII, chap. XIV, p. 413 *seq.*

October 21, 1792, the French General Custine
entered Mainz, after occupying much of the
surrounding country. There was an enthusiastic
French party in the city, chiefly composed of
" intellectuals," professors, jurists, and other
" noble dreamers " ; but the people in general
were indifferent to Revolutionary ideas, and not
unfavourable to the old *régime*, while Custine's
hauteur and violence and his heavy exactions
intensified their opposition.

On November 19, 1792, the National Convention
had decreed protection to nations struggling for
freedom. On December 15 the famous " Compulsory Liberty Decree " was passed   It imposed
on all the generals of the Republic the duty of
summoning the people of occupied territories to
primary assemblies, to organize a provisional
system of administration and justice. Eligibility
for the vote and for office was conditional on the
written renunciation of all privileges and the
taking of an oath to liberty and equality. French
commissaries were sent to the Rhineland to carry
out this decree. The primary assemblies were
convoked for February, 1793. The electors of
the deputies who were to form a National Assembly
included all citizens of 21 years of age and upwards,
who had taken the civic oath, though only those
over 25 were eligible as deputies. But the mass
of the people refused to vote, or even to take the
civic oath, influenced partly by the clergy, who
forbade their parishioners to take part in the
movement, partly by the dread of Prussian
reprisals.

The French, determined to obtain at all costs
a vote in favour of annexation to the Republic,
now resorted to intimidation and force. Their
chief opponents[1] were deported, and troops were

---

[1] *Moniteur*, No. 91, April 1, 1793. Haussman, the Commissary sent to execute the decree of December 15, at Mainz,
declared before the National Convention that " the aristocratic

called out to escort the electoral commissaries..
The voting dragged on till March 10, and the
" Convention Mayençoise " met a week later. Com-
paratively few localities were represented, but
the Republican section had a majority ; and on
March 18, 1793, a decree was passed deposing the
Emperor and all the sovereign princes between
Landau and Bingen.

On March 21 the Assembly proclaimed the union
of " free Germany " with the French Republic. A
deputation was sent to Paris ; and on March 30,
1793, the National Convention unanimously
decreed that the town of Mainz should form an
integral part of the Republic. This involved the
incorporation of a number of other towns and
communes which were represented in the Rhenish
Convention.[1]

(d) *Belgium.*—The element of compulsion was
still more marked in the annexation of Belgium.
After the French victory of Jemappes, on
November 6, 1792, the " philosopher-general "
Dumouriez overran Belgium with ease, and on
November 14 was received in Brussels as the
deliverer of the country. At Liège the enthusiasm
for France was so great that Dumouriez said it
was a " second French Nation." The French
authorities proclaimed the disinterested nature
of their interference, and assured Belgium that
she need have no fear for her independence. But
the Belgians as a whole were devoted to their
ancient liberties and to their old form of

---

clique " was plotting to prevent the execution of the decree.
The Commissaries stood firm, however, and on March 17 the
Convention Mayençoise met.

"Nous avons été forcés," said the French Commissary
Haussman, " pour soutenir ces mesures, pour déjouer les
agitateurs et les aristocrates, de faire déporter les chefs
connus des complots . . . Cette mesure a été suivie.
d'un entier succès."

[1] Heimweh, *op. cit.* Sorel, *op. cit.* *Moniteur, passim.*.

Government by provincial Estates. The people
cried both " *Vivent les Français* " and " *Vivent
les Etats.*" The priests and the Statists, wrote
Dumouriez, reigned over three-quarters of the
country.

Dumouriez himself, with the more moderate
party, wished to form an independent Batavian
Republic, but the Jacobins were resolved on
annexation. The " Compulsory Liberty " decree
of December 15 practically gave the country
into their hands, and rendered union with France
inevitable. The majority of the municipal administrations, among them the democratic representatives of Brussels, protested vainly against this
decree, as " unjust, oppressive and destructive,
an attack on the sovereignty of the Belgian people,
contrary to the solemn and repeated promises
of the French generals and statesmen." The
Belgians were not even able to form a National
Convention to defend their autonomy. The Revolutionary Clubs prepared the way for annexation
under virtual compulsion. The electors were
directly consulted in each commune, and the
voting was on different dates in the various towns.
Liège, where revolutionary feeling was strong,
led the way with a willing vote for union with
France. But elsewhere coercive measures were
taken to ensure that the voting should be in favour
of union ; and the voters were intimidated by the
clubs and by a show of military force. The
elections were not completed till the beginning of
March, 1793, when the defeat of Neerwinden restored
Belgium to the Austrians. It was not until two
years later, in 1795, that Belgium was at last
declared to be an integral part of the French
Republic.

These four instances illustrate very clearly both
the use and the abuse of the annexation plebiscite
by the Republican Government. When, as in
Savoy, and, in a less degree, in Nice, a verdict

favourable to France was a foregone conclusion, there was no difficulty in maintaining the democratic ideal in all its purity. But, as soon as opposition showed itself, the Convention took legislative action, by the decree of December 15, to force its own conception of liberty on an unwilling people. In the Rhineland, and still more in Belgium, the French annexationists won a favourable vote by coercion. In the Rhineland they worked through the orthodox channels, summoning a National Convention but influencing the popular vote. In Belgium they overrode the ordinary methods of procedure in their own interests, and appealed directly to the people in their local communal assemblies, which could be more easily terrorized than a central National Assembly. But in spite of these changes of method, the principle of the right of peoples to determine their own allegiance was never denied by the Convention. As the writer who calls himself " Heimweh " says :—

> " Plutôt que de répudier la doctrine, elle a faussé l'application. Elle a mieux aimé tourner le principe que le renverser. Aussi bien a-t-elle, par là, rendu à ce principe l'hommage le plus significatif, celui que la paix armée rend à la véritable paix, celui que l'hypocrisie rend à la vertu."[1]

(iv) *Trial of Louis XVI.*—If the exigencies of foreign policy led the Jacobins to a practical disregard of the principles of popular government to which they still paid lip-service, in the important matter of the trial of Louis XVI they frankly rejected the method of direct appeal to the people, which was supported by the Girondins, partly, it would seem, in order to shift responsibility from their own shoulders.

On November 6, 1792, the Committee of twenty-four reported on the evidence which had been collected against the king ; and on November 9 there was a debate in the National Convention

---

[1] Heimweh, *op. cit.*

on the six main points involved in the question
of the king's trial : (1) Could Louis be judged for
the crimes which he was accused of having committed as a constitutional monarch? (2) By whom
ought he to be judged ? (3) Should he be brought
before the ordinary tribunals as a common State
criminal ? (4) Should the right of judging him be
delegated to a tribunal formed by the electoral
assemblies in the departments ? (5) Was it not
more natural that the Convention itself should
judge him ? (6) Was it necessary or suitable to
submit the judgment to the ratification of all the
members of the Republic, united in communal or
primary assemblies ?

It was decided that Louis could be judged,
but it was less easy to determine the method of
trial, and who should be the judges. It was
generally agreed that an extraordinary tribunal
was needed, but there was a difference of opinion
on the constitution of this tribunal. One party
favoured trial by the Convention, another wished
to have a court formed of the whole nation. In
the long debates which followed, Saint-Just and
Robespierre emphasized the political nature of
the question at issue. Louis must be tried as an
enemy rather than as a citizen, his existence being
a constant menace to the State. He must be
condemned to death summarily, in virtue of the
right of·insurrection. The members of the Convention were not judges, but statesmen and
representatives of the nation.[1]

On December 3 it was decreed that Louis.
Capet should be judged by the Convention. On
December 28, after the king's second appearance
at the bar, Robespierre, in a famous speech,.
denounced the proposal that there should be an

---

[1] *Moniteur*, Nos. 312, 313, 314, 319, 320, 322, November 7-9,
14, 15, 17 ; Nos. 340, 341, December 5, 6, 1792 (Robespierre's.
speeches, December 3, 4). Sorel, *op. cit.*, vol. III, livre I,
chap. IV, § I.

appeal to the people. He described such an appeal as " the surest means of rallying all the royalists," and argued that the people's will had already been expressed by the insurrection of the 10th of August " Je ne vois, moi, dans ce prétendu appel au peuple, qu'un appel de ce que le peuple a voulu, de ce que le peuple a fait." He ridiculed the idea of judging the king by " a tribunal composed of 44 particular tribunals." The proposal to submit the affair of Louis Capet to the primary assemblies might lead to civil war ; the Republic was in danger ; and, in the interests of the *salut public*, Robespierre and the Extremists demanded the immediate execution of the king. Even the principle of the sovereignty of the people was here used as an argument against a plebiscite. " C'est se jouer de la majesté du souverain que de lui renvoyer une affaire qu'il nous a chargé de terminer promptement."

In spite of Robespierre's oratory, however, there was a strong feeling in the Convention in favour of referring the definitive judgment in the king's case to the primary assemblies. Vergniaud gave eloquent expression to this feeling in his reply to Robespierre. He defined the sovereignty of the people as the power of legisla-tion, a power exercised either directly or by representation, but inalienable in the sense that the sovereignty always retains an " inherent right " of declaring its will. The people had acted in conformity with these principles, but they had made a distinction between constitutional acts and acts which are purely legislative, regulative, or concerned with the general security. There could be no doubt that constitutional acts, the bases of social organization, ought to be submitted to the formal acceptance of all members of the social body ; whereas purely legislative and regula-tive acts, with those for the general security, might be submitted to a tacit ratification through the delegates of the sovereign people. Every act which emanated from the representatives of the people, however, was an act of tyranny, a usurpation of sovereignty, unless it was submitted to the ratification of the people, either formal or tacit. Tacit ratification was not suitable to the case of the judgment of Louis ; it was a judicial case ; and, in dealing with it, the representatives of the people were combining the functions of accusers, judges and legislators, a dangerous extension of powers which " ends where despotism begins."[1] The people who guaranteed the king's inviolability by individual oaths to maintain the constitution which he accepted, could only withdraw that guarantee by the direct expression of the general will. Vergniaud proceeded to discuss the method to be employed in ascertaining the general will. " You will settle a day for the primary assemblies to meet, you will settle a method of taking the poll. Every citizen will give his vote by placing it in an urn, and every primary assembly will count the votes thus polled. Each primary assembly will send the results to the district, the districts will forward to the department, and the departments to the National Convention, which will proclaim the final result."[2]

It is significant that Vergniaud seems to have assumed that the question of the King's guilt would not be submitted to the primary assemblies, but that they might be asked either to decide the penalty to be inflicted, or to confirm or alter

---

[1] *Moniteur*, Nos. 362, 363, 364, 365, 366, December 27-31, 1792 Sorel, *op. cit* vol. III, livre I, chap. IV, § VI. A motion for a *scrutin épuratoire* had been proposed and withdrawn. This would have referred the name of any deputy to his constituents in the primary assemblies, on the question of the trial of the king, and would, therefore, have been a test of public opinion. *Cf. Camb. Mod. Hist.*, VIII, p. 256 *et seq.* and Voltaire's saying : " A democrat is a potential despot."

[2] *Moniteur*, No. 368, January 2, 1793. Sorel, *ut supra.* *Camb. Mod. Hist., ut supra.*

a penalty already decreed by the Convention. Obviously, much depended on the order in which the three questions of the King's guilt, the penalty and the appeal to the people, were taken ; and by securing that the question of guilt should precede the question of popular appeal, the extreme party in the Convention won a notable victory.

The three questions, then, were put in the following order : (1) Is Louis guilty ? (2) Shall the judgement on him be submitted to the sanction of the people ? (3) What shall be the penalty ? In the session of January 15, 1793, the first two questions were put to the vote. On the first, the question of guilt, Louis was found guilty of treason against the nation, and of attacks on the general safety of the State, by 693 votes, while 26 members either refrained from voting or gave a conditional vote. On the question of an appeal to the people, of the 717 members present, 424 voted against the motion, and only 283 for it, while ten abstained from voting. The motion was therefore lost. The voting on the penalty, a few days later, gave a majority of one for death ; the motion for a respite was defeated ; and on January 21 the King was executed.[1]

In their opposition to that method of a popular appeal which they had formerly supported with ardour, Robespierre and the democratic party were undoubtedly inconsistent. But they were influenced by reasons of State, at a time when the country was at war, and the Republic seemed to be threatened by reactionary forces. It was certainly a tribute to the humanity and moderation of the French people that the politicians who had determined that the King must die

---

[1] *Moniteur*, January, 1793.   Sorel, *ut supra*.   *Camb. Mod. Hist.*, *ut supra*.

were afraid to trust the question of his fate to
the primary assemblies. The principle of the
plebiscite was honoured in its breach ; but, as a
practical administrative expedient, the appeal to
the people stood condemned by the rejection of
the motion for its use in the trial of Louis XVI.

(v) *The Constitution of 1793.*—Whatever might
be the differences of opinion on the plebiscite
as a means of settling such exceptional questions
of policy as the trial and execution of the King,
it was generally agreed that it was the only right
and democratic method of constitutional legislation ; and that, in particular, all new Constitutions
should be subjected to direct popular confirmation.
Though important constitutional changes—the
abolition of monarchy, and the establishment
of the Republic—had been effected without consulting the people, and though a motion of
October 16, 1792, for the submission of the question
of the declaration of the Republic to the people,
had been negatived, these arbitrary measures
could be excused on the plea that the war had
created abnormal conditions. But, so early as
September, 1792, the National Convention had
appointed a Constitutional Committee to frame
a new Constitution, which should give the country
a permanent system of government. This Committee laid the foundations of the Constitution
of 1793, the most democratic constitution that
France has ever known.[1]

Since this Constitution never came into operation,
it may seem to possess only academic interest,
but in the history of the plebiscite as a political
device it is of great importance. Itself ratified
by an appeal to the people, it provided for the
use of the popular vote on laws as an ordinary
instrument of legislation, on somewhat the same
general lines as the modern referendum in

[1] Aulard, *op. cit.*, Pt. I, chap. IV, p. 279 *seq.*

Switzerland.[1] By the circumstances in which it was drafted and the purposes it subserved, it affords moreover an admirable illustration of the way in which political ideals can be utilized by opportunist party leaders to further their own immediate aims.

(a) *The Girondist Scheme.*—As the Constitutional Committee, which had been entrusted with the task of drawing up a scheme for the new Constitution, was of a Girondist complexion,[2] the Jacobins formed an opposition " auxiliary Constitutional Committee," of which Robespierre and St. Just were members. In February, 1793, the Girondist Committee produced their scheme for a Constitution.[3] It began with a Declaration of Rights, which, with the Constitution itself, was founded on the earlier Declaration and Constitution of 1791, though the new scheme was more democratic in character.

Great emphasis was laid throughout on the elective principle, based on universal suffrage. The popular referendum or plebiscite, which the democratic party had long desired, was now definitely organized as the " censure du peuple sur les actes de la représentation nationale."[4] The people were given rights of petition, of criticism and of ratification. Constitutional laws and their reform were to be outside the plenary legislative power of the *Corps Législatif*, while a distinction was made between decrees, which could be executed without the popular sanction, and

---

[1] Lowell, A. Lawrence. *op. cit.*, chap. XII, pp. 245-6.

[2] It included Siéyès, Vergniaud, Condorcet, and also Danton ; there were, it is said, six Girondist members to three Jacobins. *Cf.* Rousseau, *Contrat Social*, ed. Vaughan, Note B, p. lxv *et seq.*

[3] *Moniteur*, No. 49, Feb. 18, 1793 ; *Séance du 16 fév.* Aulard, *op. cit.*, p. 280 *seq.*

[4] *Moniteur, ut supra. Constitution Française*, Titre VIII. *De la censure du peuple sur les actes de la représentation national et du droit de pétition.*

laws, which only became valid if the people did
not oppose them within a given time. Any
citizen, with 50 signatures to back him, might
demand the convocation of this primary assembly
if he wished to propose legislative changes or
reforms. By a somewhat elaborate and lengthy
process of successive reference to larger and larger
political units, a single citizen might thus set
in motion the whole legislative machine and bring
about the revocation of a law, and the resignation
of the Central Legislature. For a revision of
the Constitution, moreover, a National Convention
was to be summoned by the *Corps Législatif*,
" when this had been judged necessary by the
majority of the citizens of the Republic." In
its external relations, too, the Republic was to
annex territories when the inhabitants had freely
expressed a desire to be united to France , and
in dealings with foreign nations the Republic
might only recognize institutions which had been
" guaranteed by the consent of the generality of
the people."[1]

(b) *The Jacobin Scheme.*—The Jacobins raised a
somewhat factious opposition to this scheme ; but,
when the military reverses of the Republican
armies and the treachery of Dumouriez had
created a critical political situation, the work of
Constitution-making was resumed. In June, 1793,
after the fall of the Gironde and the triumph of the
Jacobins, a new constitutional scheme was drafted,
based, like its predecessor, on the principles of
universal suffrage and the sovereignty of the people.

The Declaration of Rights which preceded the
Constitution proper proclaimed that " the
sovereign people is the universality of the French
citizens " ; that each section of the sovereign
assembly ought to enjoy the right of expressing

---

[1] Aulard, *ut supra.* Lavisse et Rambaud, *Histoire
Générale*, vol. VIII, chap. IV, p. 178, *et seq.* (by Aulard).

its will with complete liberty ; and that a people
has the right to review, reform, and change its
constitution.[1] The popular referendum or plebiscite appeared again in this Constitution, though
in a different form from the *censure du peuple* of
the Girondist scheme. The distinction between
decrees issued by the Legislature, and laws proposed by the Legislature and sanctioned by the
people, was retained ; but the popular vote was
organized in a new fashion, and the exercise of
direct legislative power by the primary assemblies
was rendered more difficult. The section of the
Girondist Constitution on the *censure du peuple*
was omitted, but the section of the new Constitution on the " formation of law " provided that,
unless within forty days after a "proposed law "
had been sent down to the communes, in half
the departments *plus* one, a tenth of the primary
assemblies in each department had objected to
the proposal, it would become law. In case of
opposition, the *Corps Législatif* must convoke the
primary assemblies.[2] If, again, in half the
departments *plus* one, a tenth of the primary
assemblies in each department should demand
the revision of the *Acte Constitutionnel*, or an
alteration in any of its articles, the *Corps Législatif*
must convoke the primary assemblies, to decide
whether a National Convention should be summoned. The subjects which were to be treated
by law were enumerated, and also those which

---

[1] *Moniteur*, No. 178, June 27, 1793, gives the Jacobin
Acte Constitutionnel.

[2] In the *projet de constitution* drafted by Hérault de
Séchelles, on which the Constitution of 1793 was based,
the exercise of a *referendum* was rendered much more easy
than in the Constitution as it was finally adopted. The
opposition had only to come from one or more primary
assemblies in ten departments. If they did not protest
within 30 days from the sending down of the proposed law,
the *Corps Législatif* was to accept or reject it definitively.
Aulard, *op. cit.*, pp. 298, 305, note 1.

were to be settled by decree. Among the former
was the declaration of war, a power which the
earlier scheme had vested in the central Legislature,
by making it a matter for decree. In foreign
policy, the Jacobin Constitution substituted the
principle of non-intervention for the annexationist propagandism of the earlier document.

(c) *Plebiscite on the Constitution of* 1793.—On
June 21, 1793, the Convention decreed that in
eight days from the reception of their decree the
Declaration of Rights and the Constitutional
Act should be presented for the acceptance of
the primary assemblies. This meant that the
local plebiscites took place at different times in
different parts of France ; and the results in consequence came in slowly and irregularly. They
gave a large majority in favour of the acceptance
of the Constitution— 1,801,918 votes against
11,610 ; and, as out of 4,944 cantons only 424
seem to have sent in no returns, the Constitution
may be said to have been accepted with practical
unanimity. Though a large number of voters
appear to have failed to record their votes, their
abstention was probably due to carelessness and
ignorance rather than hostility to the new form
of government.[1] In certain departments of
France, moreover, in Corsica, in that part of the
Département du Nord which was occupied by
the enemy, and in the rural communes of la Vendée,
which were in insurrection, the plebiscite could not
be taken at all. The great towns, with the exception of Marseilles, unanimously accepted the
Constitution ; and, among the 40,000 communes
of the Republic, it was said that only one demanded
the restoration of monarchy, while in six departments the voting was solid for the Constitution.

---

[1] This is the opinion of Aulard, *op. cit.*, p. 319. The
above details are mainly derived from his valuable account
of the Constitution of 1793 and of the Girondist scheme, and
from the *Moniteur*.

The votes were taken either verbally or by
ballot, as the individual voter preferred ; and no
primary assembly might prescribe a uniform
method of voting. In each assembly the Constitutional Act was read aloud before its acceptance
was put to the vote. The proceedings; however,
were not uniform throughout the country. In
297 primary assemblies no individual votes were
given, but the Constitution was accepted by
general acclamation. This was the case in most
of the sections of Paris, where the voters adopted
the Constitution with loud applause, and shouts
of " *Vive la République ! Vive la liberté !* "[1]
M. Aulard[2] thinks that the Constitution was
accepted with sincere and spontaneous enthusiasm
by the Republican voters, who, if somewhat
intolerant to their opponents, gave their own
votes freely, without coercion and in a patriotic
spirit. Sone of them even sent in reasons for
their vote ; and in some of the primary assemblies
the Constitution was discussed, and amendments
were proposed.

The Constitution was proclaimed on August 10,
1793 ; and the National Convention ought then
to have appointed a date for the election of the
new National Assembly and the organization of
the new scheme of government. But the Allies
were marching on Paris ; Robespierre proposed
that the Convention should not separate until
the situation was less critical ; fears of counter-
revolution and conspiracy were expressed ; and
on October 10 it was decreed that the provisional
government of France should be " revolutionary
until the peace."

The enforcement of the Constitution of 1793
was thus indefinitely postponed ; and, while
its provisions were never put into force, it became

---

[1] Aulard, *op. cit.*, p. 311, from *Archives Nationales*, bk. II, 23.
[2] *Op. cit.*, p. 312.

in the popular imagination, a name to conjure by,
a " gospel of democracy."[1] It was doubtless,
something of a farce,[2] but it was not altogether
futile from the political point of view, since it
helped to reconcile the rival parties in Paris and
in the departments. The referendum would have
strengthened the local power of the departments ;
and they welcomed it eagerly, and in turn supported the Jacobins against both Royalists and
dispossessed Girondins.

(vi) *The Constitution of Year III* (1795).—The
Constitution of 1793 was finally set aside in the
reaction against the excesses of the Terror which
followed the downfall of the Jacobins in 1794.
In June, 1795, the Constitutional Committee,
which had been busy since April in drawing up a
new Constitution, laid its plans before the Convention. The proposed Constitution, though it was
prefaced by a Declaration of Rights, was frankly
undemocratic ; from its acceptance M. Aulard
dates the beginning of the *bourgeois* Republic
under the Directory which prepared the way for
Bonaparte.[3] Universal suffrage, in this Constitution, was replaced by a qualified franchise, based
on residence and taxability ; and a property
qualification was required from secondary electors.
The *Corps Législatif* was organized on the bi-cameral
system, with a *Conseil des Cinq-Cents* and a *Conseil
des Anciens.* The *Cinq-Cents* had the sole right
of initiating legislation, while the *Anciens* could
veto any measure for one year. The supreme
executive power was vested in the Directory, a
body of five men, appointed by the *Anciens* from
a list prepared by the *Cinq-Cents.* There was no
question of popular voting or of a referendum

---

[1] Aulard, *op. cit.*, pp. 307-8.

[2] Sorel, *op. cit.*, vol. III, p. 426, calls it " *un artifice de
construction destiné à masquer l'inévitable chute de la Révolution
dans la dictature.*"

[3] Aulard, *op. cit.*, pp. 572, 580.

on ordinary laws, but the Constitution itself was to be submitted to a plebiscite, in accordance with precedent.[1]

(a) *The Decrees of* 5 *and* 13 *Fructidor.*—Before this could be carried out, the Convention did much to nullify the practical advantages of the scheme by the " Two Thirds " decrees of Fructidor. On August 22 (5 Fructidor) it was decreed that two-thirds of the members of the existing Convention were to be retained in the new *Corps Législatif* for the first year after its convocation, and one-third for the second year. The right of nominating the two-thirds was, after much discussion, left to the electors in the primary assemblies. On August 30 (13 Fructidor) a second decree provided that the electors in the primary assemblies must nominate the two-thirds before they proceeded to the free election of the remaining third of the members of the *Corps Législatif.*

(b) *Plebiscites on the Constitution and the Decrees.*—It was decided to submit both the acceptance of the Constitution itself and the question of the decrees of Fructidor to the judgment of the people in their primary assemblies ; and plebiscites of the army and navy were also to be taken on the acceptance of the Constitution. The question to be decided by the plebiscites was whether the whole Constitutional Act should be accepted or rejected : and every voter might give his vote in the manner which seemed best to him. The meeting of the assemblies was hurried on, and the results were announced before the full returns had come in. On September 1 the Convention decreed, on the strength of the favourable vote of the " great majority " of the primary assemblies. that the Constitution and the decrees of Fructidor had been accepted, and had become laws of the Republic. A week later, more complete

---

[1] Aulard, *op. cit., Partie* III, chap. I, p. 543 *seq.*

returns were published, which showed that, out of a total of 1,107,368 votes, 1,057,390 had been cast for the acceptance of the Constitution, and only 49,978 for its rejection. The army plebiscite gave 69,567 votes for the Constitution, and 1,449 against it. The navy accepted the Constitution by 3,846 votes against 309. Among the departments which were most hostile to the proposed scheme of government may be noted the Ardennes, and the new Savoyard department of Mont Blanc, while the recently annexed department of Mont Terrible rejected the Constitution altogether by a large majority. The hostile voters, however, were probably rather counter-revolutionary than ardently democratic, for the continuance of the Republic was intimately connected with the establishment of the Constitution ; and, as M. Aulard points out, " in reality the plebiscite on the Constitution was a plebiscite on the Republic, on the Revolution itself, and they emerged victorious from the test."[1]

The plebiscite on the decrees of Fructidor gave less satisfactory results. Out of 314,282 votes, 205,498 were given in favour of the acceptance of the decrees, and 108,784 for their rejection.[2] There was a very large proportion of abstentions, which probably indicated general dissatisfaction at the attempt of the Convention to retain power by the nomination of the " two-thirds." Nineteen departments rejected the decrees altogether ; and in one, the department of Vaucluse, not a single vote was given in their favour. " France regretfully resigned herself to the decrees which retained two-thirds of the *conventionnels*, and willingly accepted

---

[1] Aulard, *op. cit.*, p. 576. *Camb. Mod. Hist.*, VIII, p. 392 *seq.*, p. 487 *seq.*

[2] M. Aulard explains that these figures are incomplete, but they are taken from the only contemporary sources available. The returns are made in a dilatory and inadequate fashion, and many details were probably omitted.

the new Constitution."[1]   If there was less
enthusiasm than in 1793, when the polls were
heavier, this was probably due to the fact that the
political situation had improved, rather than to
any dislike of the *bourgeois* character of the
Constitution. The country was no longer in
danger, and fewer citizens troubled themselves
to register their votes. ·

On September 26, the Constitution of Year III
was proclaimed ; on October 26, a month later,
the National Convention was dissolved ; on
November 3, the Directory was installed in office.

(II) PLEBISCITES OF THE CONSULATE, 1799-1804.

(i) *The Constitution of Year VIII.*—In four
years the Directory, the " bourgeois republic,"
accomplished its work of preparation for the
" plebiscitary republic " of the Consulate. In
1799 (year VIII) the French people were once
more called on to decide by plebiscite the question
of the acceptance or rejection of a new Constitution. It has been said that " a despotism resting
on a plebiscite is quite as natural a form of democracy as a republic "[2] ; and the story of Bonaparte's
rise to absolute power certainly shows with
startling clearness that popular institutions in
themselves are but feeble barriers against the
usurpations of a strong and determined autocracy.
The Constitution of Year VIII (1799) was drawn
up after the *Coup d'Etat* of 18 Brumaire (Nov. 9,
1799), which ended the Directory. It placed
the executive power in the hands of three Consuls,
elected for ten years, and practically made the
First Consul, Napoleon Bonaparte, master of

---

[1] Aulard, *op. cit.*, p. 577.

[2] Lecky, W. E. H., *Democracy and Liberty*, vol. I, chap.
III, p. 256 ; London, 1908.

France.[1] Nominally based on universal suffrage,
it really destroyed it by restricting the rights
of the people in the election of members of the
Legislature to the preparation of lists of " eligibles,"
from which, after successive reductions, the final
appointment was made by a Senate of 60 members.
The legislative power was vested in a *Conseil
d'Etat*, which alone had the right of proposing
laws ; these were afterwards submitted to a *Tribunat* of 100 members and a *Corps Législatif* of
300 members.   The *Tribunat* could discuss legislative proposals and vote their adoption or
rejection ; but the functions of the *Corps Législatif*
were restricted to voting on laws proposed to
it by the *Conseil d'Etat*, and debated before it
by deputies from both the *Conseil* and the *Tribunat*.   The three Consuls were in future to be
elected by the Senate, but in the first instance
they were nominated in the Constitution itself :
Bonaparte as First Consul, and Cambacérès and
Le Brun as his colleagues   The reality of power
was in the hands of the First Consul, who could
promulgate laws, nominate and dismiss the members of the *Conseil d'Etat* and other officials, and
appoint the judges.   It was a dictatorship, thinly
veiled in constitutional forms.

This Constitution, by its 95th Article, was to
be " offered immediately for acceptance by the
French people."[2]   Great efforts were made to
ensure a favourable popular vote.   The primary
assemblies were regarded as non-existent ; and
the votes were taken *per capita*, publicly and in
writing, without the intervention of any assembly,
in order to prevent unwelcome discussions
and the ventilation of inconvenient opinions.
In every commune a poll was opened, and the

---

[1] Aulard, *op. cit.*, p. 701 *seq.*   Cf. *Camb. Mod. Hist.*, VIII,
chap. XXII, p. 665 *seq.*

[2] *Camb. Mod. Hist.* IX, chap. I, pp. 7, 11.

citizens were called on to vote " Oui " or " Non " by signing or " causing to be signed " registers of acceptance and non-acceptance. The voting lasted for more than a month, and was taken at different times in different districts. Thus Bonaparte was able to prepare opinion beforehand in various ways. Long before the plebiscite was completed, by a law of December 23 (3 Nivôse) the new Constitution was put into force, thus strengthening the cause of the Government by enabling the question of acceptance to be presented to the remaining voters as the confirmation of a *fait accompli*. The people were also conciliated by a show of a peace policy both at home and abroad, offers of peace to England and Austria, the pacification of insurgent La Vendée, and measures of clemency towards proscribed political opponents.

This policy had the desired effect. The result of the plebiscite was the acceptance of the Constitution by a large majority. The *Bulletin des Lois* gives the figures as 3,011,007 affirmative, and 1,562 negative votes. Too much must not be made of later attacks on the plebiscite as a mere fraud, unscrupulously worked in the interests of the Government,[1] but it cannot be regarded as in any true sense an expression of the independent will of the people, unless, indeed, it be taken as an expression of their willingness to submit to political servitude.

(ii) *Plebiscite of Year X.*—In 1802, Bonaparte, when the Senate refused to make him Consul for life, determined to " consult the people " on the subject of his position. It was suggested in the *Conseil d'Etat* that two questions should

---

[1] *See* the account by Ch. Conte (*Hist. de la Garde Nationale de Paris,* 1827) of the various ruses employed to swell the lists of affirmative voters. He is, however, a late authority and gives no real proof of his statements. Aulard, *op. cit.,* p. 710, *note* 2.

be laid before the people : the Consulate for life, and the right of the First Consul to name his successor. Finally, the Consuls, " considering that the resolution of the First Consul [to appeal to the nation] is a brilliant homage to the sovereignty of the people, and that the people, consulted on its dearest interests, ought to know no limits but those interests," decreed that the French people should be consulted on the question :— " *Napoléon Bonaparte sera-t-il consul à vie ?*" It was unprecedented that a simple Consular decree should order a plebiscite ; it was rather a *coup d'état*, which was curtly notified to the Senate, the *Corps Législatif* and the *Tribunat*. The *Tribunat* and the *Corps Législatif* accepted, the *fait accompli*, and voted for the life Consulate with only four dissentient voices.[1]

The popular plebiscite was taken on the same lines as its predecessor, by direct open voting. On August 2, 1802 (14 Thermidor Year X), the results were declared in a *Sénatus-consulte*. After having heard the report of its special committee, " charged with verifying the votes given by the French citizens," the Senate, on the report of this committee, stated that out of 3,577,259, citizens who had polled, 3,568,885 had voted that Napoleon Bonaparte should be nominated First Consul for life. It therefore decreed that (1) the French people nominate and the Senate proclaims Napoleon Bonaparte First Consul for life ; (2) a statue of Peace, holding in one hand the laurel of Victory and in the other the decree of the Senate, shall attest to posterity the gratitude of the nation, (3) the Senate shall convey to the First Consul the expression of the confidence, love, and admiration of the French people.[2]

The results of the plebiscite of 1802 were a signal success for Bonaparte. He had polled

---

[1] Aulard, *op. cit.*, *partie* IV, chap. IV, p. 748 *seq.*
[2] *See* Aulard, *op. cit.*, p. 751.

half-a-million more *ayes* than in Year VIII,[1] and
this, apparently, with less conscious and deliberate
manipulation of the constituencies. Such influence as had been brought to bear on the
elections seems to have been of a semi-private
nature ;[2] and the triumph of the First Consul
was probably due, as M. Aulard states, to his
popularity on account of the conclusion of the
Peace of Amiens, to his clemency towards the
Royalists, and to the satisfaction of the clergy with
the Concordat. If, however, he was to a great
extent supported by the reactionary classes in
the State, the more devoted Republicans, with
the *idéologues* or philosophic free thinkers, were
drifting away from him ; and this party seems to
have largely abstained from voting on the Life
Consulate. There was also a small but bold
minority, 8,374 citizens, who voted in the negative, a course which, with an open register and
a public poll, demanded considerable courage.
The army, moreover, is said to have been opposed
to Bonaparte's ambitious schemes. The story
which, if not true, is at least *ben trovato*, is told
of a general who drew up his shoulders and said
to them :—" Comrades, there is a question of
nominating General Bonaparte Consul for Life.
Opinions are free, but I must warn you that the
first of you who does not vote for the Life Consulate will be shot at the head of the regiment."[3]

(iii) *Plebiscite of Year XII.*—Though in 1802
the people were only asked to pronounce on the
question of the Life Consulate, thousands of
voters added to their " *Oui* " the words " Avec le
droit de désigner son successeur." The right of
naming his successor was openly asserted by

---

[1] The number of negative votes had also increased. Cf.
Camb. Mod. Hist., IX, chap. I, p. 22.

[2] *See* Aulard, *op. cit.*, p. 751.

[3] L. S. C. X. de Girardin, *Discours et Opinions*, Paris, 1828,.
III, p. 272. Quoted by Aulard, *op. cit.*, pp. 752-3.

Bonaparte in the *Sénatus-consulte* of 16 Thermidor,
Year X, which is known as the Constitution of
Year X. It needed only one step further to
make the right hereditary,[1] and to enable Napoleon
to give himself a monarchical or imperial title.
This final step was taken in 1804, when the First
Consul of the Republic became Emperor of the
French. The momentous change was affected
by a *Sénatus-consulte*, but the following proposition was submitted to a plebiscite, to be accepted
or rejected by " *Oui* " or " *Non* " :—

"Le peuple veut l'hérédité de la dignité impériale dans la
descendance directe, naturelle, légitime, et adoptive de
Napoléon Bonaparte et dans la descendance directe, naturelle
et légitime, de Joseph Bonaparte et de Louis Bonaparte ; ainsi
qu'il est réglé par le Sénatus-Consulte organique du 28 Floréal
An XII."

This plebiscite was taken by universal suffrage,
in the same form as its predecessors, in May,
1804. There were 3,572,329 affirmative votes
and 2,569 negative votes.[2] In 11 departments
the vote went solid for the Empire ; and it is
reported, though it is hard to believe, that there
were no negative votes in either the army or
the navy. There may here, however, have been
many abstentions. In South-Eastern France, the
former home of Republicanism, the majorities
in favour of Bonaparte were enormous. Such
opposition as existed was probably due to hostile
feeling in recently-annexed departments ; to
the influence of the party among the clergy
which disliked the Concordat ; to the Royalists,
and to the more inflexible Republicans. On
the whole, however, M. Aulard is inclined to see
in the results of the plebiscite a declaration in
favour of the Revolution against the old Bourbon
régime. In any case, the French people had

---

[1] Aulard, *op. cit.*, p. 771 *seq.*, *Camb. Mod. Hist.*, IX,
chap. I, p. 32.

[2] Aulard, *op. cit.*, p. 774 and *note* 5.

abdicated their sovereignty, and resigned themselves to the will of one man.

The events of 1799, of 1802, and of 1804 had created dangerous precedents, 'and had proved the ease with which " a plebiscite vote could be secured and directed by a strong executive, and how useful it might become to screen or to justify usurpation."[1] The experience of 1802 and 1804, in particular, was all the more threatening to popular liberty, because it seemed to show that the more direct was the plebiscitary vote the greater was the triumph of despotism. When the people ceased to vote in their primary assemblies and were dealt with individually by the agents of the central authority, when they registered their votes openly and publicly, an opportunity was given for every kind of illicit influence and terrorism.

(III) PLEBISCITES OF THE SECOND REPUBLIC AND THE SECOND EMPIRE.

(i) 1848. (a) *Election of the Constituent Assembly.*
—Napoleon III was not slow to follow the precedents of the First Republic and the First Empire. It was his use of the plebiscite that made the term familiar, and connected it with the idea of Despotism posing as Liberalism. He has even been described as " a plebiscitic adventurer." During the Second Republic (1848-1852) and the Second Empire (1852-1870) the plebiscite was a favourite political device, more particularly where constitutional changes were concerned ; but it was almost always employed to obtain popular sanction for a step which had already been taken.

The Revolution of February, 1848, substituted direct universal male suffrage for a small privileged electorate, and thus restored the original foundations on which the earlier Revolutionary plebiscites

---

[1] Lecky, *op. cit.*, I, 14.

had been based. All Frenchmen over 21 years
of age were to have a vote ; and all Frenchmen
over 25 were to be eligible for election. Voting
was to be secret, by *scrutin de liste*, according
to departments. On February 26 notice was
given by the Provisional Government that a
plebiscite for the Republic would be held immediately. Both the Ministers and the revolutionary
leaders, however, were afraid of an appeal to
the people ; and the elections for the Constituent
Assembly were postponed till April 23. Early
in May the Provisional Government gave
place to the Constituent Assembly, which passed
the Republican Constitution during September
and October. It was decided to place the executive power in the hands of a President directly
elected by popular universal suffrage.

(*b*) *Election of President of the Republic.*—In
December, 1848, Louis Napoleon Bonaparte was
elected President by a direct universal vote.
He headed the poll with 5,434,226 votes, while his
three opponents polled respectively 1,498,000,
370,000 and 7,910 votes.[1]

(ii) *Plebiscite on the Coup d'Etat*, 1851.—In
the proclamation which heralded the *Coup
d'Etat* of December 2, 1851, Louis Napoleon
announced the dissolution of the Legislative
Assembly,[2] and the restoration of universal suffrage,
which had been seriously restricted by the law of
May 31, 1850, for " rectifying universal suffrage."
The Prince President had at first intended to
submit the question of the approval of the
revolution to a vote *sur des registres ouverts*,
but this method was afterwards altered to *le
scrutin secret.* A plebiscite of the army was taken

---

[1] *Camb. Mod. Hist.* XI, chap. V (Prof. Emile Bourgeois).
E. Lavisse and A. N. Rambaud, *Histoire Générale*, Paris,
(1893-1901), XI, chap. I.

[2] The Legislative Assembly succeeded the Constituent
Assembly in May, 1849.

on December 4, and the general plebiscite
followed. The electors were summoned for the
week ending December 21, to vote on the revision
of the Constitution. A verdict favourable to
the Government was practically secured beforehand by the unscrupulous use of every method
of force or of suggestion. The press was muzzled ;
risings against the *Coup d'Etat* were sternly
suppressed ; and every plausible pretext was
seized for the arrest of members of the Republican
party. Meantime, the minds of the public, even
in the remotest hamlets, were " enlightened "
by " electoral committees composed of honest
men " ; and the *préfets* were instructed to take
measures " for ensuring the free and sincere
expression of the will of the nation." The circular
of December 10, which contained directions for
active propagandism directed towards " winning
the day for the political opinions which had
prompted the *Coup d'Etat*," declared for " liberty
of conscience, but the resolute and consistent
use of every allowable means of influence and
persuasion."[1] One such " allowable means of
influence " is illustrated by the story of the *préfet*
who intimated to the mayor of a small town
that " any negative voting would occasion a
garrison of soldiers."

When the polls were opened, it is probably
true, as de la Gorce asserts, " that ' la liberté
morale du vote n'existait plus.' " The leaders of
the Republican Party were, for the most part, in
prison or in exile ; and those of them who were at
large were too well watched to do more than vote.
The Legitimist leaders advised abstention. The
clergy, as well as the army, were supporters of
Louis Napoleon. In these circumstances it is not
surprising that the general plebiscite gave an
overwhelming majority in favour of the *Coup*

---

[1] *Camb. Mod. Hist.*, *ut supra*. (Prof. Emile Bourgeois.)

d'Etat. The question on the voting paper, to be answered by " *Oui* " or " *Non* " was :—

> " Le peuple veut le maintien de l'autorité de Louis Napoléon Bonaparte et lui délègue les pouvoirs nécessaires pour faire une Constitution sur les bases proposées dans sa proclamation du 2 décembre."

The result, on December 21, 1851, including the army vote, was an affirmative vote of 7,481,280, against a negative vote of 647,292.[1]

Although a verdict obtained under conditions of despotic terrorism cannot be regarded as in anv true sense the expression of the popular will, it would be difficult to prove that the decision was antagonistic to the wishes of the French nation as a whole. The great desire was for peace at home and abroad ; and Louis Napoleon owed much of his success to the weariness of the people and to their hopes of seeing internal tranquility and social order restored under a strong but avowedly pacific autocrat, the " Napoleon of Peace." But the popular will was only called on to approve *les faits accomplis*, and the vote might have been different had there been a real choice.

(iii) *Plebiscite on the Second Empire*, 1852.— Another plebiscite was taken in less than a year after the *Coup d'Etat*, for the re-establishment of the Imperial dignity. On November 6, 1852, a *Sénatus-consulte* restored the Empire, subject to the ratification of a popular vote. The 8th article of this *Sénatus-consulte* provided that :—

> La proposition suivante sera présentée à l'acceptation du peuple français dans les formes déterminés par les décrets des 2 et 4 décembre 1851 : " Le peuple veut l'établissement de la Dignité Impériale dans la personne de Louis Napoléon Bonaparte avec hérédité dans sa descendance directe, légitime ou adoptive, et lui donne le droit de régler l'ordre de succession au trône dans la famille Bonaparte, ainsi qu'il est prévu par le Sénatus-consulte de novembre, 1852."

---

[1] These are the figures given by M. Charles Seignobos, in Lavisse et Rambaud, *op. cit.*, XI, chap. I, p. 35.

It was accordingly decreed :—(1) that the people should be convoked in the communes on November 21 and 22, " pour accepter ou réjeter le projet de plébiscite " contained in the above article ; (2) that all Frenchmen should be eligible for the vote who had attained the age of 21 years, and were in enjoyment of civil and political rights.

The voting took place by *scrutin secret* between 8 a.m. and 6 p.m. on the appointed days. It gave the Emperor an immense majority. The *Moniteur* of November 22, 1852, describes how, in spite of pouring rain, the voters flocked to the poll " to accomplish their civic duty," and how the members of the communes marched to vote with their banners displayed, or raised shouts of *Vive l'Empereur !* The returns came in somewhat slowly, but it soon became evident that the number of votes in favour of the Empire would surpass the total of the affirmative votes which had been given for the *Coup d'Etat.* On November 30, 1852, the *Moniteur* published the following summary of the results of the voting on November 21 and 22, so far as they were then known :—

	Oui.	Non.
For the 86 departments ..	7,488,130	237,244
Army	234,860	8,456
Navy	47,718	2,020
Province of Algeria (civil population)	6,269	869
Totals ..	7,776,977	248,589

There were, however, it is said, 2,062,798 abstentions.

The final totals seem to have reached a slightly higher figure than the results given in the *Moniteur*

at the end of November, though they apparently
fell short of the eight millions of *Ayes* (about half
a million more than had been given for the *Coup
d'Etat*) which had been anticipated.[1] Still Louis
Napoleon might call himself, with some show of
justification, Emperor of the French, " par la
grâce de Dieu et la volonté nationale," and claim
that his reign was " founded on the suffrages of
the People."   " A free secret ballot, open to all,"
said the President of the *Corps Législatif*, in an
official address, " had united eight million wills in
a single will."[2]

The British representative at Paris wrote to
Lord Malmesbury, the Foreign Secretary, on
November 29, that the Navy had voted on this
occasion " in much greater numbers, and much
more favourably for Louis Napoleon," than it
had done in December, 1851. The opposition
had been strongest in Paris, but even there the
affirmative majority was about four to one.
" I am told," he added, " that, however, easily
deception may be practised in the Provinces, it
is next to impossible to falsify the votes at Paris."
But, if the Paris majority in favour of the Empire
represented the true wishes of the people, it is
clear that in the country districts both coercion
and cajolery were used by the Imperial party in
order to procure a favourable decision. Notwithstanding the vast Imperialist majority and the
enthusiasm which the Government organs described as marking the process of voting, so well-
informed a witness as the British representative
at Paris was of opinion that, in point of fact,
" considerable apathy and indifference " had been
exhibited, while the dominant sentiment was
apparently that the Empire was a present necessity,

---

[1] M. Charles Seignobos (Lavisse and Rambaud, *op. cit.*,
XI, p. 36) gives the final figures apparently in round numbers
as 7,839,000, *Oui ;* 253,000, *Non.*

[2] F.O. 940, France, 15 (Dec. 1852). *Moniteur*, Dec. 2, 1852.

and that it furnished an escape from the Republic.
He noted, too, that " every conceivable engine "
had been set in motion to cause electors to make
affirmative use of their votes and that " the
abundance of employment furnished by the new
public works" had " made Imperial converts of
countless numbers of the Red Republican lower
orders."[1]

These charges of undue influence are repeated
by modern historians. " Measures of repression
and intimidations were . . . adopted," writes Prof.
Emile Bourgeois[2] ; " there were appeals from the
head of the State to Conservatives and Catholics
in the provinces, which the President visited
in September ; . . . . there was proscription of
Democrats, and suppression of the Press." In
the chorus of contemporary adulation and con-
gratulation, moreover, there were not wanting
discordant notes. The *Moniteur* of November 15,
1852, published a protest against the Empire
from " La Société de la Révolution," in which
Louis Napoleon is called " le César du guet-apens,"
and the plebiscite is attacked :—" L'exercice de la
souveraineté n'est qu'une abominable trahison et
la plus triste des comédies humaines quand la
liberté ne tient pas les urnes." " Qu'est-ce qui
sort de l'urne ? " asked another Republican
Committee, and answered : " La volonté de M.
Bonaparte. . . M. Bonaparte a les clefs des boîtes
dans sa main, les *Oui* et les *Non* dans sa main,
le vote dans sa main." The French people had
used universal suffrage, the weapon which the
Republic had put into their hands, to destroy the
Republic itself, and once more to resign their
sovereign rights to an Imperial despot.[3]

It was specially in connexion with the events of

---

[1] F.O. 939, France, 12 ; No. 21.
[2] *Camb. Mod. Hist.* XI, chap. I, p. 141.
[3] *Moniteur*, Nov. 26, 1852.

1852 that the term plebiscite, in its modern sense,
came into common use, in official documents, in
journalism, French and English, and in general
literature.   Thus the decree of 1852 for the convocation of the communes referred to " le projet
de plébiscite " contained in the 8th article of the
Sénatus-consulte.   Thus, also, the committee appointed to examine the proposed modification
of the Constitution, in its report to the Senate,
spoke of the popular petitions and acclamations in
favour of the Empire as " presque un plébiscite
anticipé."   Louis Napoleon, wrote Kingslake in
1863,[1] " knew how to strangle a nation in the
night-time with a thing he called a ' Plebiscite.' "

(iv) *Plebiscites of* 1870.—(*a*) *On the Empire*.
Under the " Liberal Empire " (1859-1870) the
discussions in the press, no longer (as in 1851 and
1852) under control, and the debates in the
Legislature, show that the plebiscite as a means of
confirming constitutional changes was losing its
popularity.

In 1860 the *Times*[2] asserted that Napoleon III
was the only man in France who retained any
belief in the utility of the plebiscite as a political
device ;   and in 1869 the *Pall Mall Gazette*[3] called
the " *plebiscitum* " an " outworn and exploded
device."   Prince Jerome Bonaparte himself, speaking in the Senate on September 1, 1869, said :—

"I do not approve of the plebiscite. It has only the
appearance of democracy. It is the legislative power
exercised by the people. Good ! But it seems to me to be,
except in very rare instances, an illusory power. It is
a mistake to take a plebiscite on changes in the Constitution.
If the people approve, the result is an illusion ; if they
disapprove, a revolution. . . . When a plebiscite is taken
. . . on a definite question of peace or war, or on the
cession of a province after a defeat, I admit its utility."

---

[1] Kinglake, *Invasion of the Crimea*, London, 1863-87, I,
XIV, 211.
[2] *Times*, April 4, 1860.
[3] *Pall Mall Gazette*, August 4, 1869.

Nevertheless, France twice resorted to a plebiscite in the eventful year 1870 ; once just before the war with Prussia, and again after the downfall of the Empire.

By a *Sénatus-consulte* of April 20, 1870, important reforms were effected in the French Constitution. The constituent authority was vested in the people, and no change in the Constitution could henceforth be made without a plebiscite. The Emperor, supported by the Senate, was anxious to revive his waning influence, and to re-assert his power by an appeal to the people.[1]

" On April 23, 1870," writes M. Albert Thomas, " the French nation was summoned to declare by plebiscite whether it approved the Liberal reforms effected in the Constitution since 1860 by the Emperor with the concurrence of the chief bodies of the State, and whether it ratified the *Sénatus-consulte* of April 20, 1870."[2] Napoleon III personally urged the people in his summons to vote *Aye*, in order " to avert the peril of revolution," to " establish liberty and order on a firm basis," and to " assure the transmission of the crown to his son." A Central Plebiscitary Committee (*Comité central plébiscitaire*) was formed, to act as the organ of the Autocratic Right against the Democratic and Republican parties. The voting, which took place on May 8, resulted in an Imperial triumph.

There were 7,358,786 affirmative votes, 1,571,939 negative votes, and 1,894,681 abstentions. On the eve of its fall the Empire seemed to have renewed its strength.

(b) *On the Republic.*—Finally, on November 5, 1870, after a rising in Paris, the provisional Government of National Defence obtained a vote of confidence in themselves by a plebiscite taken in

---

[1] *Camb. Mod. Hist.*, XI, chap. XVII, p. 492 *et seq.*
[2] *Camb. Mod. Hist.*, XI, chap. XVII, p. 493.

Paris, in which their action was approved by a large majority : 557,996 *Ayes* against 62,638 *Noes*.[1] This, the last plebiscite taken in France, is chiefly interesting because its purpose was to strengthen the hands of the Government by obtaining the popular approval of their action in the past, a *fait accompli*. With the exception of this Paris vote, the plebiscite in France ended with the Napoleonic Empire, which had discredited it by perverting its use to the service of autocracy.

(v) *General Remarks.*—Of the three main classes of plebiscite,[2] the French, then, during the last century and a half, have almost entirely neglected the plebiscite as a means of ordinary legislation, while they have used the constitutional plebiscite frequently, and the annexation plebiscite with less frequency, under the First Republic and, as is shown below,[3] under the Second Empire and the Third Republic.

In internal politics the people have acted as an extraordinary primary Constituent Assembly, not as an ordinary primary Legislative Assembly. In their constituent capacity they have, as a rule, only exercised functions of ratification or of rejection. They have approved or (rarely) disapproved of *faits accomplis*, changes already made, which they had not initiated and which they were powerless to undo. Even in this limited capacity they have shown themselves liable to be captured by plausible and unscrupulous politicians, and have become the authors of their own subjection.

Nor have the French annexation plebiscites been free from these defects, which have gone far to destroy the political efficacy of the constitutional plebiscites. The early annexation

---

[1] *Camb. Mod. Hist.*, XI, chap. XVII, p. 499.
[2] *See* above, p. 13.   [3] *See* below, pp. 60, 93-105.

plebiscites of the Revolutionary era tended to reflect the growing despotism of Republican partisans, rather than the free will of self-determining nations. With the triumphant assertion by Napoleon Bonaparte of the right of conquest, they came to an end ; and, when democracy revived after the middle of the nineteenth century, the Liberal Empire and the Third Republic saw only two cases of annexation plebiscites in which France was concerned. Italy, rather than France, was the scene of the real trial of the annexation plebiscite as a political expedient ; and, in the only question of territorial cession or annexation to France which was submitted to a plebiscite during the Second Empire, both Italy and France were involved.

(vi) *Plebiscites in Nice and Savoy*, 1860.[1]

(vii) *Plebiscite in Saint-Barthélemy*, 1877.—The last example of a plebiscite taken to sanction a cession of territory occurred in 1877, upon a very small scale. The island of St. Barthélemy, in the Antilles, was a French possession which had been ceded to Sweden in 1784, in return for some commercial privileges. The possession of the island was of small value to Sweden, which had no other interests in that part of the world ; and in 1877, the Swedish Government offered to sell it to France, subject to the consent of the population. The plebiscite resulted in 351 votes for the cession. There were some abstentions, but no votes were cast against the proposal.

No plebiscite was taken on the occasion of the annexation of Madagascar by France in 1886.

---

[1] *See* below, under " Plebiscites in Italy," pp. 93-105.

III.—PLEBISCITES IN ITALY.

(I) HISTORICAL INTRODUCTION.

(i) *Italy after the Congress of Vienna.*—The revolution that gave birth to the present kingdom of Italy had its origin not in a desire for national unity but in a desire for personal and local liberty. Without a nation there can be no desire for national unity ; and, since the fall of the Western Empire, Italy had been not a nation but a nursery of nations,[1] a mere " geographical name."[2] Indeed it is not too much to say that, on the very eve of the Risorgimento, there were in Italy as many nations as there were states ; and the Congress of Vienna, which restored the Bourbons in the south, the Habsburgs in the north and centre, cannot fairly be accused of violating Italian national feeling.

That in little more than half a century the work of the Congress was undone, and a kingdom of Italy embracing the whole peninsula created, was due not to the Restoration but to the reaction that followed it. For both, the chief responsibility lay with Metternich, who negotiated the one and approved, when he did not inspire, the other.

The settlement of 1815 had made Austria the virtual ruler of Italy ; but Metternich realized clearly that Liberalism, which would be fatal to the supremacy of the German minority in the Austrian Empire, would be equally fatal to the supremacy of that Empire in Italy. He therefore adopted in Lombardo-Venetia a policy of un-qualified absolutism, and encouraged the rulers of the other Italian states to do the same.

[1] Sismondi, *Italian Republics*, Introduction, London (1906).
[2] Metternich to Count Dietrichstein, Aug. 2, 1847.

(ii) *Liberal Parties in Italy.* (a) *The Revolutionary Party.*—The intervention of Austria, in order to suppress the risings of 1820-21 and 1831, had a wholly unforeseen effect on the Liberal movement in Italy. Hitherto, the revolutionary party had been composed almost wholly of men who had been ruined by the reaction—officials and officers of the Bonapartist administrations and armies, with a handful of professional men, lawyers, doctors, and writers, and a few nobles, who in their youth had been won by the doctrines of the French Revolution with their insistence on the rights of man. Comparatively few in number, liberty and equality had been their sole aim, secret societies and local insurrections their means. Now they were joined by men of a younger generation, whose inspiration came not from the Revolution but from the rising of the nations against it. These realized, as the older men could not, that Nationalism is the counterpart of Liberalism, and that the rights of nations are the complement of the right of man. To these men, his own contemporaries, Mazzini appealed through " Young Italy," the Society founded by him in, 1831 ; and through his influence " Union and Independence " were added to the " Liberty, Equality, and Fraternity " of the earlier revolutionaries ; the need for concerted, though still secret, action was recognized ; and revolutionary centres were organized and conspiracies set on foot all over Italy for the expulsion of the Austrian and the establishment of United Italy as a Republic.

(b) *National Liberal Party.*—At the same time Austria's intervention roused to action a Liberal party that had been growing up outside the revolutionary societies. Drawn, like them, chiefly from the upper middle classes, but with many more nobles in its ranks and among its leaders, this party derived its inspiration from a very

different source. While French thinkers were
formulating the revolutionary conceptions of a
liberty and equality independent of time and
place, and an inalienable sovereignty of the people
based on reason and the law of nature, German
scholars were reconstituting antiquity and founding
a school of thought in which the rights of men
and of peoples were based not on reason or justice,
but on history.

Thus it came to pass that, while the nations
of Western Europe demanded liberty and equality
in the name of reason, humanity, and justice,
the peoples of Central and Eastern Europe, just
awaking to self-consciousness, demanded liberty
and unity in the name of " history."[1]

Deeply as Italians differed from the Germans
and the Slavs, they could not be unaffected by
these doctrines. For, if French political philo-
sophy, which had its source in the thought of
Roman jurists, had a peculiar fascination for men
who could claim Roman Law as their own, the
appeal to history as justifying a demand for
liberty also had peculiar force for men who held
as their most precious heritage the memory of
the greatness of Rome, of Florence, of Milan,
and of Venice. Consequently, Sismondi, Manzoni
and Capponi easily did for the Italians what
Niebuhr and Gervinus did for the Germans, and
Palacky for the Slavs.

But Renaissance Italy had been a land of
city-states ; and the rise of historical and philo-
logical studies in Italy, while spreading and
intensifying the desire for liberty and reviving
the hatred of the " barbarian " once expressed
by Machiavelli, hindered rather than favoured
the growth of a desire for unity. Therefore,

---

[1] *See* Gooch, G. P., *History and Historians in the Nineteenth
Century*, London, 1913, and Bourgeois, E., *Manuel Historique
de Politique étrangère*, Paris, 1892-1906, Tome III, chap. VI.

as in the case of the party of revolution, it required
the armed intervention of Austria in the affairs
of the Italian states to rouse the party of "historic
liberty" to a recognition of the need for union.
Once this need was recognized, action speedily
followed. The societies for the scientific study
of Italian history, which had long existed at
Florence, Rome, and Turin, were really centres
of Liberalism ; and, when there met at Pisa in
1839 the first of a series of congresses to be held
annually, ostensibly for the " advancement of
natural science," but really for the exchange and
dissemination of Liberal views, the first step was
taken towards the creation of a National Liberal
party in Italy.

(iii) *Relations of the Liberal Parties in Italy.*—
The next step was taken when the Abbé Gioberto,
once a follower of Mazzini but a friend of Manzoni,
published (1843) his *Primato morale e civile
degli Italiani*, followed by Count Balbo's *Speranze
d' Italia* (1844) and d' Azeglio's *Gli Ultimi Casi di
Romagna* (1846). Agreeing with Mazzini in demanding liberty and unity, these writers differed
from him both in the meaning they attached
to these words and in the means by which they
sought their ends. Men are inevitably influenced
by the predilections of their own class ; and the
Genoese lawyer naturally had a more democratic
notion of political, as distinct from personal,
liberty than the Piedmontese nobles and eccles-
iastic. But this was of less consequence than
the fact that Mazzini held in equal distrust all
rulers, native and foreign, and looked to an Italian
Republic as his end, and to conspiracy and insurrection as his means ; whereas the others,
having no grievance against monarchy and
sympathizing with the inveterate municipalism
of their fellow-countrymen, looked to an Italian
League, in which each of the existing states might
retain its identity under its present ruler, as

their end, and to the education of public opinion
as their means. In short, while Mazzini stood
for revolution, the National Liberals stood for
reform along the lines of historical development.

This difference of opinion between the Italian
Liberal parties was fundamental and in the end
almost fatal to their common cause—the freeing
of Italy from foreign rule. For in no one state
did all the Liberals belong to the same party.
The party of revolution was naturally strongest in
the Papal States and the Two Sicilies, where the
administration was intolerable and the tradition
of liberty weak ; and, conversely, the party of
reform was strongest in the northern states,
where the administration was in general tolerable
and the tradition of liberty strong. But, as the
one party had many adherents among the middle
classes of the great cities of the North and Centre,
who distrusted as much as they envied the nobles,
so the other had many adherents among the
upper classes of the South, who feared political
revolution as the prelude to social.

Moreover, the Reformers were themselves
divided. Gioberti's book was an eloquent plea
for a return to the Guelph policy of Julius II and
the unification of Italy as a confederacy under the
headship of the Pope. The suggestion captivated
the Catholic masses and was approved by the
princes ; but it was opposed both to the traditional
Italian belief that the Papacy had ever been the
real obstacle to Italian unity, and to the ambition
of the House of Savoy, which had long cherished
the hope of uniting at least Northern Italy under
its own rule. Balbo, therefore, as became a loyal
subject of the King of Sardinia, while not
rejecting the idea of Papal headship, urged as the
first step towards independence the formation of a
North-Italian Federation under the headship of
his own sovereign ; while d' Azeglio, whose book

was otherwise one long indictment of Papal
misrule, urged that those states whose rulers
proved unwilling to grant constitutional government should annex themselves to Piedmont in
a kingdom of Upper Italy, or, in other words,
should reconstitute the Napoleonic kingdom of
Italy.   This was the idea destined to be realized ;
but, for the moment, its chief effects were, on the
one hand, to turn the thoughts of the Grand-Duke
of Tuscany towards the revival of the kingdom
of Etruria for himself, and on the other to alarm
the Dukes of Parma and Modena and bind them
closer to Austria.

(II) PLEBISCITES OF 1848.

(i) *Events leading thereto.*—It was in the midst
of this ferment of ideas that Cardinal Mastai-
Feretti ascended the Papal throne as Pius IX
(June 1846), and published an amnesty for all
political offenders and suspects.   He was at once
hailed as the ideal head of Gioberti's Italian
League ;   and throughout Italy men sought by
means of popular demonstrations to force their
rulers to grant constitutions and lead their subjects
in a crusade against the hated Austrians.   Metternich's answer was to occupy Ferrara with Austrian
troops and sign treaties of alliance, offensive and
defensive, with the Dukes of Modena (1846) and
Parma (December 1847), meanwhile ignoring the
demand of the nobles of Lombardy and Venetia
for a measure of self-government.   But the other
Italian rulers were not unwilling to fall in with
their subjects' wishes, as the one means of freeing
themselves from Austrian tutelage ;   and a rising
at Palermo on January 12, 1848, was the signal
for a general revolution.   On January 29, the
King of Naples granted a Constitution ;   and his
example was quickly followed by the King of
Sardinia, the Grand-Duke of Tuscany, and the
Pope.

At this moment, when the League of Italian
States seemed on the point of coming into existence,
the whole course of events was changed by the
revolution in Paris, whereby the Second Republic
was established. The upper and wealthier classes
looked upon the fall of the July Monarchy with
dismay, and, out of regard for order and a dread
of the extension to Italy of socialist doctrines,
were ready to give their support to the authorities,
even in Lombardy. On the other hand, the
lawyers and men of letters were ready to hail
any change with satisfaction, provided it involved
the overthrow of the Austrian rule.[1] While the
Reformers were thus hesitating and the Revolutionaries were preparing to act, there arrived
(March 17) the news of Metternich's fall. On
March 18, the Milanese rose, and after five days'
fighting drove out the Austrian garrison ; already
the Republic of St. Mark had been proclaimed
at Venice.

Both risings were the work of the revolutionaries, that is to say, the Republicans ; but
at Milan the leadership was quickly assumed by
the nobles, who at once sought the aid of Piedmont, in order, as they said, to save Lombardy
from becoming a Republic.[2] But Charles Albert
shared the dismay of the upper classes at the
events in France and hesitated to intervene.
By the time he entered Pavia (March 29) the
unity that had hitherto prevailed among the
Lombards had given place to division, the aris-
tocrats desiring that Lombardy and Piedmont
should be united, with Charles Albert for their
sovereign ; the middle classes, including the commercial and literary people, and all the promising

---

[1] Dawkins, Consul at Milan, to Lord Palmerston, March 6,
1848. F.O. Austria, 356, No. 22.

[2] Sir R. Abercrombie to Lord Palmerston, March 20, 1848.
F.O. Sardinia, No. 48.

youth, favouring a Republic.[1] In the circumstances
the Provisional Government, in which both parties
were represented, could do no more than announce
that the wishes of the people would be consulted
on the form of government to be adopted, at the
end of the war with Austria.

Despite this check, the National Liberals went
forward with their plans. The revolution was
carried out in Parma and Modena ; and the
states which had already received constitutions
joined Piedmont in what was now openly a War
of Independence. In Modena, the Duke having
fled, a Provisional Government was set up ; and
the Grand-Duke of Tuscany, whose subjects were
allowed to salute him as King of Etruria,[2] " in
the interests of quiet in his own dominions,"
occupied Massa and Carrara with the aim of
annexing all the Modenese territories.[3] The Duke
of Parma, on the contrary, granted a constitution
which his people accepted ; but renewed agitation
led to a Provisional Government being set up
in Parma also.[4] Meanwhile, the Grand-Duke of
Tuscany declared war on Austria ; while Naples
not only sent troops to Upper Italy to aid in
expelling the Austrians but sent a fleet to the
Adriatic.

At this moment, with independence in sight,
the old municipal rivalries broke out again ;
and even among the parties engaged in supporting
the cause of Italy there appeared a want of
union and a disposition to break up into sections.
The insistence of the Sicilians that their union
with Naples should be personal only, and their
subsequent deposition of the King for refusing
their demand, enabled the latter to suppress the

---

[1] Campbell (vice-consul at Milan) to Abercrombie, March
31, 1848. F.O. Sardinia, No. 44.

[2] Sir G. Hamilton to Lord Palmerston, April 1, 1848 : F.O.
Tuscany, 131, No. 43.

[3] *Ibid.*, March 24, 1848 : F.O. Tuscany, 130, No. 39.

[4] April 16, 1848 : F.O. Sardinia, 41, No. 86.

constitution he had lately granted and to order the return of his army from the seat of war (May 22). All hope of a League of Italian States had in fact already gone when Pius IX, whose favourite scheme it had been, administered the *coup de grace* by the Encyclical of April 29, in which he not only denounced the war but, both as man and as Pope, thenceforth disclaimed all part in the cause of Italy.

(ii) *Plebiscites in North and Central Italy.*—It was in these circumstances that the Lombards and Venetians were roused, by the arrival of Austrian reinforcements (April 22), from their dream of victory already won. The Republicans at once began to talk of appealing to the French Republic for aid ; but the other inhabitants of Lombardy, Venetia, Parma, and Piacenza turned with one accord to the King of Sardinia, praying for annexation to Piedmont. Modena did the same, with the exception of Massa and Carrara, which with Lunigiana turned to the Grand-Duke of Tuscany ; and only Venice, protected by her lagoons, still clung to the republican ideal. The wishes of the people were as clear as their need ; but, in face of the bitter hostility that the Republicans had already shown to union with a monarchic state, none of the Provisional Governments, bound as they were by their undertakings to consult the people on the constitution to be set up, dared to act without the express sanction of those concerned. The most direct way to obtain this sanction, and the surest way of silencing the Republicans, was to imitate the Provisional Government that had just established the Second Republic in France, and to take a plebiscite of the inhabitants of each state on the question of immediate union with Piedmont under Charles Albert as king.

Piacenza led the way, the National Guard demanding that registers should be opened for

the votes of the people on the question of union
with Piedmont, with Lombardy, with the States
of the Church, or with Parma ; and on May 13
it was announced in the Piedmontese Chamber
of Deputies that the Duchy of Piacenza had
formally proclaimed its union with Piedmont,
the numbers being as follows :—[1]

For union with Piedmont   37,000
    ,,   ,,   Lombardy   69
    ,,   ,,   the States of the Church 300
    ,,   ,,   Parma..   10

This example had already been followed by
Parma, where the Provisional Government had
arranged for registers to be opened· in all the
communes of the State in order that the wishes
of the people regarding the future destiny of the
country might be duly ascertained, but with the
view that Parma should form part of a powerful
kingdom under the name of " il Regno d' alta
Italia."[2]

At Modena the movement originated with the
municipal authorities, who addressed their fellow-
countrymen, pointing out the advantages to be
obtained from the formation of a powerful kingdom
to which Modena should belong. This demand
was seconded by the Provisional Government ;
and a register was opened at the palace of the
Municipality for the signatures of all classes.
Parma and Modena, with Reggio, followed Piacenza in voting for union with Piedmont ; but
the Duchies of Massa and Carrara, with Garfagnana
and Lunigiana, voted for union with Tuscany,[3]

---

[1] F.O. Sardinia, 42, No. 110, Turin, May 14, Abercrombie
to Palmerston.
[2] F.O. Tuscany, 131, No. 73, Florence, May 13. 37,250
votes were registered for union with Piedmont. F.O.
Sardinia, 207, No. 162.
[3] F.O. Tuscany, 131, No. 73, Florence, May 15. In April
the Provisional Governments of Massa and Carrara had
determined to elect a Chamber of Deputies by universal

and were accordingly annexed to his dominions by the Grand-Duke on May 18.[1]

Most important of all was the decision of the Provisional Government of Milan to consult the people as to the future form of government to be adopted in Lombardy, in accordance with which a decree was issued on May 12, ordering the immediate opening of registers in every parish throughout Lombardy, in which the votes of the inhabitants were to be recorded with reference to two questions, the one in favour of immediate union with the Sardinian States, the other that the discussion of the constitution should be deferred until the war should be successfully ended. The lists were to be closed on May 29,[2] the anniversary of the Battle of Legnano (1176). Clear directions were given in the decree[3] as to who should vote, and how. Every man of the age of 21 years had the right to subscribe, in the register of the parish in which he lived, his name, his age and the names of his parents, the illiterate making a cross in the presence of the parish priest and two delegates chosen by the Communal Council, preferably from among its own members, who were to superintend the signing of the Register. When closed, the registers, sealed by the parish priest, were to be sent by the Communal Deputations and the Municipal Congregations to the Provincial Congregation, which would count the registers in the presence of the Bishop, or his representative, and a Government Commissary ; and the count should then be sealed like a *procès-verbal* and sent to the Government, which should announce the result at once, a majority of

---

suffrage to decide on the fate of the duchies (F.O. Tuscany, 131, No. 54, April 17, 1848), but they abandoned this for the plebiscite.

[1] *Ibid.*, No. 74, Florence, May 18.

[2] F.O. Sardinia, 42, No. 110, May 14, 1848.

[3] Published as a supplement to *Risorgimento*, No. 117.

subscriptions constituting the vote of the nation.
Special provision was made for citizens serving
with the army, who were to subscribe, in the presence of their superior officer, a register to be
opened in each command ; also for Mantua, then
in the hands of Radetsky, and for the mainland
provinces of Venetia, whose votes were to be
collected by the Government Commissioners sent
to help them.

Of the result of the plebiscite thus taken, there
was never any doubt.[1] From the beginning, the
lower classes had regarded the war against the
Austrians as holy, since it was sanctioned by their
beloved Pio Nono ;[2] and, although his Encyclical
made some hesitate, it had less effect in Lombardy
than in any other Italian state, owing to the
secular jealousy between Milan and Rome.[3] The
middle classes were more doubtful, owing to their
republicanism ; but they were not unaffected by
the nationalist literature that had been smuggled
in from Piedmont, Switzerland, and Romagna,
long before the war began,[4] and by the Piedmontese agents who had been at work among
them. The Provisional Government also took
special pains to secure their vote by coupling with
the declaration for union with Piedmont, not only
a statement that it was for the sake of freeing
Lombardy and Italy from the stranger, but also
an announcement that in the united states there
was to be convoked a Constituent Assembly chosen
by universal suffrage which should discus and
establish the basis and form of a new constitutional monarchy under the dynasty of Savoy.
This clause is said to have been the work of the

---

[1] F.O. Sardinia, 42, No. 110, Turin, May 14.
[2] Campbell to Palmerston, April 4, 1848 ; F.O. Austria,
358, Milan.
[3] *Ibid.*
[4] Consul Dawkins to Palmerston, Milan, Jan. 5, 1848 ;
F.O. 120 Bundle, 649.

Genoese members of the Sardinian Cabinet who, desiring union with Lombardy at all costs, in order to obtain a larger market for Genoa, came to terms with both the Ultra-Liberal and the Milanese parties for a new constitution which would thus come from the people, not from the king ; and, though it was not generally approved by the Piedmontese, who feared absorption by Lombardy, nor by the aristocratic Milanese, who feared that the issue would be a Democratic Monarchy or even a Republic,[1] the event proved the wisdom of its authors. For, although Mazzini issued a violent proclamation against the plebiscite, it had no effect beyond stirring the Milanese mob to demand the indissolubility of the National Guard as then established, the right of association, the liberty of the Press, and the Constituent Assembly, all of which were granted.[2]

Such of the Republicans as did not vote for union with Piedmont and a Constituent Assembly, which might establish an Italian Republic, either voted for deferring the question to the end of the war or abstained from voting altogether, as did the few adherents of Austria. Those who took either of these courses were astonishingly few. In Milan, where 132,882 persons were entitled to vote, only 228 voted for deferring the decision, and 2,614 abstained ; in Brescia, the numbers were 35 and 3,278 out of 88,644 ; and in Pavia 9 and 1,604 out of 38,173, the percentage of abstentions being 1·9, 3·7 and 4·2 respectively.[3]

Opponents of the House of Savoy have sought to lessen the significance of these figures by asserting that forgery, pressure and coercion were freely used to obtain them ; but even they have to

---

[1] F.O. Sardinia, 42, No. 140, June 12, 1848.
[2] F.O. Austria, 358. Campbell to Palmerston, May 28, 1848. It was rumoured that this outburst was due to Austrian intrigue, and it is not unlikely (*Times*, June 10, 1848).
[3] F.O. Sardinia, 42, No. 133, June 9, 1848.

admit that, when every allowance is made for the
use of unworthy arts, there must have been among
the Lombards an overwhelming desire to escape
from Austrian rule at any cost, such as might well
lead the Republicans to accept in all honesty
and honour the compromise of a Constituent
Assembly.[1] Whatever the determining causes, it
was made known on June 8, that in Lombardy
561,000 votes had been cast for immediate union
with Piedmont against 625 for deferring the
question.[2] Two days later the agreement between
the King of Sardinia and the Provisional Government of Milan was signed and sealed, and sent to
Turin for the Chambers to ratify.

The reasons that moved the Lombards to union
with Piedmont were still more strongly felt by the
Venetians of the mainland. Even before the
Austrian advance began, the feeling in the principal
towns was unfavourable to Venice and indisposed
to acknowledge her supremacy ;[3] and, after the
fall of Udine, it became daily more hostile to the
reconstruction of the Republic of Venice.[4] The
only alternative was union with Piedmont ; and,
while the Lombard plebiscite was being taken,
another was taken in Padua, Vicenza, Treviso,
and Rovigo. Then, on May 31, the deputies of
the Departmental Committees of these provinces
addressed a letter to the Provisional Government

---

[1] The best proof that the plebiscites represented the real
wishes of the people at the moment lies in the facts that the
Republicans, aware that they were but a small minority, were
afterwards strongly opposed to this mode of ascertaining the
wishes of the people ; and that, as Manin had proclaimed the
Republic of Venice without seeking ratification by plebiscite,
so the Republics afterwards proclaimed in Tuscany and at
Rome (Feb., 1849) were not established by plebiscite but by
constituent assemblies elected by universal suffrage.

[2] F.O. Sardinia 42, No. 134.   Finali, in *Le Marche*, gives
the figures as 561,002 and 681.

[3] F.O. Austria, 356, No. 56, Venice, April 20, 1848.

[4] *Ibid.*, No. 59, April 28.

of the Venetian Republic informing it of what
had been done and why, and calling upon it to
follow their example without delay, threatening in
case of non-compliance to separate themselves
completely from Venice and to establish a new
centre of government on the mainland.[1]

In Venice the Republican Party was still fairly
strong, or at all events loud, but it was confined
to the lawyers, led by Manin, and the classes
who had money to make or none to lose.[2] The
greater part of the upper and middle classes,
with the whole of the Navy, were in favour of
a junction with Piedmont rather than the continuance of a Republican Government.[3] The
Provisional Government, therefore, sought to
temporize by issuing two decrees on June 3.
One announced the convocation of the Assembly
on June 18 for the purpose of deliberating (*a*)
whether the question relative to the present
condition of the country should be decided
then or at the end of the war ; (*b*) whether in
the event of an immediate decision being agreed
upon, it would be expedient to form an independent state or to unite with Piedmont; (*c*) whether
the members of the Provisional Government should
be changed or confirmed.   The other decree
provided for the electoral qualifications, according
to which all male persons who had attained the
age of 21 years had a right of voting, and all
persons who had attained the age of 25 years
were eligible as deputies, who were to be chosen
in the proportion of one for 2,000 inhabitants.[4]
The mainland provinces, however, were in no way
satisfied with this device—their situation was too
desperate ; and the law declaring the formal
annexation of Lombardy to the State of Charles

---

[1] F.O. 120, Bundle 649, Venice, June 4. Dawkins to
Palmerston.

[2] *Ibid.*, May 30.   Dawkins to Ponsonby.

[3] *Ibid.*, June 2.   [4] *Ibid.*

Albert, which was laid before the Sardinian Parliament on June 15, also announced the annexation of the four Venetian Provinces.[1]

The reply of the Republicans was to postpone the Assembly to July 3 and to call upon those inhabitants of Venice who were in favour of applying to the French Republic for succour to inscribe their names in registers opened for that purpose (June 13).[2] Wiser counsels, however, prevailed ; and on July 4 the Venetian Assembly, at the instance of Manin himself, voted by 130 votes against 3 for immediate decision and by 127 votes against 6 for immediate fusion with the Sardinian States, on the same conditions as Lombardy and almost in the same words.[3] The decision was generally approved, the nobles hoping that their birth might procure them that distinction under a monarchy, which their talents would never have earned for them under the Republic ; the middle classes realizing that it would have been impossible to maintain independence under the Republic, the mainland provinces being lost ; and the lower classes having been gained by money freely spent among them.[4]

The people of Piacenza, Parma, Modena, Lombardy, and Venice having thus expressed their desire for fusion with Piedmont—all, save the city of Venice, by plebiscite—it remained only for the Sardinian Parliament to consent to the annexations. This was done by 134 votes to one ; and on July 27 was completed the union of Piedmont, the Duchies, Lombardy, and Venetia in a kingdom of Upper Italy under the House of Savoy.[5] But on July 25 Charles Albert was defeated at Custozza and again on August 4

---

[1] F.O. Sardinia, 42, No. 143, Turin, June 15, 1848.
[2] F.O. Austria, 356, No. 87, Venice, June 14.
[3] F.O. Austria, 357, No. 25, Venice, July 5.
[4] *Ibid.*
[5] F.O. Sardinia, 42, No. 166.

before Milan, so that he was glad to obtain the
armistice of Salasco, which restored the *status quo
ante bellum* except in lagoon-defended Venice,
which was to hold out under a restored Republican
Government for over a year. The kingdom of
Upper Italy, created by plebiscite, had lasted
just a fortnight.

(III) PLEBISCITES OF 1860.

(i) *The Plebiscites in Central Italy.* (*a*) *Events
leading thereto.*—The state of Italy in 1860 was in
many respects very different from what it had been
in 1848. Whatever chance there once may have
been of uniting Italy as a Confederation of
Sovereign States under the presidency of the
Pope had passed away for ever ; for the Italian
princes, including Pio Nono, had reverted to
absolutism and alliance with Austria. Only Victor
Emmanuel, raised to the Sardinian throne by
his father's abdication (March 23, 1849), had
refused to revoke the constitution of 1848 ; and,
under the guidance of Cavour, Sardinia had
become the one liberal and national state in
Italy. Republicanism, too, had been discredited
by the failure of the Republics of Venice, Rome,
and Tuscany ; and Mazzini's influence had been
undermined by various causes. Liberals of all
shades of opinion had at length come to see, not
only that without union Italy could never be
free, but also that neither unity nor freedom
could be attained save through the House of
Savoy. Nevertheless, there remained a considerable difference of opinion between the two
wings of the Nationalist party as to the exact
extent and nature of the union to be effected
between the several states. The members of
the National Society (founded by three leading
Mazzinians[1] in 1857). who were drawn chiefly

---

[1] Pallavacino, La Farina, and Garibaldi.

from the lower middle classes of the towns,
advocated the formation of a unitary state by
the fusion of all the other states with Piedmont.
But, apart from her government and her army,
Piedmont compared unfavourably with the other
states.[1] So the National Liberals, who were
drawn chiefly from the upper and middle classes,
had no desire for the union of their own states
with Piedmont unless they were to form parts of
a strong Italian kingdom which might rank in
amount of population and importance with the
Great European Powers ;[2] and even then they
advocated, not annexation *to* Piedmont, but a
union *with* her of all the states of Northern and
Central Italy into one kingdom in which equal
rights would be reserved to each part.[3] So
strong, in fact, was the municipalism of the
Italians that it may safely be asserted that nothing
but the fear of foreign intervention could ever
have induced the peoples of Central and Southern
Italy to accept unconditional annexation to
Piedmont.[4]

Yet without foreign intervention Italy had no
chance of winning freedom and union. Cavour
therefore sought and found an ally in France,
the traditional enemy of Austria. But Napoleon
III, ready as he was to help the King of Sardinia
to tear up the treaties of 1815 and to turn the
Austrians out of the peninsula, was not ready to
help him to become King of a united Italy. So
the agreement for an offensive and defensive
alliance against Austria, arrived at between the
Emperor and Cavour at Plombières (July 21,
1858),[5] gave to Sardinia Lombardy, Venetia,

---

[1] F.O. Tuscany, 213, No. 23 ; Jan. 19, 1860.
[2] F.O. Tuscany, 206, No. 93 ; Aug. 1, 1859.
[3] F.O. Tuscany, 207, No. 144 ; Scarlett to Lord John
Russell, Sept. 25, 1859 ; *cf. ibid.*, 213, No. 23 ; Jan. 19, 1860.
[4] F.O. Tuscany, 207, No. 129 ; Sept. 4, 1859.
[5] *Cavour, Lettere*, ed. L. Chiala, Turin, 1913, etc., iii, pp. I, ff.

Romagna, Parma and Modena, but stipulated
that Tuscany and Umbria should form an independent kingdom of Etruria ; that Rome and
the Comarca Province should remain under Papal
rule ; that Naples—where Napoleon expected a
Muratist rising to follow the downfall of Austria—
should be left to herself ; and that the four states
thus constituted should form an Italian Confederation under the presidency of the Pope. In compensation, Savoy was to be ceded to France.

The preparations for war were not yet complete
when Europe took alarm. England, although she
sympathized with Italian liberalism, was not
prepared to weaken Austria, her traditional ally,
by furthering a union with Italy which must in
any case embarass her own position as a Mediterranean Power, unless she were forced to it
by the fear of seeing French influence replace
Austrian in the peninsula. She, therefore, offered
her mediation, while Russia proposed that the
Italian question should be submitted to a Congress
of the Powers. France approved this course, and
Napoleon III had to endorse it. At the last
moment, however, Austria, bent on settling the
Italian question once for all and in her own way,
sent an ultimatum to Sardinia (April 23, 1859),
requiring her to disarm at once. Three days
later her troops entered Piedmont ; and on May 3
France declared war on Austria.

The campaign that followed was very short.
At Magenta Lombardy was wrested from the
Austrians ; at Solferino their effort to regain it
was defeated ; and at Villafranca Napoleon III,
without consulting his ally, signed an armistice
(July 8) and a preliminary treaty of peace (July 11)[1]
by which an Italian Confederation under the
presidency of the Pope was to be created ; Lombardy, except the fortresses of Mantua and

---

[1] Hertslet, *Map of Europe by Treaty*, London, 1875, ii,
No. 298.

Peschiera, was to be ceded to the Emperor of the French, who should present it to the King of Sardinia ; Venetia, remaining subject to the Emperor of Austria, was to form part of the Italian Confederation ; the Grand-Duke of Tuscany and the Duke of Modena were to be restored,[1] on condition of granting a general amnesty ; and the Holy Father was to be requested to introduce in his States some indispensable reforms.

This abrupt conclusion of hostilities was certainly justified by the military situation ; but the Emperor's decision to make peace at once was also influenced by a well-founded fear that he could no longer control the national movement in Italy in the interest of either France or the Pope. In accordance with the plans made at Plombières the outbreak of war had been the signal for revolution in Central Italy. The very day the Austrians entered Piedmont the •Florentines rose, demanding that the Grand Duke should either make an offensive and defensive alliance with Sardinia against Austria or abdicate. He refused to do either, and left the country ; whereupon a Provisional Government was set up, which at once offered the dictatorship of Tuscany to Victor Emmanuel during the war.[2] Elsewhere, the revolution at first hung fire ; but after Magenta the Duchess of Parma and the Duke of Modena also fled,[3] and Provisional Governments were set up in both duchies as well as in Romagna, which ˉ at once proclaimed Victor Emmanuel King of Italy (June 12). At the same time the sovereignty of Tuscany was offered to him by the Provisional Government, Prince

---

[1] In the final Treaty of Zürich (November 10, 1859), their rights were reserved for the consideration of the two Emperors ; Hertslet, *op. cit.* No. 301.

[2] As France had not yet entered the war, the King would accept a Protectorate only.

[3] On June 9 and 12 respectively.

Napoleon having tacitly declined it by advising the
incorporation of the Grand-Duchy with Sardinia,.
preparatory to the union of all Italy under the
House of Savoy.[1] The Prince's views, however,.
were by no means those of the Emperor ; and.
owing to the latter's attitude, Victor Emmanuel
had to refuse the offer.[2]

To the Nationalists, who had been confident
that the end of the war would see Italy united
as well as free, the truce of Villafranca was a
crushing blow. Yet, in truth, it was to this
betrayal, as they deemed it, that they were to.
owe the fulfilment of their hopes.[3]

The unanimity of the movement for union.
with Piedmont had been apparent rather than
real. The revolutions had been the work of the
National Society, and the policy of the Provisional Governments had been inspired by it ;[4]
but at bottom the risings had been neither.
nationalist nor liberal, but simply anti-Austrian.
So long, therefore, as there was any hope of
driving the Austrians out of Italy altogether,
many inhabitants of the duchies were quite
ready to take back their late rulers, believing that,
when they could no longer count on the aid of
Austria, they would be disposed to adhere to a
liberal form of government.[5] In fact, in the

---

[1] F.O. Tuscany, 205, No. 134 ; Scarlett to Malmesbury
May 26, 1859.

[2] F.O. Tuscany, 206, No. 18 ; July 5, 1859.

[3] Cavour, *op. cit.* III, Lett. dccxxxvi.

[4] On March 1, 1859, Garibaldi, as vice-president of the
National Italian Society, gave his instructions to the chiefs
in the several provinces to revolt with the cry of " Long live
Italy and Victor Emanuel ! Out with the Austrians ! "
as soon as war began between Austria and Piedmont. When
the revolution was complete, a Provincial Commissioner was
to be appointed, and all clubs and all newspapers except an
official one to be forbidden. *Further correspondence concerning
the affairs of Italy,* 1859, No. 51.

[5] F.O. Tuscany, 213, No. 5 ; Jan. 4, 1860.

spring of 1859, the old Republican party was almost alone in desiring the union of the duchies with Piedmont ;[1] and it was not till Prince Napoleon had tacitly refused to be King of Etruria, and the Dukes had made their restoration impossible by appearing in the Austrian ranks at Solferino, that the movement for union with Piedmont gained much ground in the country at large.[2] Even so, it was only union with, not annexation to, Piedmont that was desired.

The signature of the Preliminaries of Villafranca entirely changed the state of feeling in Central Italy. That agreement left the Austrians in possession of Venetia, and promised restoration to the recently dethroned princes without reference to the wishes of their late subjects. Even if resentment at what was universally regarded as the French Emperor's treachery had not urged the Italians to thwart his plans, the fear that their late rulers would be brought back by the aid of foreign bayonets, and that there would be no amnesty for those compromised by the revolution, was strong enough to reconcile the upper and middle classes to the union of the Central Italian states with Piedmont, the only Power upon whom they could rely for assistance against the threatened restoration.[3]

Realizing that the Italian cause was doomed unless they could oppose to the will of the Emperors the will of the Italian people, the Provisional Governments were quick to take advantage of the sudden change in public feeling. Within a week of Villafranca the Electoral Law of 1848 had been re-established in Tuscany (July 14) ; and a National Assembly had been summoned, which, unanimously and without discussion, voted by ballot, that the dynasty of Lorraine should not be recalled,

---

[1] F.O. Tuscany, 205, No. 182 ; June 27, 1859.
[2] F.O. Tuscany, 207, No. 129 ; Sept. 4, 1859.
[3] *Ibid.*

and that the Grand-Duchy should form part of a constitutional kingdom under the sceptre of King Victor Emmanuel (August 20). In Parma and Modena the Provisional Governments at the outset followed the precedent of 1848 and ordered (July 16) that registers should be opened for voting by signature on the question of union with Piedmont. But, when the voting proved satisfactory—over 90,000 votes in Modena, over 63,000 in Parma, being inscribed for union with Piedmont—the Modenese Government summoned a National Assembly, which voted unanimously, first that the Duke of Modena was deposed, and then that the Modenese Provinces should be annexed to " the constitutional kingdom of the glorious House of Savoy under the sceptre of the magnanimous King Victor Emmanuel " (August 21). Shortly afterwards National Assemblies were likewise summoned in Parma and Romagna, which adopted the Modenese formula without change, the one on August 27, the other on September 10.

It was afterwards alleged that terrorism had been so freely used in the elections that the votes of the Assemblies in favour of union with Piedmont did not truly represent the national wish. It is true that Italian statesmen of that day had little respect for minorities, and were indisposed to tolerate even legitimate opposition[1] ; but there is little evidence that intimidation was resorted to during the elections. Indeed, there was little need for it, because all organized opposition had long since been made impossible, and most of the chief advocates of restoration had already left

---

[1] F.O. Tuscany, 213, No. 7, a confidential letter from Scarlett to Lord John Russell, Jan. 5, 1860. A passage in the *Souvenirs Historiques* (Turin, 1884) of the Marchioness Costanza d'Azeglio is significant. It runs :—" 16 Jan., 1860. On intrigue énormément dans les Duchés. Le Duc de Modène y dépense beaucoup d'argent, et Farini fait un peu trop le satrape ; en Toscane Bettino Bey (Ricasoli) fait de l'absolutisme."

the country.[1] When the elections took place, therefore, the opponents of union with Piedmont either obeyed the exhortations of the clergy and abstained from voting,[2] or voted in favour of a policy they disapproved.[3] It was a more valid objection that the franchise was too narrow, the whole of the peasants, for instance, being excluded, and that the Assemblies represented a minority.[4] Against this, however, must be set the facts that in Italy political life had always been confined to the towns ; and that the Assemblies, representing as they certainly did a majority of the upper and middle classes, represented the most intelligent part of the community.

That the union of the Central Italian States with Piedmont did not at once follow the vote of the Assemblies in its favour was due in the first instance to the attitude of France.

Napoleon III was very unwilling to admit that his Italian policy had failed ; and, although he would not allow the Central Italian States to be

---

[1] F.O. Tuscany, 206, No. 91 ; July 31, 1859. In the *Times* of August 10 there appeared one striking bit of news :— " In a public café (in Parma), the Café Violi, a list is now open, the subscribers of which bind themselves to shoot or stab any person who ventures to propose or in any manner to abet and promote the Duchess's restoration, the leaders being the men who murdered the Duke in 1854." We are not told how many subscribed this list, but the fact that the Government allowed it to be opened is eloquent.

[2] Of 1,200 priests in Florence, only 15 went to the poll ; F.O. Tuscany, 206, No. 100 ; Aug. 10, 1859. *Cf. ibid.*, 213, No. 30 ; Feb. 1, 1860.

[3] F.O. Tuscany, 207, No. 129 ; Sept. 4, 1859.

[4] In Tuscany, for example, in a population of 1,806,990 souls, 900,000, or nearly half, were males, but only those of 25 years of age had a vote, and the property qualification —payment of 10 Tuscan lire ($8\frac{1}{2}$ francs) of personal tax, or 30 lire (25 francs) of property tax—further reduced the number of electors to 68,311, of whom only 35,240, or 1·9 per cent. of the total population voted. *L'Assemblea Toscana* (Florence, 1859), by Leopoldo Galeotti, one of the Liberal Deputies.

coerced into taking back their former rules, since
that would benefit Austria only, he would not allow
Victor Emmanuel to accept their renewed offers
of the kingship.   At this moment Great Britain
intervened. She had watched with growing uneasi-
ness the progress of the War of Liberation, and
now took advantage of the situation created by
the Treaty of Villafranca to put herself in France's
place as the friend of Italy. Encouraged by
Palmerston to confront the Emperor and Europe
with a kingdom of Upper Italy as an accomplished
fact, Victor Emmanuel renewed negotiations with
the Governments of the Central States ; and just
before peace was formally concluded at Zürich
(November 10), the Assemblies of Romagna,
Modena, Tuscany, and Parma elected Prince
Eugene of Savoy-Carignano as Regent of the
Provinces of Central Italy.[1] This time the offer
was accepted, although the Prince did not take
up the regency in person but delegated his authority
to Boncompagni, formerly Sardinian Minister at
Florence.

Even then the Emperor did not give up all
hope that the formation of too strong a kingdom
of Italy might yet be prevented by the maintenance of Tuscany as a separate state. He was well
aware that the difference in the resolutions adopted
by the Assemblies in August reflected a real
difference of opinion between Tuscany and the
other states ; and that, as the fear of foreign
intervention declined, the desire for autonomy
had revived in Tuscany, and disunion had appeared
in Central Italy. The other states, having voted
for annexation to Piedmont, had hastened to
adopt her laws wholesale, and to abolish their
separate administrations in favour of a single
administration modelled on hers ; but Tuscany,

---

[1] This course had been approved by Palmerston in
September. (*Lettere di Cavour*, Turin, 1863-87, III, p. ccxliv,
note (2)).

although she joined her neighbours in a Military League, steadily opposed every measure that seemed to endanger her autonomy,[1] and, even when she had agreed to the appointment of one Regent for the four provinces, insisted that the Governments should remain unchanged under Boncompagni as Governor-General of the League of the Provinces of Central Italy.

Tuscan opposition to annexation was stiffened by the Piedmontese policy pursued in Lombardy by the Government of Turin ; and it is hard to say what the issue might have been, had not the formation of the Governments of Parma, Modena, and Romagna into the Government of the Royal Provinces of Emilia, as from January 1, 1860, at last convinced all but the most obstinate municipalists that Tuscany would never have the augmentation of territory without which she could not continue to stand alone, and so reconciled them to the annexation of all Central Italy to Piedmont and the formation of a kingdom able to make itself respected.

By this time, too, Napoleon III had realized that he could not prevent the union of Parma and Modena with Piedmont ; but he thought that there was still a chance of keeping Tuscany a separate state, and of saving Romagna for the Pope, at least in name.[2] He therefore accepted the British proposal (January 15, 1860) that Central Italy should be left free to determine its own fate.

He insisted, however, that the States should give their decision by plebiscite instead of through freshly elected Assemblies, believing that the influence of the priests and the landlords, reinforcing the secular antagonism of town and country, would induce the peasants to vote against annexation.

---

[1] F.O. Tuscany, 207, No. 163 ; Oct. 24, 1859.

[2] As a lay Vicariate under Victor Emanuel.

In the same belief, Ricasoli, now Dictator of
Tuscany in all but name, resisted an appeal
to the people by universal suffrage as long as he
could ; but, warned by the British Government,
he gave in at last. As the Emilian Government
had only been waiting for his concurrence, the
assurance of Cavour that Victor Emmanuel would
accept annexation, if offered (February 29), made
further delay unnecessary. On March 1, therefore, the peoples of Central Italy were invited
to express by plebiscite on March 11 and 12
their wishes with regard to " union to the constitutional monarchy of King Victor Emmanuel,"
or " the formation of a separate kingdom."

(b) *The Plebiscites in Tuscany and Emilia.*—
The form of the plebiscites taken in Central
Italy in March, 1860, followed the French mode
of procedure.[1] The appeal to the people was
made by manhood suffrage ; women and minors
were not allowed to vote[2] ; and the franchise was
restricted to males of 21 years of age and over in
enjoyment of civil rights, who had been resident
in their commune for at least six months, that is,
roughly 25 per cent. of the whole population.
Of these the municipal authorities in every
commune were to compile a list before March 11,
when the voting was to begin in the chief town
or village of the commune. The voting was to
continue for two days between the hours of 8 a.m.
and 5 p.m. and to take place in the presence of
five Councillors, or, if there were not enough for
all the booths, of five honest citizens chosen by
the Gonfaloniere, of whom two must always be
present. The voting was to be by ballot, every
voter, after his right to vote had been verified,
depositing in an urn a ticket written or printed

---

[1] The Tuscan decree is summarized in the text, but the
same procedure was followed in all the plebiscites of 1860.

[2] The Tuscan women, however, presented an address to
Ricasoli in favour of annexation.

with the words, " Unione alla Monarchia costituzionale del re Vittorio Emanuele," or, " Regno separato." Each evening the urn was to be sealed by the presiding Councillors ; and, when the voting was over, it was to be taken to the office of the *Pretore* (district judge), who was to count the votes and send the sworn result to the Prefect. In his turn the Prefect was to forward the count at once to the President of the Court of Cassation at Florence, who was also to receive the counts from the army, the total to be sent to the Minister of Justice and Grace on March 15.[1]

The plebiscites were duly taken in the prescribed manner on March 11 and 12, and on March 15 and 16 the results were made known. In Tuscany, out of a total population of 1,807,000, 504,000 were inscribed as voters, of whom 366,571 voted for annexation, 14,925 for a separate kingdom 4,949 spoiled their papers, and 117,555 abstained from voting. In Emilia, out of a total population of 2,127,105, 526,258 were inscribed as voters, of whom 426,006 voted for annexation, 756 for a separate kingdom, 750 spoiled their papers, and 98,746 abstained from voting. Taking the Emilian vote by provinces, we find that in Parma, out of 107,435 voters inscribed, 88,511 voted for annexation, 181 for a separate kingdom, and 18,743 abstained from voting ; in Modena out of 121,527 voters inscribed, 108,336 voted for annexation, 231 for a separate kingdom, 231 spoiled their papers, and 12,729 abstained from voting ; in Romagna, out of 252,727 voters inscribed, 202,659 voted for annexation, 254 for a separate kingdom, 471 spoiled their papers, and 49,343 abstained from voting.[2]

---

[1] *Further correspondence concerning the Affairs of Italy,* 1860. Part III, No. 24 and enclosure.

[2] *Ibid.,* Part IV, No. 12. These are the official figures, but they are neither complete nor satisfactory for Emilia. One official document gives 406,791 as the total number of

The opponents of Italian nationalism, mostly Clericals, have constantly asserted that this overwhelming vote for annexation was only obtained by the unsparing use of terrorism, while its friends have constantly and vehemently asserted that no official pressure of any kind was used. As usual, the truth does not wholly lie with either side. The procedure gave the authorities abundant opportunity for influencing the voting ; and, though there was no deliberate attempt at organization, it is impossible, as the *Times* Correspondent (himself an ardent Nationalist) admitted, not to feel that popular opinion was largely swayed by the attitude of the municipal authorities who had the management of it and who had just announced themselves unanimous for annexation to Piedmont.[1]   Nevertheless, it would be true to say that such intimidation as there was came, not from the authorities, but from the people themselves.

The Nationalists have always made much of the voting being by ballot ; but it was not by ballot as we understand it.   The Provisional Governments, by suppressing all newspapers, had left themselves no means of ascertaining

---

votes given there for annexation, made up of 202,659 from Romagna, 115,621 from Modena, and 88,511 from Parma ; another gives the same figures for Romagna (therein called Bologna) and Parma, but gives 108,536 for Modena, adds 23,492 for Massa, and 3,008 for Borgorato, and gives 426,006 as the total. The difference in the number of votes assigned to Modena in the two documents is very nearly 7,000—far short of the 23,492 votes assigned to Massa, which we should have expected to find included with Modena, but very nearly equal to the number of votes from Carrara (4,366) and Massa (2,875) together, as given by the British Consul at Carrara ; F.O. Tuscany, 213, No. 73. What the explanation may be cannot be ascertained without reference to documents not accessible at the present time. In the references here made to the voting at Modena, the figures given for that duchy by itself have been used.

[1] *Times*, March 8, 1860.

beforehand the real trend of public opinion ; but
with the eyes of Europe upon them, they dared
not make any attempt to influence the voting
directly. The countrymen of Machiavelli, however,
found a simple way out of their difficulty. The
two proposals on which the people were asked to
vote were printed, not on one paper but on two,
which were placed in separate baskets or salvers
on either side of the urn[1] ; and the voter had to
select his ticket and place it in the urn under the
eyes, not only of the presiding Councillors, but
also of his fellow-voters, who thus knew quite
well how he voted.   Moreover, almost simultaneously with the decree ordering the plebiscite
to be taken, there appeared thousands of tickets
printed with the annexation formula, which were
quickly bought up by the lower classes, who wore
them in their hats as badges.[2]   Thus, without a
hint of official pressure, such of the upper and
middle classes as were at heart opposed to annexation were made aware that it might be unwise
to go counter to the will of the masses by picking
up and placing in the urn a ticket for a separate
kingdom.   The movement was not confined to
the towns ;   and on the polling-days bands of
peasants headed by their curés were to be seen
marching to the parish church, which, in the
villages, served as the polling booth.[3]

By these means intimidation on the polling

---

[1] *Times*, March 19, 1860. As the correspondent of the
Times was a Nationalist, any evidence given by him against
the Italian authorities may be accepted, especially when he
seems to be unaware of its damaging nature. His evidence
for them, however, is only to be accepted when corroborated
by the British Ministers. Their evidence may be accepted
because Great Britain's policy was frankly opportunist, and
it was essential that the Government should be informed of
the whole truth without glossing.

[2] E. Rubieri, *Storia Intima della Toscana dal 1, Gennaio,
1859, al 30 aprile, 1860*, Prato 1861, p. 316.

[3] *Times*, March 19, 1860.

days was made as unnecessary as it was impolitic.
Most of the voters followed the example of their
betters, and especially that of the municipal
authorities, in voting for annexation,[1] while
those who were opposed to annexation for the
most part abstained from voting altogether ;
but those who voted for a separate kingdom
were not molested.   Any movement towards
violence was easily checked by a hint from the
better-class voters that any disturbance of the
peace would be maliciously interpreted as intimidation ;[2] and testimony to the regularity and good
order of the proceedings was freely forthcoming
from the British representatives in Italy.[3]
A much more subtle means of influencing the
voting lay in the form of the alternate proposal
for a separate kingdom.   In Emilia this proposal
had hardly any support ; chiefly, we may believe,
because its annexation to Piedmont was already
almost complete, and even five months' experience
had taught the inhabitants the advantage of
being part of a large state.   But in Tuscany, as
we have seen, the desire for autonomy was still
very strong.   Therefore, it is noteworthy that the
proposal for a separate kingdom was so vaguely
expressed that those who were in favour of preserving the autonomy of Tuscany were in many
cases prevented from voting in favour of it, from
a fear that its adoption might result in the return
of the Grand-Duke ; and, rather than do anything
which might tend to such a result, they voted
for annexation, although they disapproved it.
Conversely, many of those among the upper
classes who favoured restoration voted for annexation from a conviction that, if the formation of
a separate kingdom were favoured, the choice

---

[1] *Times*, March 8 and 19, 1860.

[2] Rubieri, *op. cit.*, p. 316.

[3] F.O. Tuscany, 213, Nos. 73, 74.

of the new sovereign would not fall on the Grand-Duke.[1]

Nevertheless, when all allowance has been made for the use of these questionable methods of influencing the voting, the fact remains that the plebiscites yielded a majority for annexation so overwhelming that it is impossible to deny that by far the greater number of those who voted for annexation did so because they really were in favour of it.   In fact, whether we compare the number of votes given for annexation with the total number of votes given or with the number of persons entitled to vote, we find that either way the majority for annexation was overwhelming, the percentages being respectively 94·8 per cent. and 72·9 per cent. in Tuscany, 99·7 per cent. and 82·3 per cent. in Parma, 99·5 per cent. and 89·1 per cent. in Modena, 99·6 per cent. and 80·1 per cent. in Romagna, and 99·8 per cent. and 80·9 per cent. for the whole of Emilia.

This is the more telling because the whole influence of the Church, as represented by the higher clergy, had almost everywhere been used against annexation ; and, although many of the country clergy in Modena, Romagna, and Tuscany, voted for it, nearly all the lower clergy in the city of Bologna followed their superiors in abstaining from voting and in exhorting their parishioners to do the same.[2]   If, then, the abstentions nowhere exceeded 24 per cent. of those entitled to vote,[3] we are obliged to admit that, whether the feeling that prompted them was a permanent one or the result of a temporary enthusiasm excited by circumstances, the vast majority of the inhabitants

---

[1] F.O. Tuscany, 213, No. 56.   March 2, 1860.

[2] *Times*, March 8 and 19.   F.O. Tuscany, 213, No. 74, March 16.

[3] The percentages were : Tuscany, 23·7 per cent. ; Parma, 21·2 per cent. ; Modena, 10·4 per cent. ; Romagna, 19·9 per cent.

of Central Italy were honestly in favour of the measure.

Any reluctance on the part of the defeated party to abide by the result of the plebiscite was removed by Napoleon himself; for he made his consent to the annexation of Tuscany to Sardinia conditional on her administration being not wholly absorbed by Sardinia; and his tone of command so wounded the self-esteem of the Tuscans that it turned into staunch unionists even the most notorious municipalists.[1] It was therefore amid universal enthusiasm that, as soon as the results of the plebiscite had been announced in the Assemblies of Emilia and Tuscany, Victor Emmanuel formally proclaimed[2] the union of the Central Italian States with his own in the kingdom of Italy. On April 2, 1860, the first Italian Parliament met at Turin.

(ii) *The Plebiscites in Savoy and Nice.* (a) *Events leading thereto.*—Almost the first business laid before the Italian Parliament was the ratification of the Treaty of Turin for the cession of Savoy and Nice to France. At Plombières Cavour had agreed to the cession of Savoy, but not to that of Nice, as the price of French aid in wresting Lombardy *and* Venetia from Austria; but the Treaty of Villafranca, by giving Victor Emmanuel Lombardy only, had made void the cession of Savoy. Now the Emperor, on the ground that Tuscany and Emilia were more than an equivalent for Venetia, made the cession of Savoy *and* Nice the price of his consent to the annexation of the former provinces to Sardinia. Cavour resisted the Emperor's demand as long as he could; but at last he had to give in and sign the Treaty of Turin (March 24, 1860), ceding both provinces to France. He made the cessions dependent, however, on the consent

---

[1] *Times*, March 14, 1860.

[2] On March 18 and 22 respectively.

both of the populations concerned and of the
Sardinian Parliament.[1]

A frank explanation of the reasons for the
cession of Savoy and Nice was made by Cavour
in the Sardinian Chamber of Deputies on May 26,
1860 :

> " All parties in France not being favourable to Italy, it
> was necessary to satisfy them by ceding Savoy and Nice,
> as otherwise the Emperor would have been unable to
> continue to manifest his sympathies with us. For a long
> time Nice and Savoy have expressed their French
> tendencies, and Nice is not an Italian province."[2]

The French Government, on their side, invari-
ably represented the cession as a reunion of
French provinces with the mother-country,
justified by the spontaneous desire of the
inhabitants.

The Savoyards, had, on the occasion of various
international agreements—in 1648, in 1713, and
in 1748—expressed a wish to be given the status
of a Swiss Canton ; and in 1814 they suggested
the creation of a neutral State between France
and Italy. The first definite suggestion of a
renewed union with France appears to have been
made in connexion with the assistance given
by Piedmont to the Allies in the Crimean War.
The treaty negotiated for this purpose met with
considerable opposition in the Sardinian Chamber ;
and the *Times* correspondent of 1860 states that,
in these discussions, the Savoyard members
objected to the use of conscription for this purpose, and suggested that they might as well
be under the French flag.[3] It is possible that
this debate inspired Napoleon III with the ambition
of procuring the cession of Nice and Savoy ; and
after the conclusion of the Crimean War the

---

[1] Hertslet, *op. cit.*, Vol. ii, No. 313.

[2] *Times*, May 28, 1860.

[3] *Times*, March 27, 1860.

possibility of the arrangement was widely discussed. In 1859, the *Courrier des Alpes* began a
French propaganda ; and on February 7, 1860,
the Marquis of Normandy asserted in the House
of Lords that there was on the Continent a universal belief in the existence of a compact between
the Emperor of the French and the King of
Sardinia for the transference to France of Nice
and Savoy. Lord Granville replied that the
Government had been assured that there was
no question of annexation at the present moment ;
but the attitude of the French newspaper press
left no room for doubt ; and on March 9 the
Opinione of Turin announced that Cavour had
written a note in which while expressing the
attachment of the King of Sardinia to the provinces of Savoy and Nice, he stated that :—

> "true to the principles which he supports in Central
> Italy, His Majesty declares his intention to interrogate
> the population in a manner to be established by Parliament,
> reserving the question of the frontiers and of the guarantees
> to be given to Savoy."[1]

Rival declarations were issued from time to
time by partisans of each policy ; and the
evidence as to the feeling of the population is,
naturally, somewhat conflicting. A demonstration against annexation took place so early as
January 29, 1860, and was followed by others.
The Municipal Junta of Nice voted against
annexation ; and the National Guard elected
by a large majority a colonel who was attached
to the old allegiance. On the other hand, a pro-
Sardinian demonstration is described by the other
side as composed of 500 children and Italian
employés. The French Emperor received a
deputation from Savoy on March 16 ; and the
Savoy correspondents of French newspapers
asserted that annexation was impatiently awaited.
Observers in this country differed in opinion.

---

[1] *Times*, March 12, 1860.

Sir Robert Peel stated in the House of Commons on February 28 that :—

> " there was a stern and determined resolution on the part of the Savoyards to resist their transfer to France, the national feeling, he knew, being absolutely antagonistic to the connection." ·

On the other hand, on March 2, Mr. Bright spoke of a popular desire for annexation.

So far as Savoy was concerned, the cession was not likely to excite much opposition either in the Duchy or in Italy. No sentiment of nationality bound the one to the other, while interest made their association a burden to each. On her side, Savoy thoroughly disliked a connexion that not only took from her every year 17,000 men for the Sardinian army and 12,000,000 lire for the Sardinian treasury, but also erected a customs barrier between her products—timber, hides and cheese—and their natural markets in France and Switzerland, as well as between Savoy and the cheap manufactured goods of those countries.[1]

The commercial interests of Savoy were certainly likely to benefit by union with France ; for the Savoyards were forced to send their products by an incomparably more difficult and expensive route to a worse market in Piedmont ; and there was no available capital in Savoy or in Piedmont to develop their own resources.

After 1848 the separatist feeling to which this divergence of interest gave rise was encouraged by the priests and the landlords, who were for the most part opposed to the Italian nationalist movement and the constitutional form of government then adopted.[2] There was, however, not one separatist party but two, one for France, the other for Switzerland, the

---

[1] *Gazette de Savoie*, April 17, 1860.
[2] *Times*, Feb. 7, 1860 ; from the Correspondent at Milan.

valleys which opened on France being for France, those which opened on Switzerland being for Switzerland.[1] Savoyard national feeling, however, was strong enough to make dismemberment unpopular ; and, until circumstances should decide the fate of the Duchy as a whole, the Savoyards clung loyally to their Duke.

With respect to Nice, the situation was very different. The province was essentially Italian by language, position and affection ; its cession to France would at once gravely affect the entire seaboard of Italy by giving the former two offensive points instead of one. Interest as well as sentiment therefore urged Italy not to cede Nice to France. As for Nice itself, sentiment was wholly on the side of Italy ; but it is not so clear that interest was. So far back as June, 1848, there had appeared in *L'Echo des Alpes Maritimes* a leading article in which it was pointed out that, while Turin, to secure the loyalty of Genoa, fostered her trade, Nice might starve behind her mountains if France closed her ports against her ; for she had no link with Turin save a route over three chains of mountains, nor with Genoa save by one cut by innumerable torrents. This article summed up the facts of the position ; and the attachment of the Nizzards to the House of Savoy was seriously shaken when its free port was suppressed in 1852 for the profit of Genoa. The French party in Nice was in fact steadily gaining ground when the events of 1859 roused to the highest pitch the Nizzards' admiration for Victor Emmanuel and for their countrymen, Garibaldi, and their anger against Napoleon III, who in deserting Italy had deserted them.

After Villafranca the separatist agitation revived

---

[1] *I.e.*, the Provinces of Chablais, Faucigny, and Annecy, which, after the annexation, were formed into the Department of Haute Savoie.

both in Savoy[1] and in Nice, but was quickly
checked by the Intendant-General sent thither by
the Sardinian Government, which thus showed
its power to defeat French designs on the Alps
until the programme on the Adriatic had been
carried out.   As soon as Napoleon III gave his
consent to the annexation of Tuscany and Emilia
to Sardinia, the separatist agitation began again.
For the whole question of the cession of Savoy
and Nice lay in this :—They had been secured to
Sardinia by the treaties of 1815, which also,
neutralized certain parts of Savoy in the interest
of Switzerland.; and it was certain that both
Switzerland, who wanted to annex those districts,
and Great Britain, who did not want to strengthen
France, would protest against the cession as an
infringement of the treaties.   Therefore, Savoy
and Nice could only be ceded and accepted if
the populations of those provinces demanded it,
as a consequence of the principle that each country
has the right of choosing its own government and
dynasty.[2]

So far as Savoy was concerned, it was certain
that, however the people might vote if left to
themselves, a popular movement in favour of
France could be got up, even in northern Savoy,
with the connivance of the Sardinian Government
and a judicious agitation by France ; but that
Nice would resist the proposed cession was made
clear by the agitation against it that began as soon
as the proposal became known.   That, nevertheless, Nice as well as Savoy voted for annexation
to France accounts for the contempt in which the
Italians thenceforth held the plebiscite as a means
of ascertaining the will of the people.

---

[1] In January, 1860, the municipal elections at Chambéry
returned the friends of annexation to France by a majority
of two-thirds of the votes, not one of the Opposition being
elected ; (*Times*, Jan. 31, 1860.)

[2] *Times*, Feb. 7 and April 17, 1860.

The treaty of Turin was made public on March 29, 1860, and on April 12 it was ratified by the new Italian parliament. The cession of Savoy was voted almost without discussion ; but to the cession of Nice there was strong opposition. This was, however, useless ; even before the treaty of cession was ratified, the plebiscites had been ordered to take place, in Nice on April 15, in Savoy on the 22nd. The rest was in keeping with this beginning.

(b) *Plebiscite in Savoy.*—In accordance with the invariable rule followed by Napoleon III, the popular vote was invoked to confirm an already accomplished fact. The Piedmontese party was necessarily deprived of its natural leaders, because the Government declared its assent before the vote was taken. The treaty of March 24, 1860, confirmed the agreement of the King of Sardinia to the transference of Nice and Savoy to France ; the Emperor and the King were to concert as to the best means of ascertaining the wishes of the people, on whose choice there was to be no kind of constraint ; the rights of the officials of the Piedmontese Government were secured ; a year was allowed for the removal of dissatisfied subjects to Piedmontese territory ; and such removal was not to invalidate their right to own land in Nice or Savoy.

The Piedmontese Government gave an unmistakable guarantee of good faith by abrogating its own powers and functions before the vote was taken. On the day of the signature of the treaty, two squadrons of Piedmontese cavalry were removed from Chambéry, the population showing no sign of emotion of any kind.[1] This was the beginning of a general recall of Piedmontese troops ; and it was announced that the

---

[1] *Times*, March 27, 1860.

military classes due to join the army at the time
were not to be called up. Not only did the
Piedmontese uniform disappear, but in the public
offices Piedmontese were replaced by Savoyards
with French sympathies.[1] Meanwhile, French
troops were passing through Savoy on their way
home from Italy, and were being received,
according to the French papers, with enthusiasm.[2]
They even established themselves at Chambéry.
Under the plea of relieving the National Guard of
the fatigue of active service, one post after another
passed into the hands of the French troops. The
whole country was inundated by secret agents in
disguise ; hosts of *commis-voyageurs*, with articles
unprecedentedly cheap, were trying practically to
convince the people of Savoy of the advantages of
union with France ; and to crown all, M. Laity,
the Imperial Commissioner, who appeared as soon
as the Sardinian Governor withdrew, undertook a
tour through the Duchy, in the course of which he
announced that Chablais and Faucigny were to
have their own commercial zone, and promised
Annecy a railway and a horse-breeding establishment.[3]

When the day of voting had been fixed, the
efforts of the annexationists were redoubled. The
form of procedure was almost the same as in
Tuscany and Emilia, but, where it differed, it
gave the authorities still more scope for influencing
the voting. All males of the age of 21 and over, born
in Savoy or out of it of Savoyard parents, who had
been living in the commune for six months at
least, and had not been sentenced to a criminal
penalty, were entitled to vote. The vote was to be
on the question, " La Savoie, veut-elle être réunie

---

[1] *Times*, April 3 and 9, 1860.
[2] *Times*, April 2 and 9, 1860.
[3] *Times*, April 19 and 28, 1860

à la France ? Oui ou Non." It was to be taken by
ballot on April 22, between 8 a.m. and 7 p.m. In
each commune a committee, presided over by the
Syndic or by the oldest assessor of the municipal
junta, and composed of four members chosen in
the junta and, if necessary, in the municipal
council, by order of seniority, was to choose a
secretary, draw up the lists of voters and post them
up on the 15th, hear claims, preside at the voting
and give the result in a *procès-verbal* signed by all
the members.[1] The poll taken, the reports were
to be sent at once to the Intendants of Arrondisse-
ments, who were to forward them to the Secretary
of the Court of Appeal through the Governor.
The Court would then proceed to consider the
votes and would publish the result in a public
sitting. Absentees and soldiers with the flag were
not to be put on the lists unless they returned
before the voting-day. To every voter was to be
sent a card with his name sealed with the municipal
seal ; and no one would be admitted to the voting-
hall without this card, which he was to give up to
the bureau when he handed his ballot-paper to the
president to put in the urn.[2]

As in Tuscany and Emilia, the balloting was
a farce. " Oui " tickets were to be seen in abundance long before the voting-day ; " Non " tickets
were not always to be obtained on the day itself.[3]
But the authorities could not, as in Italy, rely
on the people making intimidation unnecessary,
at least in the northern provinces of Savoy.
So we not only have the plebiscite taken by
communes, of which the majority were French in
sympathy, instead of by provinces, since this

---

[1] Where necessary, several sections were to be formed in
commune, each under a special bureau of five members,
chosen in the Communal Council as above, subject to the
Governor's authority.

[2] F.O. Sardinia, No. 256 ; April 14, 1860.

[3] *Times*, April 24, 1860.

would have allowed Swiss Chablais and Faucigny
to go their own way[1] ; but we also find the
Annexationist Committee at Chambéry calling
upon the municipalities, and Syndics to make the
communes vote *en masse*, enjoining the former to
take matters into their own hands in case the
Syndics were refractory.[2] Already the whole
influence of the priests was being used on their
side ; and now the appointment of French partisans
as Syndics and Intendants put the whole administration, and with it the power of inflicting
annoyance on opponents, into the hands of the
annexationists.[3] Thus every kind of influence
that could be used to hinder opposition was at
the disposal of men who did not scruple to use
it in order to bring about a favourable result.

That so much effort was thought necessary to
obtain a vote for annexation to France shows
how much opposition to it there was, at least
in Upper Savoy. For Sardinia had solemnly
renounced all her rights ; a vote for union with
Switzerland had been made impossible by the
form of the question ; the " No " had therefore
no meaning, or, rather, it meant anarchy. With
French troops already occupying the country, it
seemed wiser to make a virtue of necessity, and,
since nothing could prevent the annexation of all
Savoy to France, to seek the favour of the new
masters of the land by voting for it. The Liberals,
indeed, abstained from voting,[4] though a few
bold spirits, regardless of mobbing, voted against
annexation. But, when the result of the plebiscite
was declared, it was found that in French Savoy,
out of 71,990 persons entitled to vote, 70,636

---

[1] F.O. Sardinia, 256, No. 168.   April 9, 1860.
[2] *Times*, April 19, 1860.
[3] Five Syndics, of whom the Syndic of Chablais was one,
were deposed the day before the voting began, and their posts
taken by men favourable to France (*Times*, April 28, 1860).
[4] *Times*, April 23, 1860.

had voted—70,536 for, 74 against, annexation—
and 26 had spoiled their papers ; while in Swiss
Savoy, of 63,459 persons entitled to vote, 60,203
had voted—59,997 for, and 161 against, annexation
—and 45 had spoiled their papers ; the figures
for the whole duchy being 135,449 entitled to
vote, 130,839 voters, 130,533 for, 235 against,
and 71 null.[1] Of the Savoyards in the Army at
Turin, 3,182 voted for the annexation, and 127
against.

A correspondent of the *Times*, whose attitude
towards Napoleon III and the French claims was
unsympathetic, was present during the taking of
the plebiscite, and reported that promises had been
made and intimidation practised by the municipal
authorities. He wrote that procalamations by the
Governor of Annecy, the Syndic of Bonneville,
and the Committees of Chambéry were posted
at Bonneville, showing the advantages of the
French connexion, and ending with the words :
" Vive la France ! Vive l'Empereur ! " ; that the
Governor of Annecy announced, before the voting,
a visit of Napoleon III in the coming summer ;
and that the Syndic of Bonneville convoked the
citizens to bless the French tricolour at 7 a.m.
on the morning of the elections. " The vote,"
he asserted, " was the bitterest irony ever made
on popular suffrage—the ballot-box in the hands
of the very authorities who issued the proclamation ; no control possible ; all opposition put
down by intimidation." He described efforts
made to prevent his observing the process of
voting, and stated that Sardinian agents tried to
secure that voting-papers should not bear the
word " Non." He did not, however, say that
he actually saw any of these papers, and he did
see one which had " Non " duly printed on it.[2]

---

[1] F.O. Sardinia, 256, No. 196. Turin, April 26.

[2] *Times*, April 28 and 30, 1860.

(c) *Plebiscite in Nice.*—The story of the plebiscite in Nice was much the same. A French
frigate appeared off the town on March 23, and
was followed a few days later by a squadron from
Toulon ; troops on their way back from Italy
entered the province on April 1. A provisional
Government formed of Nizzards was nominated by
France and informed that, if the voting went
right, they would keep their places. Cavour
himself called on the civil authorities to influence
the people to approve of annexation, and asked
the Bishop, whom he had nominated, to get the
curés to do the same. Accordingly the Governor
appointed to take the plebiscite issued a proclamation urging the people to confirm by popular
consent the treaty of cession made by their king ;
and the Bishop issued a circular enjoining a
vote for France as a duty. *Il Nizzardo*, a paper
that had strenuously opposed annexation, was
seized and its editor threatened with imprison-
ment. Finally, the Governor sent agents into the
rural and mountain districts to " organize " the
vote, granting them full powers even to dissolve
the municipal councils that might happen to have
another mind than that of the Sardinian Governor,
thirsting for a French Prefecture.[1] The result was
all that could have been hoped for ; Nice,
passionately Italian as the people were, voted
for annexation to France. Out of a population
of 125,000 souls, 30,712 were entitled to vote ;
and of these 25,933 voted—25,743 for, 160 against,
annexation—and 30 spoiled their papers.[2] The
French papers treated the vote as practically
unanimous, and asserted that 100 of the 160
non-contents at Nice said that they had cast

---

[1] *Times*, April 2, 14 and 17, 1860 ; cf. F.O. Sardinia, 256,
No. 176 : a summary of Robandi's speech in the debate on the
Cession in the Italian parliament on April 12.

[2] *Further correspondence concerning the Affairs of Italy*,
1860, Part IV, No. 151.

their votes in error, and signed an address to the Emperor.[1]

The treaty of 1860 was approved in the Sardinian Chamber of Deputies on May 28, by 229 votes to 33, with 23 abstentions, and in the Senate on June 10, 1860, by 92 votes to 10. The opponents in the Lower House did not base their arguments upon any suggestions of the unreal character of the voting in the plebiscite ; but in the Senate, Signor Musio, a Sardinian, spoke of the " illegality and immorality of the vote elicited by universal suffrage in Nice and Savoy."[2]

It is quite clear that the annexation was not carried out against the popular wish, but it is also evident that the attitude of the Piedmontese Government prevented what was probably a minority from exercising its full influence. The *Times'* correspondent was probably right in describing " the immense majority " of the population as " passive in a matter which they think already decided for them."[3] The episode illustrates the importance of the *fait accompli*, and the opportunities enjoyed by the side which is in administrative control when a plebiscite is taken.

(iii) *The Plebiscite in Naples and Sicily.* (a) *Events leading thereto.*—Of the three Powers whose ambition or interest had kept Italy disunited for centuries, Austria and France had now, been forced to acquiesce in its union, at least for a time ; but there remained the third, the Pope, whose refusal to submit the fate of Romagna to a Congress of the Powers had defeated that last device of Napoleon III's for preventing the annexation of the Central States to Sardinia. When the result of the plebiscites had been

---

[1] *Times,* April 23, 1860.
[2] *Times,* May 29 and June 12. 1860.
[3] *Times,* April 9, 1860.

announced, His Holiness sent a protest to Victor
Emmanuel against his " usurpations," called on
Catholic Europe to defend the Temporal Dominions of the Church, and sought alliance with
Naples and Austria.   Cavour, aware of the danger
to the new kingdom, a danger that he would
have to meet unaided by any of the Powers,
offered (April 1860) alliance to Francis II, the
well-meaning but weak prince who had succeeded
King Bomba in May 1859. When the offer
was rejected, there remained to Cavour only
the policy that he had formulated after Villafranca :—" They have stopped me from making
Italy by diplomacy from the north ; I will make
it by revolution from the south."

    Already. revolution had begun.   The withdrawal
of the Austrian troops from Romagna after
Magenta had been the signal for revolt not only
in Bologna but in Ancona and Perugia also.   Here,
however, revolt had been crushed by the Pope's
Swiss Guards ; and in April a revolt at Palermo
had been put down.   But on May 11 Garibaldi and
his volunteers landed at Marsala ; on the 15th
he won the battle of Calatafimi ; and on the 27th
he entered Palermo.   Master of Sicily, he proclaimed his intention of crossing the Strait of
Messina to raise the standard of revolt in Naples
and Rome.

    The situation that now arose was a difficult
one for Cavour.   Summoned by the Republicans,
Garibaldi on landing had proclaimed himself
Dictator ; but he had fought in the name of
" Italy and Victor Emmanuel," and the Sicilians
had acquiesced readily enough, since all the liberal
aspirations of the island aimed first at a dissolution
of the connexion with Naples, which had for a
century been an intolerable grievance for Sicily.
But Cavour did not want Garibaldi to go to
Rome ; for an attack on the Papacy would force
Napoleon III to fight for the Pope against his

brothers-in-arms of Magenta and Solferino. At
all costs this must be prevented ; and, as the
simplest way to do this was to deprive Garibaldi
of his base of operations by having Sicily
annexed to Sardinia without delay, Cavour
sent La Farina to the island in June to urge
the Dictator to arrange this. Garibaldi's reply
was to arrest La Farina and go on with his
preparations.

In the meantime, Francis II of Naples, breaking
,at last with Austria and Russia, had turned to the
Maritime Powers, who alone could help him to
save his kingdom. They gave him nothing but
advice to do what he should have done long ago ;
but the restoration of the Neapolitan constitution
of 1848 on June 25 was regarded by his subjects
as a confession of weakness, and did not check
Garibaldi, who occupied Reggio on August 21,
and marched on Naples almost unopposed. On
Sept. 6, the king retired to Gaeta,and on the following day Garibaldi entered Naples. The situation
was now very critical. If Garibaldi's volunteers
defeated the Neapolitan troops on the Volturno,
nothing could prevent them from attacking Rome,
and French intervention must follow ; if they
were defeated, the revolution in the Two Sicilies
would be undone, and then the king of Naples
would help the Pope to recover Romagna and
undo the revolution in Central Italy. Once more
Cavour called revolution to his aid.

After the short-lived revolutions at Perugia and
Ancona, clerical misrule in Umbria and the Marches
had become even more intolerable, until the
unhappy subjects of the Pope were ready to
become royalist or republican at the bidding of
whoever would deliver them. But without aid
they were helpless, for the Pope was replacing
the Swiss soldiers, who had gone, and the French,
who were going, by an army of 20,000 foreign
mercenaries, mostly Austrian, who treated the

Pope's subjects as a conquered people.[1]   It was in
the situation thus created that Cavour saw the
way of escape from the dilemma in which Garibaldi
had placed him.

Napoleon III conceived that his duty to the
Pope did not require him to do more than defend
Rome and the Patrimony of St. Peter ; therefore,
when warned by Cavour that he would have to
forestall the Austrians by occupying Umbria and
the Marches, he merely replied : " Faîtes vite."
On September 7 the Sardinian army entered
Umbria, and a messenger was sent to the Pope
demanding the dismissal of all the foreign mercenaries in his service ; on the 18th the Papal
army was defeated at Castelfidardo ; and on the
25th Ancona capitulated. A few days' march
brought the Sardinian troops to the Neapolitan
frontier, just in time to turn the battle of the
Volturno into a victory (October 2). At last the
dreaded march on Rome had been stopped.

All that remained now was to annex Naples
and Sicily to the kingdom of Victor Emmanuel.
But how was this to be done ? By plebiscite or
by assembly ? In a plebiscite the decision would
rest with the lower classes, for the most part
illiterate and ignorant of affairs ; in an assembly
it would rest with the upper and middle classes.
Now, the rule of the Bourbons had been odious
to a vast majority of their subjects in the Two
Sicilies, but it was a majority composed of parties
having very different aims, and with the downfall
of the dynasty the differences between them came
to the fore.

In Sicily, the opponents of annexation were
split into two sections—Bourbonists, who wanted
a restoration, and Autonomists, who wanted an
independent state. The party that favoured
annexation was far the more important both in
numbers and in talent, counting in its ranks the

[1] F.O. Rome, 77, No. 66, Russell, May 11, 1860.

chief exiles and the chief non-emigrants as well
as most of the lower classes ; but it was split
into three sections : (1) Dilationists, who wished
to defer annexation till the Two Sicilies were
wholly free, and who were mostly Republican ;
(2) Fusionists, who wanted to weld all Italy into
one great whole ; (3) Conditionalists, who wanted
to annex Sicily to the other Italian States on conditions that would leave the adjustment of local
affairs to the local administrations, while securing
to the Central Government all powers necessary
to establish and uphold the unity of Italy.[1]

In the kingdom of Naples similar divisions
appeared. The lower classes in the towns, and in
the country districts through which Garibaldi
passed, shouted for Italy and Victor Emmanuel,
simply because he did so ; in the Abruzzi and
other districts not visited by him they obeyed
the priests and demanded the restoration of the
Bourbons.[2] The upper and middle classes for the
most part hated the rule of the Bourbons ; and,
so far as they were concerned, the reactionary
party was confined to the court, the army, and
the church.[3] Nevertheless, although they wanted
to have the political institutions of the north,
they also wanted to keep their own legal code
and administrative system.[4] Unwilling to see
their country sink to the level of a province,
many of them would fain have replaced the
Bourbon dynasty with a Bonapartist ; others
wanted a Republic ; and, although the greater
number realized that only union with Victor
Emmanuel's kingdom could save them from

---

[1] F.O. Naples, 321, No. 588, Consul Godwin's *Political
Journal*, Oct. 15.

[2] F.O. Naples, 321, No. 610. Elliott, Nov. 2, 1860.

[3] *Further correspondence relating to Italy*, 1861. Part VII,
No. 70. Elliott, Aug. 31, 1860.

[4] *Memoirs of Francesco Crispi*, Trans. M. Prichard-Agnetti
London, 1912. I, p. 445.

foreign intervention and perhaps restoration, they wanted the union to be conditional and to leave them a large measure of autonomy.

The opposition to unconditional annexation was expressed by Crispi[1], who urged the Dictator to submit the question of annexation to elected assemblies. His case was a good one ; and Garibaldi, who fully shared the distrust and contempt in which Italians now held universal suffrage as the clumsiest means of arriving at the real sense of the nation, was easily persuaded to issue on October 8 decrees convoking National Assemblies to meet at Palermo and Naples on October 21 to decide the fate of the kingdoms.

Neither Assembly met. Crispi's policy meant that weeks, perhaps months, must pass before annexation took place, if it ever did ; but the makers of Italy could count only on days. Austria, Prussia, and Russia were holding ominous conferences at Warsaw. Reactionary movements had begun wherever the priests could persuade the peasants to rise for Francis II. The country was falling into anarchy. Its one crying need was a regularly-constituted Government to restore order. Such a government the Neapolitans could have for the asking ; for on October 2 the Sardinian Parliament had, at Cavour's invitation, voted for the annexation of " those provinces of Central and Southern Italy which freely by direct universal suffrage may express the will of the population to be an integral part of our constitutional monarchy." Both in Sicily and in Naples the people were beginning to murmur at the delay ; and, bowing to their will, Garibaldi ordered a plebiscite to be taken on the question of annexation on October 21.

(b) *The Plebiscite.*—The form of procedure was almost, though not quite, the same as in the

----

[1] *Op. cit.*, i, 445.

plebiscites taken earlier in the year. All males of 21 years of age, and in full enjoyment of civil and political rights, were to vote. Lists of the voters, compiled by the Syndic of each commune, were to be published and affixed to the usual places by October 17. Protests were to be lodged within 24 hours before the District Judge, who was to give his decision, without appeal, by the 19th. The votes were to be collected in the chief town of each district by a committee composed of the District Judge, as president, and the Syndics of the communes of the district. At the voting places there were to be placed three urns, one to hold the " Aye " tickets, one to hold the " No " tickets, and in the middle an empty one in which the voter was to place whichever ticket he wished. When the voting was finished, the committee of the district was immediately to send the urns, closed and sealed, by means of the president, to the provincial committee. In every chief town of a province there was to be a committee composed of the Governor, as president, the President and Procurator-general of the Grand Criminal Court, and the President and Procurator-Royal of the Civil Tribunal. This committee was to examine the votes collected by the district committees and immediately send the result, closed and sealed, by means of a municipal agent, to the President of the Supreme Court of Justice. The general scrutiny of the votes was to be made by the Supreme Court ; and its President was to announce the result from a rostrum placed for the purpose in the square of St. Francesco di Paula.[1]

So far there was but little difference between the southern and northern plebiscites, although the substitution of the district for the commune was nicely calculated to keep away from the

---

[1] *Further correspondence relating to Italy*, 1861. Part VII, No. 130.

voting urns the peasants of the outlying communes
who, under the influence of their priests, might
have voted against annexation. But there was a
notable difference in the formula on which the
people were to vote. Instead of " Annexation to
the constitutional kingdom of Victor Emmanuel,"
they were asked to vote on the question : " Do
the people wish that Italy be one and indivisible,
with Victor Emmanuel as her constitutional king,
to be followed by his legitimate descendants ?
Yes or no." This was a concession made by
Pallavicina to meet Crispi's contention that the
southern kingdoms, owing to the special conditions
under which their revolution had taken place
and in consideration of the importance of their
position as regards the rest of Italy, could not
accept the formula that Tuscany and Emilia had
accepted. " Our country," he said, " must not
give herself to another, must not *annex* herself,
which verb savours over-much of servitude, but
must rather express her desire that union be
achieved."[1] In the end, however, the difference
in the formula was of no importance, save in so
far as it may have caught the votes of some
who were separatist at heart and grudged sorely
to see their country become a mere province of
the *parvenu* Sardinia. In fact, as the British
Minister at Naples wrote, " the terms of the vote
and the manner in which it is to be taken are
well calculated to secure the largest possible
majority for the annexation, but not so well
fitted to ascertain the real wishes of the country."[2]

This criticism was fully justified by the event.
The situation in Naples and Sicily was in fact
just like that in Nice and Savoy, with the one big
difference that in the southern provinces it was the
lower classes that were for, and the upper and

---

[1] Crispi, *op. cit.*, I, p. 443.
[2] F.O. Naples, 320, No. 579. Elliott, Oct. 16, 1860.

middle classes that were against, unconditional
annexation. It was, therefore, easy for the
authorities to act correctly. since the people
themselves could be trusted to supply all the
pressure needed to secure the vote desired. The
voting in Naples itself was typical of the whole
country. The Sardinian army occupied the
country, but was not in evidence on the day of
voting ; and the voting urns were placed under the
care of the National Guard, who had orders to
protect anyone who was maltreated for voting
as he chose. The presiding officials also insisted
on the right of a free vote ; but the risk run in
exercising it was considerable. Popular feeling
was very strong against those who were suspected
even of a wish to throw in a negative ; some
people even received letters threatening them if
they voted " No." Many were undoubtedly kept
away by fear or by diversity of opinion ; the
gentry especially abstained. Some " Noes " were
given, but very few ; and the wonder was that
even a few could be found in Naples who had the
moral courage to vote " No." We can but repeat
the words of the correspondent of the *Times* :—
" I cannot call the great drama which has just
terminated a national expression of opinion,
because the moral obstacles to freedom of voting
were undoubtedly great. . . . It was, however,
a grand demonstration of the Liberal party."[1]

The result was all that could have been hoped
for. On November 6, it was officially announced
that the votes given were in Naples 1,302,064 for
and 10,312 against, annexation ; and in Sicily
432,054 for, and 667 against. As the number of
persons entitled to vote in each kingdom is not
available, it is impossible to say how many abstained
from voting ; but the fact that in Naples, out of a
population of over 7,400,000, only 19·17 per cent

---

[1] *Times*, Oct. 30, 1860.

voted as against 21·83 per cent. in Tuscany where
the number of abstentions was 119,555, suggests
that in the Two Sicilies it was very large.[1]

(iv) *The Plebiscite in Umbria and the Marches.*
(*a*) *Events leading thereto.*—Clericals have always
maintained that the inhabitants of the States of
the Church were quite contented with the Papal
Government, and would never have sought to
change it but for the intrigues of Piedmont. But,
as Odo Russell pointed out, " this happy conviction
scarcely explains the revolution in Romagna after
the departure of the Austrians, the presence of a
large army of foreigners under General de
Lamoricière in the Adriatic Provinces, and the
French occupation of Rome for the last ten years."[2]
Nor is there really any need to look outside the
States of the Church for an explanation of the
discontent of the Pope's subjects with his rule.
Pius IX himself supplied all the explanation
needed when he said, " We are advised to make
reforms, and it is not understood that those very
reforms, which would consist in giving this country
a Government of laymen, would make it cease
to exist. It is called the States of the Church,
and that is what it must remain."[3]

The Papal Government, in fact, was hated not
only because it was absolute, but because it was
foreign, as foreign as the Austrian was in Lombardo-
Venetia. That hatred was to be met in every
class. The middle classes, in whom were chiefly
to be found the intellect and energy of the nation,
were of course opposed to the Pope's rule.[4]

---

[1] F.O. Naples, 321, Nos. 609, 619, 621.

[2] F.O. Rome, 77, No. 131. Russell, Sept. 17, 1860.

[3] *Queen Victoria's letters*, ed. 1907, III, p. 397 : a letter
from Odo Russell to Edwin Corbett, Secretary of the Legation
at Florence, Jan. 14, 1859.

[4] F.O. Rome, 78, No. 148. Russell, Oct. 2, 1860.

The aristocracy were " as distant from the throne as all the other lay subjects of the Sovereign Pontiff ; and the majority of them were Italian in their sympathies."[1]   Even the clergy, elsewhere the most determined opponents of Italian unity, were here largely in favour of it.   The Pope had long ceased to consult the Sacred College of Cardinals, and, having dismissed the financial Consulta, governed his States despotically with the aid of Cardinal Antonelli.   So it came to pass that among the Italian Cardinals in 1860, nine at least were in favour of a spiritual Church under the Protectorate of a United Kingdom of Italy. In this opinion they were supported by a · large majority of the lower Italian clergy, jealous of the favour shown by the Pope to the foreign prelates around him.[2]

Well aware of the existence of these feelings in the inhabitants of the Papal States, Cavour hoped that, when the Sardinian army was actually accupying Umbria and the Marches, Pius IX would realize that the Temporal Power was doomed, and would accept the understanding with United Italy summarized in the formula, " A free church in a free state."   But, when the men he sent to negotiate with His Holiness on that basis were imprisoned, he recognized that in the Papacy he had found the most implacable foe of Italian unity, and without loss of time appealed from the Pope to the People.   On October 21, a decree was issued for taking a plebiscite in Umbria and the Marches on November 4 and 5.

(b) *The Plebiscite.*—The form of procedure was practically the same as in Emilia and Tuscany. All males of 21 years of age and over, enjoying full civil

---

[1] F.O. Rome, 78, No. 148.   Russell, Oct. 2, 1860 and F.O. Rome, 77, No. 131.   Russell, Sept. 17, 1860.

[2] F.O. Rome, 78, Nos. 170, 190 ; Russell, Nov. 11 and Dec. 26, 1860.

rights, were entitled to vote. The Municipal Commissions were to make up the list of voters. The voting, which was to be secret, was to take place in the chief town or village of each commune, the Commission being empowered to form the voters into sections of at least 500 wherever there were more than 1,000. The votes were to be counted by the Pretore, who would send the count to the Commissary of the Province. He would transmit them to the President of the Tribunals of First Instance, which were to meet on November 9, at Ancona in the one case, at Perugia in the other, under the presidency of the Chief of the Court of Appeal, who would make the final count and announce the result.[1]

The formula differed from both the Tuscan and the Neapolitan formulæ, but was equally well devised to attract votes. The people were simply asked to answer " Aye " or " No " to the question, " Volete far parte della monarchia costituzionale di Vittorio Emanuele II ? " But the issues involved were put clearly before the voters in a proclamation issued with the decree ordering the plebiscite to be taken.

> " To be part of a great nation, or a province of a little state ; to be fellow-soldiers of Victor Emanuel, or soldiers of Lamoricière ; to be equal before the laws which your deputies have helped to make, and which you yourselves will administer, or to obey the arbitrary will of a privileged class ; to belong to a civil state in which you will have justice, security, education, industry and commerce, or to have none of these things. Yours is the choice."[2]

To such a question so put there could be but one answer. In the Marches, out of 135,255 persons entitled to vote, 123,783 voted for and 1,212 against annexation, 205 spoiled their papers, and

---

[1] G. Finali, *Le Marche* (Ancona, 1896), pp. 187 *et seq.*
[2] *Ibid.*

10,055 abstained from voting ; in Umbria, out of
133,011 persons entitled to vote, 97,040 voted
for and 380 against annexation, 205 spoilt
their papers, and 35,386 abstained from voting.[1]
That the abstentions were so many in Umbria
—26·45 per cent. of those entitled to vote—
is really less surprising than that they were
so few in the Marches—7·43 per cent. of those
entitled to vote. For many of the country
labourers had been persuaded by their parish
priests that eternal damnation would be the consequence of such a wicked act as voting on such
a question.[2] Many also did not seek the voting urns
because they were too few to form a separate
section, and would not journey to the chief town
of their commune. Something, too, must be
allowed for the influence of the women and the
minors, who were very angry at not being allowed
to vote, although they had been neither too weak
nor too young to suffer for Italy.[3] Nevertheless,
contempt for the administration of the priests was
deep enough and general enough to produce an
overwhelming vote for annexation to the kingdom
of Victor Emmanuel.

On December 26, 1860, the National Parliament at Turin voted the annexation of the Two
Sicilies, the Marches, and Umbria, and then gave
place to a new assembly, the Italian Parliament,
which on March 13, 1861, gave Victor Emmanuel
the title of King of Italy.

(IV) THE PLEBISCITES OF 1866 AND 1870.

(i) *The Plebiscite in Venetia :* (a) *Events leading
thereto*—The kingdom of Italy had been made ;
but it lacked its historic capital, Rome ; and Venice

---

[1] F.O. Sardinia, 259, No. 458. Hudson, Nov. 11, 1860.
[2] F.O. Sardinia, 259, No. 459. Consul at Ancona, Nov. 6,
1860.   [3] Finali, *loc. cit.*

was still under the Austrian yoke. Without the
goodwill of France neither could be won ; and that
goodwill was wanting. Even French Liberals were
reluctant to make Italy stronger, while French
Catholics were determined to maintain the Temporal Power, believing that without it the spiritual
freedom of the Pope would be lost, and that,
when Rome became the capital of Italy, the Vicar
of Christ would become nothing more than an
Italian bishop ready to further the interests of
Italy in every way. Napoleon III saw more
clearly, but he could not go against the will of
France. Therefore, before Victor Emmanuel could
obtain the withdrawal of the French troops from
Rome, he had to undertake (Sept. 15, 1864), not
only not to attack Rome himself, but also to
prevent anyone else from doing so. Nevertheless,
Napoleon III's personal goodwill to Italy remained ; and of this Austria availed herself in
1866, when on the eve of war with Prussia, using
him as the medium of an offer of Venetia as the
price of the neutrality of Italy. It was too late.
On April 8, a treaty of offensive and defensive
alliance against Austria had been concluded between Prussia and Italy. Refusing to betray her
new ally, Italy declared war on Austria, only to be
defeated once more at Custozza. On July 3, however, Austria was defeated at Sadowa, and renewed
her offer of Venetia in exchange for an armistice
that would allow her to concentrate her forces
against Prussia. Again Italy refused, and extended
the war to the Adriatic, only to be defeated at
Lissa.

Even now Italy would not make peace ; for
beyond Venetia lay *Italia Irredenta*—Italian Tirol,
Istria, and Dalmatia, once part of the Republic
of Venice. But Bismarck's plans required that,
when war began between France and Prussia,
Austria and Italy should remain neutral ; and,
to that end, Austria must keep something that

Italy wanted to take. He therefore concluded
(August 23) the Treaty of Prague. As after
Villafranca, Victor Emmanuel, abandoned by his
ally, could not continue the war. So he accepted
the good offices of Napoleon III and signed an
armistice on August 12, followed on October 3
by the Treaty of Vienna, whereby the Emperor
of Austria agreed to the union of the Lombardo-
Venetian Kingdom to the Kingdom of Italy.[1]

Italian pride was sorely hurt by having to take
Venetia as well as Lombardy as a gift from the
Emperor of the French ; and it was partly to
soothe the smart that Napoleon, when offering
Venetia to Victor Emmanuel (Aug. 11), made the
cession conditional on the people expressing their
desires by means of universal suffrage. But
nothing could make the whole transaction other
than humiliating, whether to the king, who had
already signed decrees for organizing the Venetian
provinces in the name of national right and for
promulgating the Italian constitution in Venetia,
or to the people, who, contemptuous as ever of the
plebiscite, called it " a hard, an absurd, and a
humiliating thing." They found fault with everything. The plebiscite, they declared, would be a
mockery, because in the first place no one under
21 years of age was to vote, which would cut off
that part of the population which was most
ready to receive new ideas ; in the second place,
the lists were to be compiled by the parish priests
who would avoid the houses of those not in the
pale of the Catholic Church. " Does liberal and
progressive France," they asked, " count non-
Catholics as excommunicated dogs to whom civil
rights are to be denied ? "[2] They even talked
wildly of refusing to vote at all ; but gradually

---

[1] Hertslet, *Map of Europe by Treaty*, III, Nos. 383, 388,
392.

[2] A letter from Venice to the *Corriere della Venezia*,
quoted in the *Times*, Sept. 18, 1866.

wiser counsels prevailed, as they came to see how the plebiscite might be used to show the whole world how whole-heartedly they desired to form part of the kingdom of Italy.

(b) *The Plebiscite.*—It is probably for this reason that the plebiscite taken in Venetia on October 21, 1866, corresponds more nearly than any of the others to our idea of what a plebiscite ought to be. For the voting was really secret. Every voter went up to the bureau alone, gave his name and address, which were verified, received a voting paper, marked and folded it, and put it in a metal box through a slit in the top.[1] No one knew how his neighbour voted ; and there was no disturbance of the peace, save at Padua, where there was almost a revolution among the women demanding to vote. Otherwise, the procedure did not differ materially from that followed in the other provinces, though a change in the formula is noteworthy, the voter being asked, " Do you desire union with the kingdom of Italy under the constitutional monarchy of Victor Emmanuel II and his successors ? " Evidently, the Government was still afraid of the Republicans, who had waived their demand for a republic for the king's lifetime only. Nor were their fears wholly groundless. The result of the plebiscite was an overwhelming vote for union, 641,758 votes being given for, and only 69 against it ; but the 273 spoiled papers included certain votes for annexation to Italy under Victor Emmanuel as constitutional king but not his successors.[2]

(ii) *The Plebiscite in Rome.* : (a) *Events leading thereto.*—Rome had still to be won ; and in October, 1867, Garibaldi entered the Papal territory, hoping that a revolution in the city would follow. But he was now too closely identified with

---

[1] *Times*, Oct. 29, 1866.
[2] *Times*, Oct. 29 and 30 and Nov. 2, 1866.

" revolution," for which the Italians had lost their
taste ; so the Romans looked on quietly while the
French troops, who had hurried back to the defence
of the Pope, crushed the Garibaldians at Mentana
(Nov. 3).   The French remained in Rome till
July, 1870, when Napoleon III had to recall them
to meet the Prussians.   The German victories set
Victor Emmanuel free at last ; and on Sept. 8, the
Italian Government announced its intention to
occupy parts of the Roman territory in the
interests of peace, allowing the inhabitants of the
same to choose their own government.   Then an
ultimatum was sent (Sept. 14) requiring the
Pope to renounce his Temporal Power under
pain of seeing Rome invaded.   On Sept. 22,
the Italian troops entered the Eternal City ;
and, two days later, orders were issued for a
plebiscite to be taken on Oct. 2.

(*b*) *The Plebiscite.*—The form of procedure was
that now familiar to us.   All males of 21 years of
age and over enjoying full civil rights were entitled
to vote.   The lists were prepared by the Giunta
appointed by the Italian General, Cadorna.   Voting
began at 8 A.M. and closed at 6 P.M.   In Rome a
bureau, where a member of the Giunta with two
citizens and a guard of firemen[1] watched over the
voting urn, was set up in each of the twelve
quarters of the city.   Each voter was offered two
tickets by the presiding member of the Giunta,
one " Aye " and one " No," one of which he had to
choose as his answer to the question, " Do you
desire union with the kingdom of Italy under the
constitutional monarchy of Victor Emmanuel II
and his successors ?"[2]   At 6 o'clock the urns
were sealed by a notary and taken to the Capitol.
The same form was observed in the Roman
Provinces.

[1] There was no National Guard in Rome.
[2] *Correspondence respecting the Affairs of Rome*, 1870-71,
No. 52.

Nearly the whole male population over 21 took part in the voting, led by the aristocracy and the middle classes, but not to any extent by lawyers or professors. There was more organization of the voters than in any other Italian plebiscite except those in Savoy and Nice, the corporations, trade guilds, and districts having agreed that the voters should muster under their respective banners and so march to the voting booths ; but the sole basis of the charge that voters were imported from other parts of Italy seems to be the return to Rome of 4,300 Roman soldiers in the Italian army, whose expenses were paid by the Government.[1] The count, however, showed that the voting had not been appreciably affected by these devices. In the Roman Provinces, out of 167,548 persons entitled to vote, 133,681 voted for, and 1,507 against, union with the kingdom of Italy, 103 spoiled their papers, and 32,257, or 19·25 per cent. abstained from voting. In Rome itself 40,805 votes were given for and only 46 against union.[2]

When all allowance has been made for the presence of the Italian army, for the influence of the anarchy into which Rome seemed to be falling in the two days that elapsed between the entry of the troops and the appointment of the Giunta by Cadorna, for the organization of the voters, and for the fear of some of the Papalists and the apathy of the rest, it remains undeniably true that a majority of the Romans, at least of the upper and middle classes, did wish their city to be part of the kingdom of Italy.

(V) THE ITALIAN PLEBISCITES AND THE RIGHTS OF NATIONS.

If the Italian Plebiscites had done no more than facilitate the formation of a strong kingdom of Italy out of the petty states of the Italian

---

[1] *Times*, Oct. 10, 1870.   [2] *Times*, Oct. 4 and 8, 1870.

peninsula, they would be of first-rate importance
in the history of Europe. But they did much
more than that ; for they initiated a change in
the principles regulating international relations
and international law, the meaning of which we
are only now beginning to perceive.

For over four centuries—from the rise of the
New Monarchy, in fact—international relations
and international law have been regulated by one
principle only, the interest of the sovereign state,
which knows no limitation of its powers but self-
interest and acknowledges no right that does not
emanate from itself. Even the advocates of the
rights of man and of the sovereignty of the people
could conceive no other principle by which international relations could be regulated ; for, whether
vested in one man or in a whole people, sovereignty
remains the same, illimitable save by self-interest,
non-moral, and without need of any justification
for its acts other than the reason of state.

As a matter of fact, the first result if the
application of the principle of the sovereignty of
the people to treaties and international relations
was the violation of the Treaties of Westphalia
and Utrecht and the annexation of the lands
between the frontier of France and her " natural "
boundaries, whose inhabitants had been induced
by skilful propaganda to demand union with the
French Republic. It is not surprising, therefore,
that European statesmen should have regarded the
doctrine of the sovereignty of the people with
abhorrence as one subversive of all law and order,
nor yet that they should afterwards have sought
to restrain all states from action injurious to their
neighbours by making the maintenance of treaties
the guiding principle of European policy, even
forming the Concert of Europe for that purpose.

Yet the treaties in the maintenance of which
men saw the only security for peace had in themselves no element of performance ; for they were

based on reasons of state and had no other aim than to establish a balance of power. Neither the treaties nor the international law that grew up around them recognized the existence of any right not created, or at least admitted, by the state. The treaties " cut and pared kingdoms and duchies as though they were Dutch cheeses," without regard to the wishes of the inhabitants ; and the law denied that persons resident in a conquered or ceded territory had any right to withhold their allegiance from the new sovereign.[1] It made no difference that some of the states recognized the rights of man and the sovereignty of the people in their relations with their own members ; their relations with other states were still regulated by the reason of state. Thus, the United States of America, although they justified their own declaration of independence by an appeal to the rights of man, annexed Louisiana, Florida, New Mexico, California, and Texas by conquest and treaty, with as little heed to the wishes of the populations concerned as the Prussians showed when they annexed Hanover, Schleswig-Holstein, and Alsace-Lorraine.

The recognition of such states as Greece and Belgium did not constitute a real exception to the rule. On the one hand, they were recognized as having become states by a successful revolution, not as having had a right to do so in any case ; on the other hand, recognition was accorded to them only because it served the interests of the Great Powers most nearly concerned ; and assuredly it would never have been accorded if they had sought to annex themselves, the one to Russia, the other to France. As the reason of state required the modification of the treaties on which the peace of Europe depended, so the reason of state determined the limits of such

---

[1] W. E. Hall, *International Law*, 2nd ed., Oxford, 1884, p. 567 note.

modification ; international law was modified
to the extent only of admitting that, when a
Government constituted by a successful revolution
is found to be possessed of the rights of sovereignty
over those whom it claims to govern, it must be
recognized by other states as a state with all
the rights of a state.[1]   " Might " was still " right."

The first serious challenge to this principle
and to the underlying conception of the state
as the whole source of right, came from the
Lombards in 1848, when they laid claim to " the
inalienable right that all peoples have to be
independent and to be masters of their native
land, the right to be not only Lombards but
Italians ; " and declared that, while " treaties
may settle questions between nations, they cannot
dispose of the right of a people, as they cannot
blot out a history, abolish a language, and establish that a transient act created by force should
prevail over the laws fixed by Providence."[2]
That nations, as such, have rights was not to
be admitted by any of the Powers in 1848, the
year of the revolutions. It even seemed to
them less dangerous to recognize the sovereignty
of the people, since that at least had been shown
to be not incompatible with the continuance of
the reason of state as the regulating principle
in international relations and law. And it was
on this ground rather than on the other that the
kingdom of Italy was ultimately recognized.
The distinction may be subtle, but that it is real
becomes clear when we consider how little the
principles of international law have been modified
in consequence of that recognition. Few writers
on international law deny that, by itself, conquest

---

[1] P. Fiore, *International Law Codified* ; trans. E. M.
Borchard, New York, 1918. Tit. II, § 91.

[2] Memorandum of the Provisional Government of Lombardy to the Nations of Europe, April 12, 1848. F.O. Austria,
No. 358.

gives a just title to sovereignty over the conquered territory, or contend that a cession of territory requires the consent of the inhabitants to make it valid. They are not even agreed that the old principle of a forcible transfer of allegiance should be abandoned in favour of that of an express or implied consent[1] ; and, although the better opinion now seems to be that those who wish to retain their former allegiance may do so on condition of leaving the country, it has not yet been established that they may keep their property if the treaty of cession does not expressly stipulate for this.[2]

It is in the sphere of politics that the Italian plebiscites have had most influence. However willing the Powers might still be to treat the rights of nations as non-existent, they could not well continue to do so when once Italy had taken her place among them. But, indeed, with the single exception of Austria, they were not unwilling to adopt the principle of nationality as soon as they saw how it could be made to serve the state. It was in the name of nationality that Germany seized Schleswig-Holstein and Alsace-Lorraine, and the Concert of Europe broke up the Ottoman Empire. Nevertheless, some of these applications of the principle of nationality were so loudly denounced by those most concerned as being really violations of it, that it became

---

[1] In 1866 Count Hallemund, who left Hanover with his late sovereign, was condemned by the Prussian Kammergericht to 15 years' penal servitude on a charge of high treason for acts committed by him as " a Royal-Prussian subject " after ceasing to reside in Hanover. Halleck, *International Law*, ed. Sir Sherston Baker, 1908, ii, chap. xxxiv, § 8.

Hall, *loc. cit.*, likewise denies that persons resident in a conquered territory have a right to withhold their allegiance from the conqueror, on the ground that they have no right to keep their property.

[2] Halleck, *op. cit.*, ii, chap. xxxiv, §§ 6, 7 ; cf. W. J. Westlake, *Private International Law*, 5th ed., London, 1912, §27.

clear that much hard thinking and more goodwill
were needed before the principle could pass
from policy into law.

Uncertainty as to what constitutes a nation
makes it very necessary that there should be some
recognized means of ascertaining whether populations that seem to be parts of one nation are
really so to the extent of desiring to unite with
one another as a political body. At first sight
there seems to be no method more suitable than
the plebiscite ; but the Italian plebiscites, especially those of 1860, give us reason to doubt this.
The Italians themselves deride the plebiscite
as the clumsiest of devices for ascertaining the
will of the people. A plebiscite, if it does not
yield an overwhelming majority one way or the
other, is worse than useless ; for it serves only
to emphasize the division of opinion among the
people, and to open the way for intrigue, perhaps
for civil war. We have only to think what the
consequences of a narrowly contested vote in
Tuscany or Naples would have been, to realize
that there is some excuse for the men who made
the plebiscites there, though nominally secret,
virtually open, in order to " manage them."

Again, the plebiscite is a suitable means of
determining only the simplest issues ; but those
affecting the destiny of a people are never simple.
What could seem simpler than the issue laid before
the voters in Savoy ? " Do you wish Savoy
to be annexed to France ? " Every one who
voted for this knew exactly what he was voting
for. Savoy would be merged in France ; Savoyard
law would give place to French ; and the voter
would share all the privileges and all the burdens
of Frenchmen. But there was not the same
certainty as to what was being rejected. If
not, annexed to France, would Savoy remain
part of a Sardinia that was fast becoming Italy ?

If so, would her identity be merged in that of
Italy, or would she recover a large measure of
autonomy? Or would she become independent
and free to join the Swiss Confederation? Only
when these questions had been answered could
the Savoyards decide for or against annexation
on its own merits. Not one, but four plebiscites
were really needed here.

But it is seldom that an annexation plebiscite
can be taken on so simple an issue. When the
question is one of uniting several fragments of a
nation in a single state, there must always arise a
further question of the constitution to be adopted;
and this can never be simple. How difficult it
is to get a decision for or against annexation on its
own merits, and how easy it is for those taking
the plebiscite to obtain the decision they want
by confusing the issues, becomes clear when we
consider the Neapolitan plebiscite. The question
submitted to the voters looked simple enough :
" Do you wish for Italy one and indivisible under
the constitutional monarchy of Victor Emmanuel
and his lawful descendants? " Really, it was
very complex. Many who wanted Italy one and
indivisible did not want a monarchy, constitutional or otherwise ; others were prepared to accept
Victor Emmanuel as king for his own lifetime
but wanted to re-open the question of his death.
Others who were ready to accept the whole formula
were by no means agreed as to what was meant
by " Italy one and indivisible." Was it simply
an expansion of Sardinia, or was it a new state?
In the latter case, was it to be unitary of federal?
Conversely, those who were opposed to union
were in grave doubt as to what would follow
if it were rejected. Would the Bourbons be
restored unconditionally, or on condition of
maintaining the constitution? Would a Muratist
government be established ; or would a republic
be created? Not one, but half a dozen plebiscites

would have been needed to determine all the issues involved. And behind all, there was the conviction that it was waste of time to vote for anything but annexation, as the withdrawal of the Sardinian troops would be the signal for the arrival of the Austrians, who would assuredly pay no heed to the result of any plebiscite.

The Italian plebiscites also bring out another defect of the annexation plebiscite ; it submits the destiny of a whole people to the decision of the classes most easily swayed by passing considerations and least fitted by education and experience to deal with the complex issues involved. Serious in any circumstances, this defect is particularly so where there is so much illiteracy as there was in Italy in 1860. It is quite clear that in the central states the masses voted for annexation because they hated the Austrians, and in the southern states because they worshipped Garibaldi ; and that the one thing that could have made them vote against it would have been the influence of the priests. In neither case was annexation voted for or against on its own merits. It is also clear that a large majority of the upper and middle classes desired union but not annexation, though they were willing to accept it rather than run any risk of renewed Austrian intervention in the affairs of Italy. But the desire of these classes for autonomy was quite overborne by the demand of the masses for annexation ; so the Italian states were annexed *to* rather than united *with* Sardinia, and the Sardinian constitution and law became the constitution and law of the whole kingdom of Italy.

How much this was to be regretted became clear before many years had passed. In the north no great harm was done, because the states there were fairly homogeneous, not only in origin and speech but in manners and customs. Only historical tradition had kept them asunder, and that only in part. For the very municipalism that had held them asunder was rooted in a common passion for self-government that had again and again brought them into alliance against the foreigner, albeit for a time only. Fear of Austria and resentment against France had led them to give their latest alliance a more permanent form by annexing themselves to Sardinia ; and the persistence of the Austrian menace kept them together until they became fully conscious of a community of interest based on a common political ideal and a common economic life which made separation unthinkable.

In the south it was very different. Between Naples and Sicily and the rest of Italy there was indeed substantial community of origin, speech, and culture, but there was no community of historical tradition. Under a long line of French or Spanish kings their political and economic development had been very different from that of the northern states. While the northern were industrial and commercial, urban and democratic, the southern were agricultural, even pastoral, and feudal. Four-fifths of the land was held by a small number of nobles, who had surrendered their feudal rights with reluctance and still shared with the priests a strong influence over the peasants. The nobles had steadily resisted the attempts of their foreign rulers to impose on them a foreign administration, and had maintained the rights of the local Estates ; but there were very few towns, and the middle class was small and weak, even in the middle of the nineteenth century. Where the mass of the people was so backward, representative constitutional government was hardly possible ; and, if only the Bourbons could have brought themselves to observe the constitution of 1848 and to make alliance with Sardinia, all the aspirations of the Neapolitans for liberty and unity would have

been fully satisfied, as would those of the Sicilians,
if, at the same time, the bond that held them to
the Neapolitans had been severed or made merely
personal.

Cavour's insistence on the formal annexation
of Naples and Sicily was natural in view of the
attitude of his own country, where his ministry
would probably have fallen if he had followed
any other course, and of the need for establishing
a stable government in the Two Sicilies before
the spread of anarchy gave Austria and Russia a
reasonable pretext for intervention. But it is
none the less regrettable, for the gulf between
north and south was too wide to be easily bridged.
Cavour himself recognized that the Kingdom of
Italy ought to be regarded, not as an expansion
but as a new State requiring a new constitution ;
but, after his death, Italy was constituted as a
unitary State with a highly-centralized administrative system, by the simple process of extending the
Sardinian constitution and laws to the whole
kingdom. This course, by forcing into too close
a union peoples at such different stages of political
and economic development as were the Italians
of the north and the south, encouraged a Bour-
bonist reaction that very nearly wrecked the new
kingdom in 1866, when the declaration of war
against Austria was the signal for revolt in Sicily,
and left a legacy of brigandage that has hindered
the economic development of the south, as the
corruption introduced from Naples into national
politics hampered for a time the political development of the country.[1] Union was politically
necessary ; but, if the question had been determined by assemblies instead of by plebiscite,
it would have taken place in a form more
consistent with historical circumstance.

---

[1] R. de Cesare, *La Fine di un Regno*, 2 pt. Città di
Castello, 1901.

The contrast between the consequences of the annexation policy in the centre and in the south suggests (1) that community of origin, speech, and culture is not by itself sufficient to constitute a nation, and that without community of historical tradition national unity is incomplete ; and (2) that this ought to be reflected in the degree of .political union established between parts of a nation that have long been severed.   We may also infer that nationality is a matter not of the past but of the present ; and that, therefore, no nation has the right to insist on a population that once belonged to it being again united with it on that ground only.[1]

This becomes still clearer if we consider the history of Nice since its annexation to France. The existence of the shore road round the end of the Alps has always made intercourse between the people on either side of the mountains easy here ; and in origin there is practically no difference between Provençals and Genoese. Accident made Nice Italian in speech and culture ; but geographically, and therefore economically, the district west of Cap Martin belongs to France, and, as soon as the artificial barriers erected by historical circumstances had been removed by the plebiscite of 1860, it began to follow its natural line of development and became French in interest, as it is becoming French in speech. Would it be reasonable to contend that, because all Nice was once Italian, Italy has a right not only to the part of Nice east of Cap Martin which has remained Italian, but also to the part which has become French ?

---

[1] There are interesting discussions of these matters in the *Revue de Droit International*, 1870-71, by von Holtzendorff, *Le principe des nationalités et la littérature italienne du droit des gens*, 1870, p. 92 ; F. Lieber, *De la valeur des plébiscites dans le droit international*, 1871, p. 139 ; and G. Padelletti, *L'Alsace et la Lorraine et le droit des gens*, 1871, p. 464.   The last is the most interesting.

The fact that here the national boundary now almost coincides with the geographical boundary between France and Italy, that is, with the water-parting of the Alps, suggests that in the making of a nation geographical circumstance is more effective than historical. This suggestion is fully supported by the history of Savoy, annexed to France at the same time as Nice. In speech and culture all Savoy is and always has been French ; but geographically, and therefore economically, only the southern part belongs to France ; the northern part belongs wholly to Switzerland. On the ground that Savoy was a political unit and ought not to be dismembered, Napoleon III insisted on the whole Duchy being annexed to France, with the result that, whereas southern Savoy is now wholly French, northern Savoy, in spite of its French speech and culture, is so essentially non-French in interest that France has had to withdraw her tariff boundary to the watershed and make Haute Savoie, like the Pays de Gex, economically as well as militarily neutral. The inference to be drawn is that, as community of origin, speech, and culture are not enough to constitute a nation without the community of interest that comes from having a common past, so they are not enough without the community of interest that comes from living in the same environment ; and that, of the two, geographical circumstance is more effective and therefore more important than historical circumstance.

IV.—THE NORWEGIAN PLEBISCITES
OF 1905.

(i) *Introductory*.—In 1905, when the dissolution
of the Union between Sweden and Norway was
under consideration, the authorities of the latter
country resorted on two occasions to the expedient of a plebiscite.   As the special committee
appointed to consider the question of the first
plebiscite reported, such an expedient was un-
known to the Norwegian constitution, but it was
considered a rapid and convenient way of
obtaining an expression of public opinion.

The earlier plebiscite, which was held on August
13, 1905, was concerned with the question of the
dissolution of the Union.   A proposal was made in
the Storthing to incorporate with this the question
of the future constitutional form of the Norwegian
Government ; but it was considered inconvenient
to combine the two matters, and the proposer
seems to have been the only member who voted
in favour of the amendment.   The fate of the
monarchy was therefore deferred for later consideration, and formed the subject of the second
plebiscite above referred to, which was held on
November 12 and 13.

The basis of both plebiscites was the existing
parliamentary franchise, which included all males
over 25 years of age, with five years' residence in
the country, unless disqualified by the receipt of
parish relief or other specified cause.   Facilities
were provided whereby men who had qualified
since the last electoral register should have an
opportunity of being included in the electorate.

(ii) *Causes of the Separation from Sweden*.—The
events leading up to the dissolution of the union

with Sweden may be briefly stated. Since their union in 1815 the relations between the two countries had never been very cordial; their commercial interests and political ideals were widely different; and the language of Norway, though akin to that of Sweden, differs far more from the latter than from that of Denmark. The position became critical in consequence of the introduction of what was known as the " consular question." Norway desired a separate consular service, a project which was persistently opposed by the king, under pressure of Swedish opinion. On May 23, 1905, the Storthing, without a dissentient voice, passed a bill for the establishment of an independent consular service. King Oscar, however, contrary to general expectation and the advice of his Norwegian ministers, refused his assent to the measure, thereby bringing about the immediate resignation of the ministry. This resignation he refused to accept, on the ground that it was clearly impossible, in the circumstances, to form an alternative government. Accordingly, on June 6, the ministry pointed out to the king that " according to the fundamental law (*grundlov*) of Norway, it is incumbent upon Norway's king to provide the country with a constitutional government. In the same moment that the king's policy prevents the formation of a constitutional council, the Norwegian monarchy is thrown out of function." As a sequel to this protest the Storthing, on June 7, passed, unanimously and without debate, the following resolution :—

" Since the members of the state council have all resigned their offices ;

" Since His Majesty the King has declared himself not in a position to provide the country with a new government ;

" And since the constitutional power of the monarchy is thus thrown out of gear ;

"" The Storthing authorizes the members of the state council which ceased to operate to-day to exercise until

further notice the authority vested in the King, in conformity with the fundamental law of the Norwegian
kingdom and the relevant laws, with the changes
necessitated by the fact that the Union with Sweden under
one king is dissolved, as a result of the King's cessation
to function as a Norwegian king."

(iii) *Reasons for the Plebiscite.*—The dissolution
of the union was thus, from the Norwegian point
of view, a *fait accompli*. In confirmation of this
attitude, the Storthing passed on the same day
resolutions adopting a national flag for the navy
and deleting from the church services the prayers
for the king and royal family. There was therefore
from a constitutional standpoint no necessity
for any further expression of the national will.
Sweden, however, as was to be expected, refused
to concur in such a point of view ; and, on the
address from the Swedish Chambers to the king
presented on July 28, 1905, the expedient of a
referendum is thus suggested :—

> " In certain bills laid before the Riksdag it is maintained
> that Sweden should not give her consent to the dissolving
> of the Union before the Norwegian people should have had
> an opportunity of declaring their will, either, as one
> mover proposes, by the election of a new Storthing, or,
> as it is suggested by another, by a referendum to the
> people. The Riksdag considers that in a matter of such
> importance as that of the maintenance or dissolution of
> the Union, a surer expression of the will of the Norwegian
> people must be obtained than that which is to be found
> in the decision of the Storthing of the 7th of June, 1905.'

At the same time a vigorous propaganda had
been begun by both nations with a view to influencing opinion abroad. Norway desired to settle
matters, if possible, on a friendly footing, and was
also anxious to obtain the favourable opinion of
other countries. Accordingly, on July 27, the
Norwegian Department of Justice issued a report
recommending that a plebiscite should be held,
upon the following grounds :—

> " In the extraordinary decision, necessitated by the
> circumstances, which has been taken by the Storthing on

the nations' behalf by its resolution of the 7th of June, 1905, the national assembly has proceeded with the authority which is secured to it by its position and with the consciousness of acting with the full accord and approval of the Norwegian people. Outside Norway, however, there has been an attempt to raise a doubt as to the existence of such a popular feeling. In particular, this state of doubt may be presumed to be the reason for the desire for a further demonstration of the will and opinion of the Norwegian people, which has been expressed in the committee's report now presented to the Swedish Riksdag, and in the Riksdag's resulting resolution with reference to the dissolution of the Union and the questions connected with it . . . .

" A free plebiscite of Norwegian citizens with reference to the question of the dissolution of the Union, with the answer to which the said doubt is evidently connected, will make the matter fully and widely clear, and get rid of the effects of the mistaken opinions which may have made an impression abroad. And for our fellow-citizens such an extraordinary personal demonstration of their feeling and desire may serve in itself to strengthen patriotic affection and devotion, and further awaken their sympathy and consciousness of the common responsibility."

On the grounds stated above, a plebiscite was accordingly decided upon, and a special committee appointed to consider the draft resolution. This committee still further emphasized the *fait accompli* by altering the original question " whether they (the voters) are in agreement with the dissolution of the union or not " to read " whether they are in agreement with the dissolution of the union, which has taken place, or not."

(iv) *The first Plebiscite.*—The interval before the voting was taken up with an energetic canvass of the nation, in which all parties worked together. The Conservative Union issued a manifesto in which, as " old friends of the union," they proclaimed their conversion. The Church lent its support ; and even among the resident Swedes resolutions were passed and manifestoes issued in favour of the dissolution of the Union.

The Norse Woman's Suffrage Union, doubtless with an eye to the furtherance of their cause, which obtained recognition not long afterwards, also made arrangements whereby the women of Norway might have an opportunity of recording their agreement with the national point of view, since, as they said, " even if our votes cannot be counted, they may yet be weighed." On the day of the plebiscite the newspapers all brought out special " Ja " numbers ; the country was decorated with flags ; and the strains of the national anthem could be heard issuing from many churches. The result was what might have been expected from the measures adopted to excite popular en- thusiasm—368,211 votes were recorded in favour of separation, and only 184 against it. The canvass was probably justified in the circumstances, as the opinion of the country was never really in doubt, and the only thing to be secured was that the electorate should take the trouble to give proof of the views they indisputably entertained.

(v) *The second Plebiscite.*—The question had still to be decided whether Norway should continue to exist as a monarchy or should change her constitution to that of a republic. An address from the Storthing to King Oscar, dated June 7, 1905, had suggested his support of the proposal that a prince of his house should be elected to the Norwegian throne, after resigning his right to the succession to the crown of Sweden. On October 27, however, the King of Sweden declined this offer, the acceptance of which, he thought, might give rise to mistrust and suspicion. After a long debate in the Storthing on the question of the future constitution, the following resolution was passed on October 31.

" The Storthing authorizes the government to initiate negotiations with Prince Carl of Denmark to accept election as King of Norway, on condition that the Norwegian people supports the resolution of the Storthing by a majority of the votes given in a plebiscite carried out in essentials according to the same rules as were employed in the plebiscite of the 13th of August, 1905."

The Government thereupon issued a manifesto
to the people, in which the advantages of continua-
tion as a monarchy were not obscurely indicated.
The republican party, on the other hand, sent out
a strong appeal with over 200 signatures inviting
the people to reject the proposal.   In the result
the monarchy obtained a majority of 259,563 votes
against 69,264.   Prince Carl immediately asserted
his willingness to be elected, and he ascended
the throne of Norway as King Haakon VII.

V.—THE REFERENDUM IN NATAL, 1909.

THREE of the four South African colonies that
sent delegates to the South African Convention
of 1908-9—Cape Colony, the Transvaal, and the
Orange River Colony—were content to accept the
new Union Constitution on the vote of their
respective Parliaments.   The fourth—Natal—
insisted on a referendum to all the voters in the
Colony.   There were special reasons for this
decision.   Natal was not originally enthusiastic for
union in any form.   More purely British than the
other colonies, she feared that with union she
might be ruled by Dutch Ministries, and her
children forced to learn Dutch at school—in a
word, that she would lose her British tone.
Moreover, Natal had always been somewhat apart
from the other colonies for geographical reasons,
and had thus been comparatively unaffected by
the movements and ideas prevalent in the rest of
South Africa.   There was much more hesitation
in Natal than elsewhere about sending delegates to
the Convention ; and, when it had been decided to
send them, considerable anxiety was displayed
lest the Colony should lose its full liberty to
reject any decisions arrived at by that body.
Mr. Smythe, himself one of the delegates and
leader of the opposition, in September, 1908, a
month before the Convention met, introduced a
Bill into the Natal Parliament providing for a
referendum on any scheme to be proposed by the
Convention.   This Bill was rejected as inopportune
for the moment, though not before the Prime
Minister had promised that a Referendum Bill
should be subsequently introduced.

The first draft of the Constitution for the
Union of South Africa was submitted to the

Natal Parliament in the following March. It found many critics there, all the more as it was found to contemplate, not the loose federation on the Australian model, such as the Natal delegates had proposed, but a close union more after the model of Great Britain, which entirely abolished the legislative independence of the four colonies as such. Certain amendments were proposed, with a view to strengthening and more amply securing Natal's provincial powers. Moreover, in fulfilment of the Prime Minister's promise of the preceding year, a Referendum Act was passed, whereby Natal's acceptance of the scheme, as finally agreed to by the Convention after the consideration of various amendments, was to depend on the result of a vote by all those on the Colony's electoral roll.

The chief points to notice in the debates on the Bill are the following :—

(1) Some discussion arose as to whether a minimum of votes should be polled to make the decision valid. It was suggested, for example, that, out of the total roll of 25,463 electors, a minimum of 11,000 should be required. But it was decided, without much objection, that the people of the Colony could be trusted to vote in sufficient numbers on so important a question.

(2) More difference of opinion arose as to the need of stipulating for a majority of a certain size to make an affirmative decision valid. There were two contradictory precedents in Australia. The 1898 Referendum Act of New South Wales on the Commonwealth Constitution had required a large affirmative majority, while that of 1899 only demanded a bare majority. For Natal, Mr. Smythe had in 1908 proposed a majority greater than a bare majority ; but, though some members asked in the 1909 debate for a majority of 2,000 it was finally decided to adopt the precedent set in 1899 by New South Wales.

(3) The provision for plural voting, under which

parliamentary elections were held, was dropped on this occasion with general consent.

(4) Special precautions were enacted to secure that the voters should know for what they were voting and where they should vote. The Draft Bill of Union, as finally approved by the Convention, was to be published not only in the Government Gazette but also in every newspaper of the Colony at least 20 days before the polling; and notice of the polling-stations was to be given at least 7 days before.

(5) All the voting was to take place on one day between the hours of 8 A.M. and 4 P.M. In parliamentary elections the voting was not all confined to one day.

The Convention met again at the beginning of May, and, after making certain amendments, approved of the final draft to be submitted to the four Colonies. In accordance with the Referendum Act, the draft was submitted to the electors of Natal on June 10, 1909.

The ballot papers were in this form :—

Referendum Act, 1909.

Are you in favour of the proposed Draft South African Act ?

Yes ..   ..   [   ]
No ..   ..   [   ]

If you are in favour of the Draft Act, make your **X** in the square opposite the word Yes.

If you are against the Draft Act, make your **X** in the square opposite the word No.

Before the polling day the members of the House of Assembly had toured their constituencies, explaining the Draft Act to the electors. Other advocates and opponents of the measure, some from other Colonies, had held public discussions about it, and the newspapers were full of it. On the whole, the public discussions did not seem to augur well for the prospects of the scheme. One of the two chief Natal papers was strongly against

it, and the other seemed rather undecided. Great
capital was made by the opponents of the Act
out of the recent dismissal of three English
inspectors in the Orange River Colony; and,
partly owing to some delay in explaining the
recent commercial treaty between the Transvaal
and Delagoa Bay, which was really not unfavourable to Natal, some apprehensions were aroused
amongst commercial people. Undoubtedly, the
opponents were more vociferous, and created a
feeling outside the Colony that Natal might very
possibly reject the Union. But two strong forces
were working in a contrary direction. The Dutch
in the districts of Greytown, Vryheid, and
Newcastle had said little, but were almost solid
for union with their brothers in the Transvaal
and the Orange River Colony, while the German
colonists in New Hanover were on the same side.
Moreover the English trading and farming community, though politically anxious to remain
separate, saw that they stood to lose enormously
in trade by setting themselves up against the
rest of South Africa. If high tariff walls were
erected against them, they were in danger of ruin.
These considerations proved decisive; and, in
spite of newspaper and platform talk, which gave
an entirely wrong impression of public feeling,
the voting showed an overwhelming majority for
the Draft Act.

Altogether, out of an electorate of 25,463
14,822 voted; 11,121 in favour of the Draft Act
and only 3,701 against. Not only was the majority
for the whole Colony decisive, but in every one of
the 17 voting districts there was a majority, the
smallest being at Pietermaritzburg (1,122 for,
722 against). The percentage of voters who
recorded their votes varied between 55·63 per
cent. and 99·27 per cent. (in the Vryheid district).
It must be remembered, however, that the electorate in Natal was exceedingly small compared

with the whole population, as white males only had the vote : the figures of the 1904 census being :—

Europeans	.. ..	97,109
Indians and Asiatics	..	100,918
Natives ..	.. ..	910,727
Total population	..	1,108,754

This referendum was certainly amply justified in Natal. In the other Colonies there was no need for it, as there was no considerable opposition to union ; and, though there was a half-hearted demand for a referendum in some quarters in the Transvaal, the scheme had been so fully discussed there and in the other two Colonies that nobody felt it a grievance that the electors were not specifically consulted. But in Natal it was very different. The Colony had not wished for union at first ; and, though the objections to refusing, when the other Colonies intended to unite, were obviously strong, the opponents of union did their best to prove their own importance. Had no referendum been held, the numerical weakness of these men would never have been demonstrated, and Natal would undoubtedly have felt that she had been driven into union against her will. After the referendum, Natal felt that she had entered the Union with her eyes open, and became much more disposed to make a success of the new venture.

VI.—THE REFERENDUM IN AUSTRALIA.

The value of the Referendum as a part of the
legislative machinery was discussed in various
States of Australia almost from the dawn of
responsible government. In its theory and practice
there have been so many good examples under the
Federation that no record need be made of facts
earlier than those of 1897-98.

(i) *Referenda on the Constitution.*—The Federal
Convention sat in three sessions in 1897-98 to
draft a constitution for the Union of Australia.
The States represented sent ten delegates each.
The Convention agreed upon a Federal Constitution modelled on American lines rather than
on those of the Canadian Constitution   " State
rights " were reserved ; and the Senate was
constituted as a Second Chamber, not only with
the ordinary functions of a revising Chamber, but
with the special responsibility of safeguarding
" State rights."

A proposal to settle disputes between the two
Houses by means of the Referendum was defeated.
It was recognized that this would make the Second
House practically powerless to defend the interests
of the less populous States in conflict with
those having a larger population. The Referendum
was, however, adopted as a final reference in
cases of any proposed change in the Constitution.

Such an amendment must secure an absolute
majority of both Houses of Parliament and must
then be referred to a direct vote of the people.
At this vote the amendment, to take effect, must
be endorsed by a majority of the voters in a
majority of the States and by a majority of the

total poll of the Commonwealth. There are six States in the Commonwealth. A proposed change of Constitution must thus be endorsed not only at the total poll, but also at the poll of at least four States. If Tasmania, West Australia, and South Australia by small majorities voted " No," and New South Wales, Victoria, and Queensland by large majorities voted " Yes," the " No " would have effect, though the total poll of the Commonwealth would be overwhelmingly " Yes."

This referendum system acts as a very conservative check on constitutional changes. It is made still more conservative by the provision that, if a proposed alteration in the Constitution affects the boundaries of any particular State or its representation in the Federal Parliament, the referendum in that State must give a majority in favour of the alteration.

The purpose was to safeguard " State rights " and " self-determination." This extremely jealous care as to State rights is remarkable in view of the fact that the States were almost identical in types of population, commercial interests, language, etc.

The Federal Constitution, as agreed to by the Convention of 1897-98, was submitted to a Referendum in the various Australian States. The New South Wales Parliament had imposed, as a condition of its acceptance of the decision of the Referendum, the proviso that a certain minimum number of affirmative votes should be cast. This number was not reached. The Federal Constitution was then slightly amended and again submitted to the Referendum in 1899. There was no condition in any State as to a minimum affirmative vote. The Constitution was accepted by New South Wales, Victoria, Queensland, South Australia, and Tasmania. Subsequently West Australia gave its adhesion. In 1901 the Federal Constitution was proclaimed.

To understand the subsequent Referenda of 1911 and 1913, it is necessary to have in mind the fact that the Australian Commonwealth Constitution (following therein the Constitution of the U.S.) gives to the High Court of Justice the right to veto State laws that trespass on the Federal Constitution and Commonwealth laws that trespass on State rights. A great deal of the " Labour legislation " of the Federal Parliament was declared unconstitutional by the High Court. A Labour Government in Power carried through both Houses of Parliament proposed amendments of the Constitution which gave to the Federal Legislature increased powers in dealing with trusts and monopolies. The figures of the Referendum poll taken on April 26, 1911, were :—

Total electors enrolled ..	2,341,624
Total ballot papers issued...	1,248,226
Affirmative votes for proposed first amendment to Constitution	483,356
Negative ditto	742,704
Affirmative votes for proposed second amendment to Constitution	488,668
Negative ditto	736,392

In all the States the vote was negative. On May 31, 1913, certain proposed amendments to the Constitution were again submitted to a Referendum. They covered a wider range this time, but all had the same design, to increase the power of the Federal Legislature in matters of Labour legislation. All the proposed changes were negatived, though they had all been approved by both Houses of Parliament.

(ii) *Other Referenda.*—On October 28, 1916, the Australian Government, by a special Referendum, asked the voters whether they were in favour of compulsory enlistment for service abroad (compulsory service for home defence already existed in Australia). The answer was " No," by a majority in the total poll of 72,426. Three States voted " Yes " by a majority, and three States voted " No." Experience of the Referendum in the Commonwealth of Australia shows that it does not follow the vote of Parliament.

Several of the States of Australia have a regular Referendum on the question of the sale of alcoholic liquor, taken at the time of a General Election. At such a Referendum the electors, voting on this direct issue, can vote for a continuance of the existing number of licensed houses, or for a reduction, or can vote " no licence." New South Wales, in 1916, had a special Liquor Referendum to decided the hour at which public-houses should close during the continuance of the war. Electors could vote for any hour from 6 P.M. to 11 P.M. The decision was for 6 P.M.

VII.—THE REFERENDUM IN SWITZERLAND.

As now understood in Switzerland, the Referendum means that certain bills must (Obligatory Referendum) and that other bills may (Facultative Referendum) be submitted to a popular vote for acceptance or rejection. But, in another form, the Referendum had existed for hundreds of years in certain of the Swiss cantons, where

> " certain matters which the assembled deputies of the people could not decide, either from want of the necessary powers or from lack of instructions, were reported on by them to their constituents, who, after discussing and considering them in their local assemblies, accepted or rejected the proposed measures, their decision being conveyed by their deputies to the large assembly, and the law finally rejected or approved by the majority of the communes or *Gemeinden* and not by the general assembly."

The earliest examples of this use of the institution are to be found in the history of the Valaisan and Rhætian Leagues, which were allied with, but were not part of, the Swiss Confederation. The Communes or Zenden of the Upper Valais sent, so early as 1399, representatives to the *concilium* or Landrath of the Bishop of Sion. These deputies brought back reports of proposed measures which were discussed in the Zenden, and the decision was announced to the Landrath. No measure was binding unless it was approved by all the Zenden.

The institution of the Referendum is more fully developed in the Swiss cantonal constitutions than in the federal constitution ; and its corollary, the

---

[1] Coolidge, in *English Historical Review*, October, 1891. *See* above : Introduction, pp. 12, 13.

Initiative, by which representative assemblies can be compelled to take proposals into consideration, was introduced in the Cantons before it was adopted by the Federation. By the federal Constitution of 1848, as amended in 1874 and 1891, it is provided (a) that a revision of the Constitution shall always be submitted to a popular vote ; (b) that the question of the desirability of a revision shall be submitted, if either House of the Legislature or 50,000 qualified voters demand this step ; (c) that eight cantons or 30,000 voters can demand a vote upon any measure not being urgent ; and (d) that the Initiative may be applied to any partial revision of the Constitution on the demand of 50,000 electors. Apart from the acceptance of the constitutions of 1848 and 1874, there were, between 1848 and 1907, 30 Obligatory Referenda on amendments of the federal Constitution, 30 votes on bills (since the introduction of the Facultative Referendum in 1874) ; and, since the introduction of the Initiative in 1891, seven votes have been taken in accordance with the provisions then made. Of these 67 appeals to the people, only 28 have resulted in approval of the proposed changes, and only one of these approvals was given in the period from 1848 to 1874. These figures seem to suggest that, in contrast to the French plebiscites, which, as we have seen, tended to be taken after the accomplishment of the facts which they confirmed, the Swiss Referenda, taken while the event was still doubtful, tended towards conservative decisions. On the other hand, it must be remembered that, while in the 26 years between 1848 and 1874 there was only one approval, in the 33 years between 1874 and 1907 there were 27 ; and the experience of the last few years does not necessarily confirm the theory that the Referendum is essentially a conservative institution. In 1908, by the Facultative Referendum, the Swiss people procured the passage of a law authorizing the

Federal Legislature to legislate about trades and
professions ;[1] and by the Initiative they secured
the adoption of a resolution authorizing the Federal
Legislature to pass laws for the utilization of
hydraulic power, and of a decree prohibiting the
manufacture and sale of absinthe (the latter by
237,665 votes to 136,254). In 1910, an Initiative
in favour of proportional representation in the
National Council was rejected by a small majority
(265,000 votes to 240,000). In 1912, a Facultative
Referendum on a Sickness and Accident Insurance
Bill approved the new measure by 287,566 votes
to 241,416 on a poll of 63·04 per cent. of the
electorate. In 1913, a bill giving the Federal
Government power to deal with dangerous and
widespread diseases of human beings and animals
was prohibited, on a Referendum, by a majority
of about 57,000 votes. These approvals illustrate
a marked tendency of recent Swiss politics
towards the transference of administrative
authority from the Cantons to the Confederation.
The only important innovation which falls outside
this category—the proposed introduction of proportional representation—was, as we have seen,
rejected.

A very important vote has recently been taken
in Switzerland on the question whether the Confederation should join the League of Nations or
not. The voting took place on Sunday, May 16,
1920. The votes were : for adhesion 416,870
votes ; against it 323,719, showing a majority of
93,151 in favour. But, according to the law,
a majority of cantons was also required ; and here
too a majority, but a very narrow one, was secured,
11½ cantons voting for adhesion, and 10½ against it.

---

[1] The voting was 228,670 against 90,182.

VIII.—THE REFERENDUM IN
THE UNITED STATES.

" The Referendum, in the restricted sense of a submission to a vote by the whole electorate of measures passed by the representative body, has been introduced in three different forms at three different (though to some extent overlapping) periods of American history."[1] These three forms are (1) the Constitutional Referendum ; (2) the Referendum as a check on the Legislature ; (3) the General Referendum on ordinary laws.

The Constitutional Referendum, which was the earliest form of the modern Referendum to appear in America after the Declaration of Independence, resulted from an attempt to place the fundamental law of the State on a different basis from the ordinary law.   By it State constitutions were submitted to the people for ratification.   In 1778 Massachusetts rejected a " Frame of Government " by a direct popular vote ; two years later a constitution was accepted by the same procedure. New Hampshire rejected a constitution in 1779, and accepted one in 1783, by the same procedure. After 1820 it became the common practice to submit State constitutions to a popular vote. It is possible, too, to amend, or partially revise, a constitution by this method, without rejecting or revising it as a whole. This is effected by inserting a provision in the constitution itself whereby the Legislature is empowered to enact amendments

---

[1] Lowell, A. Lawrence, *Quarterly Review*, April, 1911, art. 11, *The Referendum in Operation*. This article gives an admirable summary of the subject. *See also* Viscount Bryce, *The American Commonwealth.* 2 vols. New York, 1910.

subject to ratification by popular vote. A provision of this kind, which appeared in Connecticut in 1818, has since been almost universally copied.

The use of the Referendum as a check on the Legislature has arisen from a practical demand. A clause was inserted in several State constitutions providing that the action of the Legislature on certain subjects should not be valid unless ratified by popular vote. The subjects to which this test was applied were those in which the Legislature was supposed to be peculiarly susceptible to local influences or external pressure. The practice of thus checking the Legislature by the direct action of the people in particular circumstances began about the middle of the nineteenth century. It has been chiefly used in the smaller States, and has not spread very widely either in local extension or in the range of subjects affected by it.

The General Referendum on ordinary laws, the most comprehensive of the three forms of Referendum, is of very recent introduction. It is brought into being by inserting a general provision in a constitution that, " upon the petition of a certain number of citizens, any law, not declared urgent by the Legislature, shall be submitted to popular vote."[1] . . . . " It is a conscious imitation of Swiss models, and has usually been coupled with the Swiss Initiative, whereby a fixed number of citizens can propose a law and require a popular vote thereon."[2]

The General Referendum was adopted by South Dakota in 1898, and has since spread to many of the newer and less populous States. The Initiative has been little used in America, except in Oregon, where it has been very popular.

---

[1] Lowell, A. Lawrence, *ut supra*.
[2] *Ibid.*

IX.—THE PROMISED PLEBISCITE IN NORTH SCHLESWIG, 1866.

Article V of the Treaty of Prague (1866) provided for a plebiscite in Schleswig :—

" His Majesty the Emperor of Austria transfers to His Majesty the King of Prussia all the rights which he acquired by the Treaty of Vienna of October 30, 1864, over the Duchies of Holstein and Schleswig, with the condition that the populations of the northern districts of Schleswig shall be ceded to Denmark if, by a free vote, they express a wish to be united to Denmark."

Prussia not only refrained from consulting the people of North Schleswig, but sternly repressed any expression of Danish sympathies, and declared that the execution of the treaty was a matter that affected the signatories alone, and that any effort to bring this provision into effect was treasonable. A petition with over 27,000 signatures was ignored.[1] Bismarck, in a speech in the Diet, insisted that the clause in the treaty gave no right to any inhabitant of Schleswig ; that only the Emperor of Austria could exact its fulfilment ; that the treaty itself gave a wide latitude to the Prussian Government, entrusting the decision to its good faith and to its realization of the interests of the Prussian State ; and that in no circumstances could Prussia accept a frontier which compromised its own strategic security.[2] In 1879 the clause in question was cancelled by the Treaty between Germany and Austria which laid the foundation of the Triple Alliance ; and no plebiscite was taken in Schleswig under Prussian rule.

---

[1] *Revue de Droit International,* vol. ii (1870), pp. 325-6.
[2] *Ibid.,* p. 722, and *Les Discours de M. le Comte de Bismarck,* 2 vols., Berlin (1870), vol. i, pp. 322-5.

AUTHORITIES.

GENERAL.

Articles in *Le Moniteur Universel*, 1789-1804, 1848-70.

Article *Plebiscitum* in *Smith's Dictionary of Greek and Roman Antiquities.*

COOLIDGE, W. A. B. *Early History of the Referendum* : *English Historical Review*, vol. vi. London, 1891.

DICEY, A. V. *The Referendum and its Critics :* *Quarterly Review*, April, 1910.

HEIMWEH, J. (pseudonym). *Droit de Conquête et Plébiscite.* Paris, 1896. *(Questions du Temps présent.)*

LECKY, W. E. H. *Democracy and Liberty.* London, 1908.

LOWELL, A. LAWRENCE. *Governments and Parties in Continental Europe.* London, 1904.

ROUARD DE CARD, E. *Etudes de Droit International.* Paris, 1890.

ROUSSEAU, J. J. *Du Contrat Social*, ed. C. E. Vaughan. Manchester, 1918.

FRANCE

AULARD, A. *Histoire Politiqu. de la Révolution Française.* Paris, 1901.

BODLEY, J. E. C. *France.* London, 1898.

Cambridge Modern History, vols. viii, ix, xi.

DUGUIT, L., and MONNIER, H. *Les Constitutions et les Principales Lois Politiques de la France depuis* 1789. Paris, 1898.

LA GORCE, P. de. *Histoire de la Seconde République Française.* Paris, 1911.

SOREL, A. *L'Europe et la Révolution Française.* Paris, 1911.

ITALY.

KING, BOLTON. *A History of Italian Unity*, 1814-71, 2 vols., London, 1899 (ii, pp. 121 ff., 175 ff.) ; and THAYER, W. R. *The Life and Times of Cavour*, 2 vols., New York, 1911 (ii, p. 415), contain very brief accounts of the plebiscites. Fuller accounts of particular plebiscites are to be found in the following works :—

CADORNA, R. *La Liberazione di Roma nell' anno* 1870 *ed il Plebiscito.* Turin, 1898. (Rome.)

CESARE, R. de. *La fine di un Regno.* 3 vols. Città di Castello, 1909. (Naples and Sicily.)

CESARE, R. de.   *Roma e lo Stato del Papa.*   Rome, 1907.
(Rome.)

FINALI, G.   *Le Marche: Ricordanze.*   Ancona, 1897.
(The Marches, esp. ch. xiii.)

RUBIERI, E.   *Storia intima della Toscana, dal 1 Gennaio*
1859 al 30 aprile, 1860.   Prato, 1861.   (Tuscany.)

There is, however, no detailed account of the Italian
plebiscites as a whole ; and the account given in the text is
almost wholly based on the correspondence of the British
Ministers and Consuls accredited to the Italian States, 1848-60,
much of which has been printed in the Parliamentary Papers
relating to the affairs of Italy, *viz. :—*

Correspondence respecting the Affairs of Italy, 1846-9.
4 pts.   1849.

Correspondence relating to the Affairs of Italy, 1860.

Further Correspondence relating to the Affairs of Italy.
7 pts.   1861.

Correspondence respecting the Affairs of Rome.   1870-71.

These have been supplemented by the reports of the
correspondents of the *Times* and the *Morning Post.*

NORWAY.

HEIBERG, J. V.   *Unionens opløsning,* 1905.   Kristiania, 1906.

NANSEN, F.   *Norway and the Union with Sweden.*   London,
1905.

NORDLUND, K.   *The Swedish-Norwegian Union Crisis.*   Stock-
holm, 1905.

The Union between Sweden and Norway.   Address presented
to the King by the Swedish Parliament, 1905.

NATAL.

Debates of House of Assembly, Natal, 1908-9.   Parliamentary
paper Cd. 5099 (1910), *Correspondence respecting an Act*
of Referendum in Natal.

Edinburgh Review, July, 1909.   " The South African Union."

AUSTRALIA.

MOORE, W. HARRISON.   *The Constitution of the Commonwealth*
of Australia.   Melbourne, 1910.

QUICK, SIR JOHN, and GARRAN, SIR ROBERT R.   *Annotated*
Constitution of the Australian Commonwealth.   Sydney,
1901.

Official Year Book of Australia.

SWITZERLAND.

Article *Switzerland* in *Encyclopædia Britannica*, 1911.

HEUSLER, A. *Rechtsquellen des Cantons Wallis.* Basle, 1890.

LOWELL, A. LAWRENCE, and Professors MOORE and OECHSLI. *The Referendum in Operation* (The Referendum in Switzerland, the United States, and Australia). *Quarterly Review*, April, 1911.

Rapport du Conseil fédéral . . . concernant le résultat de la votation populaire du 16 mai 1920.

SIMLER, J. *De Helvetiorum Republica*, Zurich, 1576. (Reprints, 1577-1735).

VULPI, J. A. *Historia Rætica translatada et scritta in lingua vulgara ladina.* Coira, 1866.

SCHLESWIG.

Revue de Droit International. Brussels, 1869, etc., vol. iii.

Printed by H.M. STATIONERY OFFICE PRESS, Dugdale Street, S.E.5

HANDBOOKS PREPARED UNDER THE DIRECTION OF THE
HISTORICAL SECTION OF THE FOREIGN OFFICE.—No. 160

SCHEMES FOR MAINTAINING

GENERAL PEACE

BY

The Right Hon. LORD PHILLIMORE,
D.C.L., LL.D.

LONDON
PUBLISHED BY H.M. STATIONERY OFFICE

1920

TABLE OF CONTENTS

Wt. 9157/860. 1000. 6 20. O.U.P.

SCHEMES FOR MAINTAINING GENERAL PEACE

PRELIMINARY

THE task undertaken in the following pages is to tabulate and discuss the various measures which have been suggested for the peaceful settlement of disputes which may arise in future between States, so that they may be, if possible, decided without recourse to war. The schemes to this effect, if we go through the history and literature of the world, seem to fall into four classes :

(1) The provision of a single Universal Superior who would settle in the last resort as between his subordinates or feudatories.

(2) The substitution of a Republic for a single Universal Superior, and the making of a Federation of States which, through its organ or organs, should decide disputes between its component members.

(3) The provision and promotion of International Arbitration.

(4) A sort of composite between (2) and (3), which has found favour with writers of quite modern date, mostly since the War began.

I. ONE SUPREME POWER

From time to time, since Europe began to settle down after the break-up of the Western Roman Empire, there have been thinkers who have devoted their attention to schemes for the prevention of war. Scholars in particular have referred with regret to the times when the *Pax Romana* prevailed, when the great Roman Empire, or the

B

two halves of it acting in conjunction, embraced the whole of the civilized world for those who were ignorant of the civilization of the Far East, and when the Empire by its strength imposed quiet upon its uncivilized neighbours, and reduced frontier wars with them to the category of mere border forays, to be dealt with as matters of police.

One of the earliest exponents of the idea of a universal monarchy—that is, literally, of there being one supreme ruler over all princes and States—was Dante, who published his treatise *De Monarchia* in the year 1311.[1] He felt the need of a superior tribunal to decide between warring nations, and contemplated, for this purpose, a monarchy so universal that there could be no enemies, only rebels. With a bold neglect of historical detail, and a contempt for all the world outside his narrow knowledge of geography, he considered that the monarchy of the Emperor Augustus was such a universal monarchy; that the right to it was vested in the Romans; and that this right had passed to the Emperors of his own day. The point on which he felt most doubt was whether the Emperors held immediately from God or mediately through the Pope, and he concluded in favour of the immediate jurisdiction of the Emperor in matters temporal.

Other writers looked for their Universal Monarch in the Pope; and there is no doubt that from time to time he exercised a valuable mediating influence, and sometimes received complete submission. Leibnitz, in the preface to his *Codex Iuris Gentium Diplomaticus*, published in 1693, expresses himself, in a remarkable passage,[2] as follows:

---

[1] There is a good summary in J. A. Symonds's *Introduction to the Study of Dante*, pp. 71–5.

[2] Dr. Darby (*International Tribunals*, p. 100) gives a translation of the greater part of this passage. He also quotes (p. 98) a letter

' But Christians have another common bond, that is, the positive Law of God which is contained in the Holy Scriptures. To which should be added the sacred Canons which have been received by the whole Church, and afterwards, in the West, the Papal Laws to which kings and nations submitted themselves. And I find that before the schism of the last century it had long been universally accepted (and not without reason) that there should be understood to be a sort of Commonwealth of Christian Nations, whose heads should be in sacred matters the Pope, in temporal matters the Roman Emperor, who was thought to have retained as much of the rights of the old Roman Monarchy, as might be needful for the common good of Christianity, without prejudice to the rights of Kings and the liberty of Princes. . . . Nothing was more common than for Kings to submit themselves, in the making of treaties, to the approval and correction of the . Pope, as in the Peace of Bretigny. . . . But as human things, even the best, tend to become corrupt, the Popes began to extend too much the limits of their authority and to make a too unrestrained use of their power.'

Calvo, in his work on International Law, treats of the Pope as an International Arbitrator.[1] The claims of the Popes to dispose of newly discovered territories, hitherto occupied by infidels, are well known. One of these Bulls is set out in the *Codex* of Leibnitz.[2] Another, dated May 4, 1493, was in the nature of an award between Spain and Portugal, and was confirmed by the Treaty of Tordesillas, 1494.[3]

Though it is inconceivable that the majority of nations would recognize any jurisdiction in the See of Rome, it might be useful to have a sovereign who, by virtue of his position, was a perpetual neutral, and could be

from Leibnitz to Saint-Pierre. It should be remembered that Leibnitz was not a papist.

[1] Sect. 1487.

[2] And see Fleury, *Histoire Ecclésiastique*, vol. 24, Lib. 117, Sect. 73.

[3] Calvo, sect. 1487; Prescott, *History of Ferdinand and Isabella*, vol. i, p. 544.

applied to for his services as an intermediary. The
present Pope brought about some mitigation of the
cruelties of the Great War,[1] and it is perhaps unfortunate
that Leo XIII was denied admission to the first Hague
Conference.

After the Western Empire, as refounded by Charlemagne, had become entirely dissociated from, and often
came into conflict with, the Eastern Empire, and after the
rowth in strength and organization of the Mohammedan
Powers, the idea of a universal monarchy under the
Emperor became untenable. After the failure of the
Council of Florence (A. D. 1437) to heal the rupture
between the Eastern and Western Churches, and the
development of the Reformation in the next century,
the Pope (however some might think of him as a supreme
power *de jure*) ceased to have any position as a generally
recognized superior.

II. A FEDERATION OF STATES

A Republic or Federation of States was a natural
substitute for the idea of a Universal Monarchy. The
first approach to it was the 'Grand Design' of Henry IV
of France. Somewhere about the same time the expedient of Arbitration began to present itself. While
the object of both these schemes is the same, their
principles are different, indeed inconsistent.

The idea of a Federation is the formation of such
a Unity that war between any two of the federated
States partakes of the nature of Civil War, and is to be
suppressed in some way by the sovereign authority of
the Federation. The idea of Arbitration is that two

---

[1] His Circular Note, issued in August 1917, is mentioned in
Section III (p. 21).

independent Sovereign Powers submit, *pro hac vice* only, some particular dispute to the determination of an authority chosen *ad hoc*, to which they were under no obligation *a priori* to submit themselves, and to which they, of their own free will, submit for the moment. The two ideas have kept their place in the literature on this subject ; but, while Federation was the favourite scheme of the 17th and 18th centuries, Arbitration took the leading place throughout the 19th. Now, however, as will be seen hereafter, the idea of Federation is the one which specially commends itself to writers of the present time.

There is a possible combination of the two ideas, if for Arbitration before a Tribunal formed *ad hoc*, in virtue of previous consent, recourse to a Permanent Court be substituted, and the main object of the Federation be to constitute and support such a Court, with an Executive and a Police to enforce obedience to its orders.

The idea of a wide Federation of States seems to have been suggested by the success of such Confederations or Leagues as the Amphictyonic League, the Swiss Confederation, the Hanseatic League, and the States-General of Holland. Later writers have fortified their views by reference to the Confederation of the United States of North America.

The idea of a European Federation is generally supposed to have first seen the light in the 'Grand Design' of Henry IV of France. This scheme is to be collected partly from Sully's *Mémoires*, and partly from the works of the Abbé de Saint-Pierre. Henry IV contemplated a rearrangement of Europe. The five principal points treated of with Elizabeth of England were, according to Sully : [1]

---

[1] Sully, *Mémoires*, ed. 1814, vol. iii, pp. 54, 55 ; and see generally vol. vi, Book XXX.

1. Restoration of the freedom of the election of an Emperor;

2. Making the States-General independent of Spain and perhaps giving them some addition of territory from Germany;

3. Making Switzerland completely independent and adding to it Alsace and Franche-Comté;

4. Dividing Christianity into sovereignties of about equal importance;

5. Reducing the religions or the forms of Christianity in Europe to three: the Catholic, the Protestant or Lutheran, and the Reformed or Calvinist.

Henry IV proposed to secure the internal peace of the Federation, but he contemplated external war. Indeed, the principal object of the Federation was the reduction of the power of the House of Habsburg. Another object being to reduce the religions of Europe to three, the Turk was to be expelled from Europe; and it was expressly provided that, if the Grand Duke of Muscovy or Tsar of Russia would not come into the alliance, and apparently if he would not accept one of the above-named forms of Christianity, he was to be treated like the Sultan, and cast out of Europe.[1]

The scheme of Saint-Pierre (see Authorities, p. 68) is conveniently summarized by Wheaton[2] and by Dr. Darby.[3] His views have also been given by De Molinari (see Authorities).[4] His own publications, *Projet de traité pour rendre la Paix perpétuelle entre les Souverains Chrétiens*, and *Abrégé du projet de Paix perpétuelle*, are not easy of access. According to Wheaton his main articles were:

1. An alliance for mutual security against foreign or civil war, and for guaranteeing the possessions of the several States as established by the Treaty of Utrecht.

2. A provision for contributions to a common fund.

[1] Sully, ed. 1814, vol. v, p. 296.
[2] Wheaton, *Histoire des Progrès du Droit des Gens*, fourth edition.
[3] *International Tribunals*, p. 70.   [4] See below, p. 10.

3. Establishing peace among the Allies. Any differences to be submitted to the arbitration of the other Powers of the League, and to be decided provisionally by a majority, and finally by a plurality of three to one. For this purpose nineteen Powers whom he mentions were to have single votes; all other Powers were to be associated to make up a vote.

4. Provision for offensive action against recalcitrant members who did not conform to the rules made by the Alliance, or contravened treaties, or prepared for war.

According to quotations in Dr. Darby's *International Tribunals*, Saint-Pierre provided for each State in the Confederation sending a quota of forces, and for the appointment of a generalissimo. At the end of his scheme there is a suggestion of an Asiatic Union similar to that of Europe, with a hope that the two Confederations would be at peace with each other.

Saint-Pierre is a decided advocate of force. Thus he says:

'Le Souverain qui prendra les armes avant la déclaration de guerre de l'Union, ou qui refusera d'exécuter un règlement de la Société ou un jugement du Sénat, sera déclaré ennemi de la Société, et elle luy fera la guerre, jusqu'à ce qu'il soit désarmé, et jusqu'à l'exécution du jugement et des règlemens.' [1]

And:

'Si après la Société formée au nombre de quatorze voix un Souverain refusoit d'y entrer, elle le déclarera ennemi du repos de l'Europe, et lui fera la guerre jusqu'à ce qu'il y soit entré, ou jusqu'à ce qu'il soit entièrement dépossédé.' [2]

A scheme for a European Diet, Parliament or Estates, was published by William Penn in 1693-4 (see Authorities). It was limited to European States, and its object was that peace should be established and maintained in Europe. Penn expresses his general adhesion to the

[1] Dr. Darby, *International Tribunals*, p. 75.

[2] *Ibid.* Voltaire called it, in his poem *La Tactique*, 'L'impraticable Paix de l'abbé de Saint-Pierre', *Works*, vol. xii, p. 232.

'Grand Design'. As between the various members of the Federation, obedience to the decisions of the Supreme Diet or Senate was to be enforced by arms. Thus he says that,

'If any of the Sovereignties constituting this Imperial Diet should refuse to submit their claims or pretensions to the Diet, or to accept its judgment, and should seek their remedy by arms, or delay compliance beyond the time specified, all the other Sovereignties, uniting their forces, should compel submission to, and performance of, the sentence and payment of all costs and damages.'

No one of these schemes, as will be observed, was wide enough for 'the Parliament of man, the Federation of the world'. They are only schemes for large and comprehensive alliances, and for regulating disputes between the Allies. Penn points out many of the difficulties which would attend upon even his limited Federation. In this he is followed by Kant in a work which is about to be quoted, and in which the idea may be traced that, the larger the Federation, the less its value as an expedient for preserving peace between the Allies.

Kant, in 1795, published a tract on *Perpetual Peace*. It is very short, and consists of a series of Articles or Propositions, with a running commentary for the amplification of each. He proposed that standing armies should, in the course of time, be abolished; that no State should interfere by force with the constitution or government of another State; that the civil constitution in every State should be republican, by which he carefully explains that he does not mean democratic;[1] and

[1] 'Republicanism (says Kant) is the political principle of severing the executive power of the government from the legislature. Despotism is that principle in pursuance of which the State arbitrarily puts into effect laws which it has itself made; consequently it is the administration of the public will, but this is

that 'international right should be founded on a federation of free states'.

As to the completeness of this Federation he seems to be somewhat hazy. In one part of his observations upon this proposition he says that a 'State of Nations' would be a contradiction; a little farther on he says:

'For States, in their relation to one another, there can be, according to reason, no other way of advancing from that lawless condition which unceasing war implies, than by giving up their savage lawless freedom, just as individual men have done, and yielding to the coercion of public laws. Thus they form a State of Nations (*civitas gentium*), one, too, which will be ever increasing and would finally embrace all the peoples of the earth.'[1]

His mind is perhaps to be gathered as much from other parts of his writings as from the actual treatise itself.[2] From his *Rechtslehre* one gathers that he thought that a Universal Union of States was impossible, and that therefore perpetual peace, the final goal of International Law, was really an impracticable idea.

In the passage in the *Rechtslehre* he proposed a Union of Nations, to be termed a Permanent Congress of States, to which every neighbouring State might be at liberty to associate itself, on the model of the Diplomatic Conference which used to exist, as he says, at The Hague during the first half of the 18th century. The Association was to be voluntary, and adhesion to it would be at all times revocable. He had no scheme for a tribunal, and had worked out no details. The material passage from the *Rechtslehre*, and the actual propositions of *Perpetual*

identical with the private will of the ruler. Of these three forms of a State, democracy, in the proper sense of the word, is of necessity despotism.' *Perpetual Peace*, by I. Kant, 1795, p. 125. Translation by Miss M. Campbell Smith, 1915

[1] *Ibid.*, p. 136.

[2] *Rechtslehre*, Pt. ii, sect. 61. Translation by Miss M. Campbell Smith, p. 129.

Peace, without the running commentary, are given by Dr. Darby in his work.[1]

In the translation of the whole *Essay on Perpetual Peace*, published with Introduction and Notes by Miss Mary Campbell Smith, the translator's Introduction is well worth study as a more complete contribution than Kant's own Essay. Miss Campbell Smith points out the inability of Arbitration to deal with disputes which arouse the passions of nations, and the practical objections to any scheme of disarmament; and, while advocating Federation as the only thing that 'can help out the programme of the Peace Society', says, nevertheless, that it cannot be pretended that it would do everything.

In 1857, shortly after the Crimean War, De Molinari, who had been much moved by that war, and especially felt the injury which it had occasioned to neutrals, published a work on Saint-Pierre, and prefixed to it an Introduction which stated his own views. He referred also to a work by Ancillon,[2] called *Tableau des Révolutions du Système politique de l'Europe* (see Authorities, p. 68).

De Molinari is perhaps the first writer who contemplated a Federation, the object of which would be confined to the establishment of an International Tribunal with International Police. The Tribunal was not to be an accident of the Federation; but the Federation was to be made in order to constitute it a real Court, and not a mere Arbitral Tribunal. He called his Federation 'concert universel', and was not even afraid of the expression 'une Sainte-Alliance universelle'. He observes:

'S'il existait, pour les gouvernements comme pour les particuliers, des tribunaux devant lesquels ils fussent tenus de porter leurs différends, avec une force publique organisée pour faire

---

[1] *International Tribunals*, pp. 150–63.

[2] The 'Discours préliminaire' to Ancillon's book is pessimistic, but worthy of study. He wrote in French, but was in fact a German.

respecter les décisions de ces tribunaux ; s'il existait, pour tout dire, une justice et une police internationales, les différends des gouvernements ne troubleraient pas plus la paix du monde que les procès des particuliers ne troublent aujourd'hui l'ordre intérieur des États.

‘ Malheureusement, ces cours de justice et cette force publique internationales n'existent point. Pour nous servir de l'expression des jurisconsultes, les gouvernements se considèrent comme étant les uns vis-à-vis des autres dans l'état de nature ; ce qui signifie qu'ils s'attribuent le droit de juger leurs propres causes, comme aussi de poursuivre par la force la revendication de leurs droits ou de leurs prétentions abusives ou fondées. De là, la guerre ’ (pp. 47, 48).

Bluntschli also had a scheme for a European Federation, the decisions of which were to be carried into execution by the Great Powers. He frankly says of his scheme that the possibility of a European War would not be completely excluded by its organization, and that a disarmament and disbanding of all standing armies would by no means be an immediate consequence of it. His scheme, as set forth in Dr. Darby's book (p. 194), is very fanciful.

A few years before the Great War, the idea of a United States of Europe commended itself to Sir Max Waechter, who visited, as he states, every European country, and interviewed a number of Sovereigns and Ministers, delivered a lecture at the Royal Institution in February 1909, and wrote on the subject numerous letters to the papers, especially one which appeared in *The Times* of January 31, 1914. He founded a European Unity League, and developed his scheme in a pamphlet, privately printed, date November 1, 1916 (see Authorities, p. 71).

III. INTERNATIONAL ARBITRATION

States unwilling to diminish aught of their sovereignty and independence by submission to a paramount Power, or by entrance into a Confederation, can nevertheless get the advantage of some form of neutral intervention to assist in the conciliation of their warring claims. Thus, from early times, it has been a convenient practice to invoke the good offices or mediation of a third State.

The Treaty of Teschen, 1779, between Maria Theresa, Empress and Queen of Hungary, and Frederick II, King of Prussia, was concluded under the mediation of France and Russia. These Powers not only mediated but guaranteed the stipulations of the Treaty and of certain ancillary Treaties.

The Treaty of Szistowa, 1791, between the Emperor and Turkey, was declared to have been concluded under the mediation of Great Britain, France, and the States-General.

The Treaty of 1850, between Prussia and Denmark, was declared to be concluded with the concurrence of Great Britain as a mediating Power.

Pufendorf,[1] Vattel,[2] Wheaton,[3] Bluntschli,[4] Heffter,[5] Klüber,[6] Phillimore,[7] and Calvo,[8] treat of 'good offices'

[1] *De Iure Naturae et Gentium*, Book V, ch. 13. sect. 7 ; Book VIII, ch. 8, sect. 7.

[2] *Le Droit des Gens*, Livre II, sect. 328.

[3] *Elements of International Law*, sects 73, 288.

[4] *Le Droit International Codifié*, Introduction, p. 31 ; sects. 485-7.

[5] *Le Droit International de l'Europe*, sect. 88.

[6] *Droit des Gens moderne de l'Europe*, sect. 160.

[7] *Commentaries upon International Law*, vol. iii, sect. 4.

[8] *Le Droit International*, sects. 686, 687, 1456-70.

and mediation. Diplomatic sanction to the general idea of mediation was given by Article VIII of the Treaty of Paris, 1856, and by Protocol 23 of the Congress by which the Treaty was framed.[1] Good offices and mediation form the subject of Section 2 of the Convention for the pacific settlement of international disputes, framed at the Hague Conference of 1899, and reaffirmed at the Conference of 1907.[2]

A further step is taken when States agree to submit differences to arbitration. Arbitration, as at least an occasional means for avoiding war, has been contemplated by most writers on International Law—by Grotius,[3] Pufendorf,[4] Vattel,[5] Phillimore,[6] Heffter,[7] Klüber,[8] Bluntschli,[9] and Calvo.[10] Passages from other writers, such as Bentham and James Mill, are quoted by Dr. Darby, in the work already referred to. as having treated of arbitration as a means of avoiding war.

As Calvo says, arbitration was rare in the 16th, 17th, and 18th centuries. It has been well observed that the 18th century was the century of mediation, and the 19th that of arbitration. Since the Franco-German War of 1870–1 and the formation of the Institut du Droit International and the Association for the Reform and Codification of the Law of Nations, afterwards styled The International Law Association, projects for international arbitration have been very numerous. They are to be found in Dr. Darby's book on International Tribunals. The most fully developed of these projects is that of the International Law Association accepted at the Conference at Buffalo, August 31, 1899 (op. cit., p. 592).

[1] Darby, *International Tribunals*, p. 299.
[2] *Ibid.*, p. 606 ; Pearce Higgins, *The Hague Conferences*, p. 102.
[3] *De Iure Belli et Pacis*, Book II, ch. 23, 8 ; Book III, ch. 20, 46.
[4] Book V, ch. 13, sects. 3-6.   [5] Sect. 329.
[6] Vol. iii, sects. 3, 5.   [7] Sect. 109.
[8] Sect. 318.   [9] Sects. 488–98.
[10] Sects. 1481–1565.

As regards the appearance of arbitration clauses in Treaties, the germ is to be traced to clauses in Treaties of Peace referring claims for compensation by the subjects of one of the two States at war against the other State to Commissioners for adjudication and assessment. The next step was to provide in similar Treaties for Arbitrations *de futuro* in the event of new disputes arising. Then came a series of Treaties of modern date, some ratified and some not, being not Treaties of Peace after war, but Treaties framed in time of peace solely for the purpose of avoiding war in the case of future disputes by means of some form of arbitration.

Into these Treaties there gradually enters the idea of a Tribunal or Court. The phrase occurs in the plan of the International American Conference of 1890, which ultimately lapsed for want of ratification by the individual American Republics. The Anglo-American Arbitration Treaty, 1897, also not ratified, and the Treaty between Argentina and Italy, 1898, speak of an Arbitral Tribunal. But all these Courts or Tribunals were to be created *ad hoc*, and to be merely bodies of Arbitrators chosen for the purpose of deciding some special controversy, whose commission would end as soon as they had awarded on that controversy.

In the Convention for the specific settlement of international disputes framed at the Hague Conference of 1899, a further step was taken by the organization (on paper at any rate) of a ' permanent Court of Arbitration accessible at all times and working, except there be contrary stipulation of the parties, in conformity with the Rules of Procedure inserted in the present Convention'. If this Court had had a real existence, with ascertained judges, and an obligation on the States party to the Treaty to refer differences, even differences of one class only, to it, and to abide by its decision, it might be said that the contracting States were tending towards

the position of the United States of America, with one
Supreme Court to decide differences between different
States or between their respective inhabitants.

But, on examination, very little that is effective remains
of this idea. There is, no doubt, an International Bureau
established at The Hague, which is to act as the Clerk's
Office or Registry of the Court (Art. 22). Each of the
Signatory Powers is to nominate certain persons to be
Arbitrators, so that the Bureau will have a list of
Arbitrators (Art. 23). Further, when two Powers desire
to apply to the Permanent Court for the settlement of
a difference, the choice of Arbitrators to form the Tribunal
should be made from the general list of the Members of
the Court. And, if the States, having applied to the
Permanent Court, and so far submitted to it, fail to
agree upon the constitution of an Arbitral Tribunal,
there is a procedure in the Treaty for effecting the composition of the Tribunal (Art. 24).

But no State binds itself to apply to the Permanent
Court. If States do apply, they are not discouraged from
choosing their own Arbitrators, either within, or outside
of, the list of Members of the Permanent Court : and if,
failing to agree otherwise, they allow the procedure of
the Court to be applied, that procedure helps them very
little, for it only provides that each party shall name two
Arbitrators, and that these Arbitrators together shall
choose an Umpire. It is only by suggesting a list of
Arbitrators and providing in the case of disagreement
for the choice of an Umpire that the rules of the
Conference help them (Art. 24).

Moreover, no power is given to a State to have recourse
ex parte to the permanent Court of Arbitration or to its
Bureau at The Hague with a statement that it has a
dispute with another State which it wishes to have
referred to Arbitration, and to get the assistance of the
Court to have it so referred. Nothing comes before the

Court unless and until the two States 'sign a special agreement or *compromis* clearly defining the objects of the dispute as well as the extent of the powers of the Arbitrators' (Art. 21).

Article 32 contemplates the conferring of Arbitration functions upon a single Arbitrator, or several Arbitrators, named by the parties at their discretion, or chosen from among the Members of the Permanent Court. The Signatory States in fact set up a model form or pattern of arbitration proceedings, but bind themselves to nothing except the establishment of an International Bureau at The Hague, to which they are to communicate information as to any Arbitration Proceedings to which they are parties (Art. 22), and the expenses of which they are to bear in certain proportions (Art. 29).

In addition to the Procedure by Arbitration there are some useful provisions for International Commissions of Inquiry, under which the North Sea Commission sat in 1905 to inquire into the recent episode at the Dogger Bank.[1]

The second American International Conference, meeting at Mexico in 1902, effected a Treaty that was not only signed but ratified by a sufficient number of American States to give it force; but the Treaty did little more in this respect than adhere to the Hague Conference, with a provision (Art. 4) that

' Whenever it may be necessary, from any cause whatever, to organise a Special Tribunal, either because any one of the parties may desire it or by reason of the Permanent Court of Arbitration at The Hague not being open to them, the procedure to be followed shall be established on the signing of the Arbitration Agreement.'

The second Hague Conference of 1907 went some way farther. The Convention is at any rate a much more

---

[1] Pearce Higgins, *The Hague Peace Conferences*, p. 167. And see later the Anglo-American Treaty of 1914 (p. 21).

elaborate document, having ninety-seven Articles as against sixty-one. The subject of International Commissions of Inquiry is much farther elaborated. This Convention was not intended to be supplementary to the old Convention, but to replace it; and many of the Articles are mere re-enactments.

The old Convention stated that

'In questions of a legal nature, and especially in the interpretation or application of International Conventions, arbitration is recognized by the Signatory Powers as the most effective, and at the same time the most equitable, means of settling disputes which diplomacy has failed to settle' (Art. 16).

The new Convention repeats this, and adds:

'Consequently, it would be desirable that, in disputes regarding the above-mentioned questions, the Contracting Powers should, if the case arise, have recourse to arbitration, in so far as circumstances permit' (Art. 38 of 1907).

There is an improvement in detail as to the appointment of the Umpire (compare Art. 24 of 1899 with Art. 45 of 1907); and there is a noteworthy step towards the conversion of the International Tribunal into a Court to which any aggrieved Power may apply *ex parte*, in the additional clause which appears at the end of Art. 48:

'In case of dispute between two Powers, one of them may always address to the International Bureau a note containing a declaration that it would be ready to submit the dispute to arbitration. The Bureau must at once inform the other Power of the declaration.'

A similar indication is found in Chapter III, 'On Arbitration Procedure', where this new provision is introduced by Art. 53:

'The Permanent Court is competent to settle the *compromis*, if the parties are agreed to have recourse to it for the purpose. It is similarly competent, even if the request is only made by one of the parties, when all attempts to reach an understanding through the diplomatic channel have failed in the case of

' 1. A dispute covered by a general Treaty of Arbitration concluded or renewed after the present Convention has come into force, and providing for a *compromis* in all disputes and not either explicitly or implicitly excluding the settlement of the *compromis* from the competence of the Court. Recourse cannot, however, be had to the Court if the other party declares that in its opinion the dispute does not belong to the category of disputes which can be submitted to obligatory arbitration, unless the Treaty of Arbitration confers upon the Arbitration Tribunal the power of deciding this preliminary question ;

' 2. A dispute arising from contract debts claimed from one Power by another Power as due to its nationals, and for the settlement of which the offer of arbitration has been accepted. This provision is not applicable if acceptance is subject to the condition that the *compromis* should be settled in some other way.'

This is supplemented by Articles 54 and 58 :

' ART 54.   In the cases contemplated in the preceding Article, the *compromis* shall be settled by a Commission consisting of five members selected in the manner laid down in Art. 45, paragraphs 3 to 6.   The fifth member is *ex officio* President of the Commission.'

' ART. 58.   When the *compromis* is settled by a commission, as contemplated in Art. 54, and in default of agreement to the contrary, the Commission itself shall form the Arbitration Tribunal.'

In the Convention of 1907 a new Chapter (Chap. IV) on Arbitration by Summary Procedure is added.   This is an alternative form, the utility of which it is not very easy to see ; at any rate, no new matter or principle is introduced.

In the final Act of the Conference of 1907 it is stated that the Conference is unanimous—

' 1. In admitting the principle of compulsory arbitration.

' 2. In declaring that certain disputes, in particular those

relating to the interpretation and application of the provisions
of international agreements, may be submitted to compulsory
arbitration without any restriction.

'Finally it is unanimous in proclaiming that, although it has
not yet been found feasible to conclude a Convention in this
sense, nevertheless the divergencies of opinion which have come
to light have not exceeded the bounds of judicial controversy,
and that, by working together here during the past four months,
the collected Powers not only have learnt to understand one
another and to draw closer together, but have succeeded in the
course of this long collaboration in evolving a very lofty
conception of the common welfare of humanity.'[1]

And there is added a wish or *vœu* to the following
effect:

'1. The Conference calls the attention of the Signatory
Powers to the advisability of adopting the annexed draft
Convention for the creation of a Judicial Arbitration Court,
and of bringing it into force as soon as an agreement has
been reached respecting the selection of the Judges and the
constitution of the Court.'[2]

The draft Convention referred to in this *vœu*[3] goes
farther, as it contemplates the appointment of salaried
and permanent judges, who are to enjoy diplomatic
privileges and immunities, and who are to form a special
Delegation of three judges annually. The Court is to
meet once a year, unless the Delegation considers it
unnecessary. The Delegation is to be competent to
decide cases if the parties agree to arbitration by summary procedure, to settle the *compromis* of Art. 52 of
the Hague Convention, if the parties are agreed to leave
it to the Court, and, in certain cases at the request of one
party only. And a procedure for the Court is established.
The result is that there is in the actual Convention
a suggestion of a skeleton Court and a procedure for any

[1] Pearce Higgins, p. 67.   [2] Pearce Higgins, p. 67.
[3] Pearce Higgins, p. 498.

c 2

cases which States at variance may desire to refer to
arbitration; there is a distinct recommendation to refer
certain classes of cases to arbitration without restriction ;
though no recourse to the Hague Court of Arbitration
can be made except by mutual consent, there is the
power to use the International Bureau as a formal vehicle
for announcing the readiness of one State to go to arbitration ; and lastly, there is the more trenchant provision
in Art. 53, enabling the Permanent Court in certain cases
to frame a *compromis* or reference to Arbitration.

But this is more in seeming than in reality ; for the
vehicle for framing the *compromis* is to be a Commission,
the members of which are to be nominated as in Art. 55,
that is by each party appointing two Arbitrators, with
provisions for the choice of an Umpire.   If, therefore,
one State is unwilling to go to Arbitration, even though
it has obliged itself beforehand to submit questions to
Arbitration, it can effectively prevent a compulsory
reference by refusing to appoint its members of the
Commission.

When facts are looked in the face, it remains that
Arbitration under the second Hague Conference, as under
the first, is only for those who agree to submit to it.
The draft Convention carries matters a little farther, but
not much.

As Sir Thomas Barclay [1] has truly observed :

'It is obvious that a Treaty of Arbitration, to fulfil its
purpose of avoiding any break in the amicable relations between
States, must be at the same time general, obligatory, and automatic. It must be general, because its purpose would be defeated
if, when the crisis came, one or the other party were driven to
dispute the applicability of the treaty to the matter at issue.
It must be obligatory, because, if it is not, a treaty of submission
must be negotiated at the worst moment for negotiations,

---

[1] 'The Hague Court and Vital Interests,' *Law Quarterly Review*,
April 1905.   Reprint, pp. 9, 10.

viz., at a moment when the state of feeling threatens to suspend negotiations altogether. . . . For the same reason it must also be automatic.'

But the Conference of 1907 could not attain this desirable object.

By the Treaty of Washington of September 15, 1914, between Great Britain and the United States, provision is made for the appointment of a Permanent International Commission, to investigate and report upon disputes between the two countries when diplomatic methods of adjustment have failed. The composition of the Commission is to be as follows :

'One member shall be chosen from each country by the Government thereof; one member shall be chosen by each Government from some third country ; the fifth member shall be chosen by common agreement between the two Governments, it being understood that he shall not be a citizen of either country.'[1]

The reference to the International Commission is compulsory. The Commission may also spontaneously, and by unanimous agreement, offer its services. A great number of Treaties[2] on this model have been effected between the United States and other countries. This procedure may be considered as an adoption or extension of the provisions as to International Commissions of Inquiry framed by the Hague Conferences. It is the latest application of the principle of International Arbitration.

In August 1917 the Pope addressed a Note 'To the Heads of the Belligerent Peoples',[3] in which as his first

---

[1] League of Nations Society Publications, No. 4, November 1916 : 'Treaty between the United Kingdom and the United States of America with regard to the Establishment of a Peace Commission. Signed at Washington, September 15, 1914.'

[2] Known as the Bryan Treaties.

[3] *The Times*, August 16, 1917.

suggestion towards a 'just and lasting peace' he placed
the following:

'The fundamental point should be that the moral force of
right should replace the material force of arms; hence a just
agreement between all for the simultaneous and reciprocal
diminution of armaments, according to rules and guarantees
to be established, to the extent necessary and sufficient for the
maintenance of public order in each State; then, in the place
of armies, the establishment of arbitration with its exalted
pacifying function, on lines to be concerted and with sanctions
to be settled against any State that should refuse either to
submit international questions to arbitration or to accept its
awards.'

To this the German Government apparently
answered:[1]

'The Imperial Government welcomes with special sympathy
the leading idea of the peace appeal, in which his Holiness
clearly expresses his conviction that in the future the material
power of arms must be superseded by the moral power of right.
We also are convinced that the sick body of human society can
only be healed by the fortifying moral strength of right. From
this would follow, according to the view of his Holiness, the
simultaneous diminution of the armed forces of all States and
the institution of obligatory arbitration in international disputes. . . . The task would then of itself arise of deciding
international differences of opinion, not by the use of armed
forces but by peaceful methods, especially by arbitration, the
great peace-producing effect of which we, together with his
Holiness, fully recognize. The Imperial Government will, in
this respect, support every proposal which is compatible with
the vital interests of the German Empire and people.'

The Austrian Emperor replied as follows:[2]

'With deep-rooted conviction we greet the leading idea of
your Holiness that the future arrangement of the world must be
based on the elimination of armed forces and on the moral force
of right and on the rule of international justice and legality.

[1] *The Times*, Sept. 24, 1917.   [2] *The Times*, Sept. 22, 1917.

We, too, are imbued with the hope that a strengthening of the sense of right would morally regenerate humanity. We support, therefore, your Holiness's view that negotiations between the belligerents should and could lead to an understanding by which, with the creation of appropriate guarantees, armaments on land, sea, and air might be reduced simultaneously, reciprocally, and gradually to a fixed limit, and whereby the high seas, which rightly belong to all the nations of the earth, may be freed from domination or paramountcy, and be open equally for the use of all.

'Fully conscious of the importance for the promotion of peace of the method proposed by your Holiness—namely, to submit international disputes to compulsory arbitration—we are also prepared to enter into negotiations regarding this proposal.'

The United States had previously, in a communication signed by their Secretary of State, regretfully pointed out to His Holiness that 'the word of the present rulers of Germany could not be taken as a guarantee of anything that is to endure'.[1]

IV. RECENT SCHEMES OF FEDERATION

1. *Summary of Views*

Since the Great War began, there have been a number of publications by individuals and by associations submitting schemes for the prevention of future war. Some writers lay stress upon recourse to Arbitration, others upon a European or World Federation or League. The various proposals will be given with some fullness in the latter part of this section; but the following is a convenient summary :

All agree in dividing disputes between nations into disputes which are justiciable and those which are not, and suggest that the former should go before some form

---

[1] *The Times*, August 30, 1917.

of Tribunal, whether called a Court or a Body of Arbitrators, and whether established in permanance or appointed *ad hoc.* The general idea is that it should be a permanent body.

All agree in referring all other disputes to some body which will not proceed upon legal principles which are *ex hypothesi* inapplicable, but will act—as it is sometimes expressed—as a Council of Conciliation. Some would give to this Council quasi-legislative powers, that is to say, powers to add to the existing rules of International Law. Some would give the Council a power to supersede, or to take the place of, the Court, by amending or repealing the existing rules of International Law or the existing terms of Treaties, and, having thus established new law, either remitting the case to the Court or dealing with it as a Court. The source of this last idea is the Alabama Convention, by which Great Britain and the United States, before submitting their disputes to the Arbitration Tribunal at Geneva, agreed that certain principles should be applied, as if they were International Law, by the Tribunal.

All these writers agree that it should be incumbent upon every State party to the League to submit, or to consent to the submission of, any dispute either to the Court or to the Council; and that there should be a *moratorium* (to use a convenient application of a word hitherto employed in. commerce), that is to say, that no State should have recourse to war pending the decision of the Court or Council, as the case may be.

As to the constitution of the Court and of the Council, there are varieties in detail. All the writers would admit that, to some extent, every State party to the League should have some voice in the appointment of the Court and of the Council; but they differ widely as to the extent and as to the weight to be given to the smaller States.

Most of them would create an artificial body of eight
Great Powers—the old six European Great Powers, with
the United States and Japan added, but China excluded,
and would eliminate from the League, and therefore from
voice in the Court or Council, what they call backward
or half-civilized States.   Some hesitate about the admission of any of the South American States,[1] forgetting
that, if their schemes are to be of any use, they must at
least contemplate what is likely to happen during the
next fifty years, and that during that period the A. B. C.
States [2] are likely to become some of the most important
in the world.   Most of them would divide States in
the League into two classes only—(a) the Great Powers,
(b) all the rest, putting the eight Great Powers on an
equal footing *inter se*, and all the others, however much
they differ in importance, also on an equal footing
inter se.

As to the enforcement of the duty to go to the Court
or Council, and to refrain from war in the interval, most
of those who have written since the War began accept
the necessity of constraint by force.   Many of them do it
with reluctance, and most of them suggest that the
primary and most suitable use of force would be by
some form of international boycott, in lieu of an actual
recourse to arms.   Many writers have persuaded themselves that, if the international boycott be used, it would
be sufficient, and that it would not in its turn provoke
war.

On the question of enforcing the Order or Award of
the Court or Council, there is more difference of opinion.
Few go the length of saying that it should be the duty of
the several States parties to the League to compel the
State against which an Order of the Court has been

---

[1] e. g. Hobson, p. 158 ; Woolf, *International Government*, p. 58 ;
Framework of a Lasting Peace, p. 55.

[2] Argentina, Brazil, and Chili.

made to comply with that Order. None go the length
of saying that it should be a duty of the States to enforce
obedience to the recommendation or award of the Council.
Where obedience is to be enforced, some would make it
the duty of every State to contribute to the enforcement;
some would leave it to the Great Powers alone; some
suggest that, if a State not content with non-performance
of the Order or Award takes up arms in contradiction
of it, it should be resisted by all the States. Some would
leave the injured State to enforce its right, or protect
itself against invasion, assisted only to this extent, that
the wrongdoer will be driven to fight without allies,
because all Treaties of Alliance are to be deemed in such
an event to be dissolved. Some, again, have been content with a general outline, and have not worked out in
detail the machinery by which force, whether economic
or military, is to be decided upon and applied. Some
would create for these purposes an Executive of the
League, and suggest that there should be a scale of
contributions in men and money, such as there was
among the States of the old Holy Roman Empire and,
it is believed, among those which formed the German
Confederation of 1815.

The next question that arises concerns the relation of
the League to States outside the League, and the duty
of States inside the League to assist one of their number,
if attacked from outside. Opinions vary as to this, and
as to the possibility of having anything like a large
League to start with, some being so modest in their
aspirations that they anticipate that the League, in its
initiation, will consist of the 'Entente' Powers with
a few neutrals added. Others deprecate anything like
a League which would exclude Germany and her Allies—
an exclusion which would result in the formation of a
second League, more or less hostile to the first.

Most of the writers to whom reference will be

made published their books before the United States
joined in the war; and many of them are now out
of date.

Some see a great instrument of peace in absolute, unconditional Free Trade; others are violent Protectionists
in the sense that they would artificially regulate trade
for the benefit of particular national industries. But
they seek to reconcile their scheme with international
harmony, by setting up some international or supernational body that would play the part of Providence
to the several States, and, while protecting the national
industries, would compel the various nations to facilitate
the supply of raw materials and advantages of transit to
all others in need of them.

Some think that the panacea is to be found in what
they call Democratic Control, by which they mean not
merely that a people should elect its Parliament—
Parliament choosing the Ministers and leaving it to
them to settle such matters—nor even that they would
have confidence in Parliament, but that every diplomatic
question should be decided in the face of day, after
general public discussion. It is as if, in matters of
business, when two bodies of men were treating with each
other, neither were to be allowed to discuss between
themselves in private what line of action they should
take with regard to the other.

Another school is so anxious for regulation of all
kinds that it would press forward from regulation by
the State of most of the actions of individual citizens
to regulation by a super-State of the actions of individual
States. This school would have, not merely a supernational Executive to determine how the forces of the
League should be used to prevent war, but a Legislature
which would regulate all relations of States *inter se*, and
of citizens of one State with another State or the
citizens thereof, in peace as well as in war, as to the

course of trade, the rules of occupation and development of unsettled countries, grants and concessions, trusts, cartels, changes of nationality and domicile, and so forth, with a supernational Executive to enforce the enactments of this supernational Legislature.

2. *Particular Organizations*

The organizations which have thus far taken this matter in hand appear to be those of—

(*a*) Viscount Bryce and his friends.

(*b*) The British League of Nations Society.

(*c*) The (American) League to Enforce Peace.

(*d*) The Fabian Society.

(*e*) The Union of Democratic Control.

(*f*) L'Organisation Centrale pour une Paix durable (The Hague).[1]

(*a*) *Lord Bryce's ' Proposals for the Prevention of Future Wars'*.—These have been revised to April 1917. Under this scheme, summarily described, the six Great Powers of Europe, the United States and Japan, and all other *European* Powers which may be willing, shall enter into a 'Treaty Arrangement'. China and the other American and Asiatic Powers may apparently be admitted later (Art. 1). Disputes are divided into those which are of a justiciable character and those which are not (Arts. 2, 4).

' Disputes of a justiciable character ' are to be defined as

'Disputes as to the interpretation of a treaty, as to any question of international law, as to the existence of any fact which, if established, would constitute a breach of any inter-

---

[1] The outlines of the schemes of these organizations have been filled up in several cases by members writing on their own behalf, who sometimes carry the proposals of their particular body a good deal farther.

national obligation, or as to the nature and extent of the reparation to be made for any such breach.'

Justiciable disputes are to be referred to 'the Court of
Arbitral Justice', or to the Court of Arbitration at The
Hague; and the Powers are to agree 'to accept and to
give effect to the Award of the Tribunal' (Art. 3). For
other matters, and for the question whether a dispute
is of a justiciable character or not, reference is to
be made to the Permanent Council of Conciliation. On
this Council all the signatory Powers are to have representatives; each of the Great Powers so called—that is,
the eight mentioned—is to have, it is suggested, three
members, the other Powers at least one (Introd., p. 21).
Apparently the whole Council is to sit, though it is to
have power to appoint Committees to report. No executive power is conferred on the Council; but it is to have
power, of its own initiative, to consider disputes and
invite the Parties to submit them with a view to conciliation (Art. 10), and even to make suggestions before
disputes arise (Art. 12).

'MORATORIUM FOR HOSTILITIES.

'ART. 17. Every signatory Power to agree not to declare war
or begin hostilities or hostile preparations against any other
signatory Power before the matter in dispute has been submitted
to an arbitral tribunal, or to the Council, or within a period of
twelve months after such submission; or, if the award of the
arbitral tribunal or the report of the Council, as the case may
be, has been published within that time, then not to declare war
or begin hostilities or hostile preparations within a period of six
months after the publication of such award or report.

'LIMITATION OF EFFECT OF ALLIANCES.

'ART. 18. The signatory Powers to agree that no signatory
Power commencing hostilities against another, without first
complying with the provisions of the preceding clauses, shall be
entitled, by virtue of any now existing or future treaty of
alliance or other engagement, to the military or other material
support of any other signatory Power in such hostilities.

'ENFORCEMENT OF THE PRECEDING PROVISIONS.

'ART. 19. Every signatory Power to undertake that, in case any Power, whether or not a signatory Power, declares war or begins hostilities or hostile preparations against a signatory Power, without first having submitted its case to an arbitral tribunal or to the Council of Conciliation, or before the expiration of the prescribed period of delay, it will forthwith in conjunction with the other signatory Powers take such concerted measures, economic and forcible, against the Power so acting as in their judgment are most effective and appropriate to the circumstances of the case.

'ART. 20. The signatory Powers to undertake that, if any Power shall fail to accept and give effect to the recommendations contained in any report of the Council or in the Award of the Arbitral Tribunal, they will at a Conference to be forthwith summoned for the purpose consider, in concert, the situation which has arisen by reason of such failure, and what collective action, if any, it is practicable to take in order to make such recommendations operative.'

(b) *The British ' League of Nations Society'*.—This Society published its *Project of a League of Nations* in August 1917. The programme is short, and is as follows :

'1. That a Treaty shall be made as soon as possible whereby as many States as are willing shall form a League binding themselves to use peaceful methods for dealing with all disputes arising among them.

'2. That such methods shall be as follows :

(a) All disputes arising out of questions of International Law, or the interpretation of Treaties, shall be referred to the Hague Court of Arbitration, or some other judicial tribunal, whose decisions shall be final and shall be carried into effect by the parties concerned.

(b) All other disputes shall be referred to and investigated and reported upon by a Council of Inquiry and Conciliation; the Council to be representative of the States which form the League.

'3. That the States which are members of the League shall

unite in any action necessary for ensuring that every member shall abide by the terms of the Treaty ; and in particular shall jointly use forthwith both their economic and military forces against any one of their number that goes to war, or commits acts of hostility against another, before any question arising shall be submitted as provided in the foregoing Articles.

' 4. That the States which are members of the League shall make provision for mutual defence, diplomatic, economic, or military, in the event of any of them being attacked by a State not a member of the League which refuses to submit the case to an appropriate Tribunal or Council.

' 5. That conferences between the members of the League shall·be held from time to time to consider international matters of general character, and to formulate and codify International Law, which, unless some member shall signify its dissent within a stated period, shall hereafter govern in the decisions of the Judicial Tribunal mentioned in Article 2 (a).

' 6. That any civilised State desiring to join the League shall be admitted to membership.'

It will be seen that this scheme accepts the same division of disputes as that adopted by Lord Bryce. It contemplates forcible action by the States which are members of the League. They are to use economic or military force against any one of their number that goes to war before submitting the question either to arbitration or for conciliation. It binds the parties, when the case is referred to arbitration, to carry out the award. But it makes no provision for force being brought to bear upon the party unwilling to obey the award or to accept the Report of a Council of Conciliation. Force is only to be used to secure the *moratorium* while the dispute is under consideration. It will be further seen that the scheme is so far from contemplating a world-wide League that it provides in Art. 4 for mutual defence by members of the League against outside Powers in certain events.

(c) *The American 'League to Enforce Peace'.* — The

proposals of this League are set out in an article by the chairman, Dr. Marburg, in a publication of the Society. The four articles of its platform are as follows :

' 1. All justiciable questions arising between the signatory Powers, not settled by negotiation, shall, subject to the limitations of treaties, be submitted to a judicial tribunal for hearing and judgment, both upon the merits and upon any issue as to its jurisdiction of the question.

' 2. All other questions arising between the signatories and not settled by negotiation shall be submitted to a Council of Conciliation for hearing, consideration, and recommendation.

' 3. The signatory Powers shall jointly use forthwith .both their economic and military forces against any one of their number that goes to war, or commits acts of hostility, against another of the signatories before any question arising shall be submitted as provided in the foregoing.

' 4. Conferences between the signatory Powers shall be held from time to time to formulate and codify rules of international law, which, unless some signatory shall signify its dissent within a stated period, shall thereafter govern in the decisions of the Judicial Tribunal mentioned in Article 1.' [1]

It will be seen that this platform is less drastic than that of the British League, because it omits the contractual duty to carry into effect the decision of an Arbitral Tribunal, and also contains no clause corresponding to Article 4 of the British platform, which makes the League into an Alliance against any State, not a member of the League, that attacks a member. [2]

The American League has published a collection of speeches made at a meeting held by it in Philadelphia, June 17, 1915, and, under the title ' Enforced Peace ', the Proceedings of the first Annual National Assemblage at Washington, May 26–7, 1916.   Dr. Lowell, President of Harvard University, who was a speaker

[1] *The Project of a League of Nations*, p. 18.
[2] One speaker, however (Dr. Clark), at their first meeting, took the line of the British League.

at both meetings, published a separate pamphlet in
September 1915. The purport of these publications is
to show the need of an organization to enforce peace,
and to induce the authors' countrymen to take an active
part in promoting it. They are very eloquent, but they
do not go into detail, and they contribute little towards
the development of the general idea or to meet criticisms.[1]

Dr. Lowell's pamphlet, however, has useful observations
upon the impracticability of an international police, upon
the probable feebleness of a Conference of Powers called
upon to restrain a recalcitrant State, and upon the
difficulties of an economic boycott. One point is insisted
on which has more novelty, namely, that, as balancing the
moratorium which prevents a State from having recourse
to arms pending the reference to Court or Council, that
State should be able to get an injunction from Court or
Council restraining its opponent from continuing its
aggression *pendente lite*. This suggestion is also made by
Mr. Lowes Dickinson.[2] How far it would be understood
and accepted by nations whose systems of jurisprudence
are not Anglo-American may be a question.[3]

(*d*) *The Fabian Society.*—A work of some importance,
entitled *International Government*, has been published by
this Society. It contains two reports (Parts I and II)
by Mr. L. S. Woolf, and a project (Part III) by a Fabian
committee 'for a Supernational Authority that will
Prevent War'.[4] Part I is well worthy of consideration.

---

[1] The papers which go into most detail are *The League Program*,
by Thomas Raeburn White; *Preparedness and Ultimate Reduction of
Armaments*, by Hamilton Holt; and *A Reply to Critics*, by Theodore
Marburg.

[2] See below, pp. 51 *seq.*

[3] Mr. Robert Goldsmith has written a book, published at New York
in 1917, to support the views of the American League.

[4] Mr. Woolf has more recently published a second book called
The Framework of a Lasting Peace (1917). The body of the work

Mr. Woolf attempts to classify the causes of war, and he analyses them under four heads:

' 1. Disputes arising from legal or quasi-legal relationship, e. g. (a) as to interpretation of treaties; (b) as to contractual rights and duties; (c) as to definitions of boundaries; (d) as to delicts.

' 2. Disputes arising from economic relationship, trade, and finance.

' 3. Disputes arising from administrative or political relationship, e. g. as to questions of territory, subject races, expansion, nationality, supremacy, and predominant influence.

' 4. Disputes arising from what may be called social relationship, e. g. as to questions of honour.' [1]

The classification is not satisfactory; and, though Mr. Woolf attempts to bring two of the recent great wars, the Spanish-American and the Russo-Japanese, under one or other of these heads, he fails. He does not deal with the Boer War or attempt to classify the Great War. He is a believer in International Law, and expresses himself to the following effect:

' A large number of its rules are quite definitely admitted, are acted upon every day, and really do help to regulate pacifically international society. On the other hand, much of it is vague and uncertain. This is due largely to two facts: there is no recognized international organ for making International Law, and no judicial organ for interpreting it. The consequences are two: whenever new circumstances arise which require a new rule of conduct for nations, the nations concerned have to set about making the new rule by bargaining and negotiation. If they cannot agree, either it remains uncertain what the law is or the question has to be settled by war. Secondly, when there

is a useful reprint of the schemes of the several organizations, including a translation of the Minimum Programme of the Central Organization for a Durable Peace and the Draft Treaty framed by the Dutch Committee. The introduction makes little or no new contribution to the study of the subject.

[1] *International Government*, p. 10.

is already a rule, but nations disagree as to its interpretation, they again have to attempt by bargaining and negotiation to come to some agreement as to how it shall be interpreted.   And again, if they cannot agree, the only method left is to cut the knot by war ' (*op. cit.*, p. 13).

Mr. Woolf makes some acute reflections on the difficulty of combining respect for the *status quo* with the legitimate desire of nationalities, now by force included in different States, to obtain separation and possibly amalgamation. He thus expresses himself :

' The Union of Democratic Control urges the adoption of the principle that "no province shall be transferred from one Government to another without consent, by plebiscite or otherwise, of the population of such province ".   The adoption of this principle as part of the international constitution would indisputably be a great step forward, but one may point out that really to ensure a permanent peace it would be at least necessary to add : " Nor shall any province be compelled to remain under any Government against the consent of the population of such province " ' (*op. cit.*, p. 29).

He summarizes his historical conclusions as follows :

' 1. A new system of international relationship began to appear in the last century.   The pivot of the system was the making of international laws and the regulation of certain international affairs at international Conferences of national representatives.   The important part of the system was the expressed or unexpressed acceptance of the principle that such affairs could only be settled by the collective decision of the Powers.

' 2. The functions of these international Conferences may be of three different kinds, which in practice have not been clearly recognized and distinguished.   Their function may be :

(*a*) To come to a decision binding upon the States represented, i. e. to legislate ; or

(*b*) To examine facts and express an opinion or issue a report ; or

(*c*) To act as a Council of Conciliation or Mediation between two or more disputing States.

' 3. The efficacy of Conferences in preventing war and in settling international questions has been remarkable. It has, however, been limited by the fact that the submission of any question to a Conference has always been a subject for negotiation, and, therefore, only a move in the diplomatic game. The first step towards the peaceful regulation of international affairs would be to remove this question of submission altogether from the sphere of negotiation and diplomacy, and to define the cases in which a Conference must be called or could be demanded.

' 4. Little progress in the making of international laws by Conferences can be expected unless the rights of an international majority to bind a minority—if only an exceptionally overwhelming majority, in specific cases—are admitted and defined.

' 5. The development of Conferences into full international legislative bodies depends principally upon the possibility of :

(a) Agreement as to what are international questions which are to be submitted for collective decision to Conferences.

(b) Agreement as to the rights of an international majority to bind a minority ' (op. cit., pp. 42, 43).

His constructive scheme is based upon the following principles. There are two classes of national disputes : the first, fitted for a Tribunal whether the members of it be called Judges or Arbitrators, where there is a dispute as to facts or the construction of Treaties and similar documents, or upon the construction and application of recognized International Law ; and a second, in which the Arbitrators may, or may not, have to determine the facts and there is no law to guide them, and where, as he expresses it :

' Certain persons must be selected by States as likely to be reasonable and open-minded, and such disputes will be referred to their decision, which will represent a fair and reasonable settlement or compromise ' (op. cit., p. 44).

He presumes that disputes of the first class will generally be referred to a Permanent International Court of Arbitration, and disputes of the second to an International Conference. But he thinks that there

would be certain cases in which it would not be right
to insist upon the *status quo* or rights thereby acquired ;
and that the existing principles of International Law
may favour certain Great Powers—particularly his own
country, Great Britain—too much. In cases of the latter
sort it ought (he thinks) to be the right of a disputing
State to have it considered by the International Conference whether the law ought not to be altered first, and
then the case decided on ; or, as the reference to the
Tribunal of Arbitration would probably be unnecessary,
he would allow the disputing State to claim that the
whole matter be determined by the Conference, which
would first make the law, and then adjudicate upon the
law which it had made. He gets this idea from the
Alabama Arbitration.[1] It will probably be thought that
this scheme is impracticable ; and, as Mr. Woolf con-
fesses, the State most likely to suffer would be his own.

For the constitution of his Tribunal of Arbitration
he divides the States of the world into two classes : the
eight so-called Great Powers, and the rest. He would
have a Tribunal of seventeen Judges, each Great Power
appointing one and the other States collectively electing
nine ; and he would exclude from the Court the representative or representatives of any disputing State. This
might give a lesser Power, in case it were not directly
represented by a subject of its own on the Tribunal,
some advantage in a contest with a Great Power.

The international rights and obligations which would be
defined and acknowledged under his system are as follows :

' 1. The obligation to refer all disputes and differences not
settled by negotiation either to a tribunal or to a Conference.

' 2. The obligation in certain defined disputes and differences [2]

[1] See above, p. 24.
[2] ' i. e. those which would not affect the independence or the
territorial integrity, or which would not require an alteration in
the internal laws, of a State.'

referred to a Conference, to accept and abide by the decision of the majority of the representatives.

' 3. The obligation to accept and abide by the judgment of a tribunal.

' 4. The obligation of a State to abide by every general rule of law and every decision made by a Conference and agreed to or ratified by that State.

' 5. The obligation to abide by certain defined general rules of law made by a majority of the representatives in a Conference' (*op. cit.*, p. 75).

Of these he regards the first, third, and fourth, as of primary importance. He insists that there shall be what has above been called a *moratorium*. He says that the nations which compose the International Authority are to

'agree to enforce, and actually enforce by every means in their power, the obligation of each individual State to refer a dispute or difference to tribunal or Conference before resorting to force of arms' (*op. cit.*, p. 77).

He shrinks from definitely saying that force should be employed, but he seems to contemplate that either war or ' economic and social pressure' would be used if necessary. He then passes to what he calls the ' construction of some International Authority', and with a good deal of elaboration suggests a scheme of International Legislation by the Powers assembled in Conference, with a considerable predominance given to the eight Great Powers, and the right of a sufficiently large majority to bind the recalcitrant rest.

Part II is devoted to an elaborate analysis of the extent to which, under existing conditions, nations are united and interpenetrated, and to an enumeration of a number of Unions, Postal and Telegraphic, Sanitary, and so forth, official or otherwise, which at present exist. Here and there the writer shows that he has not much

knowledge of practical business; and this part will
hardly repay perusal.

One idea, however, can be drawn from it. He points
out, as is the fact, that in some of these Treaties the
States with large Oversea Dominions are allowed
additional votes. Thus, in the General Postal Union
Treaty of June 1, 1878,[1] by Art. 21, Great Britain has
one additional vote for British India and the Dominion
of Canada; and votes are given to the Danish, Spanish,
French, Dutch, and Portuguese colonies, one vote to
each group. By the Telegraphic Convention of June 15,
1897,[2] separate votes are given for India, Canada,
Australasia, and the other British Colonies (afterwards
declared to be South Africa); to the German, Danish,
Spanish, Dutch, and Portuguese Colonies—each collectively; to the French Possessions in China, and a
second vote to the other French Colonies. These cases
seem to form precedents to be borne in mind, if any
numerical Court of Arbitration should be hereafter
established.

Part III of *International Government* is the work of the
Fabian Committee. It contains a draft code for the
'establishment of a Supernational Authority'.

There is to be an International High Court for the
decision of justiciable issues, and an International
Council to secure 'by common agreement such International Legislation as may be practicable', and to
promote the settlement of non-justiciable issues, with
an International Secretariat or Bureau. All the constituent States are to bind themselves to abstain from
war till they have first submitted their claim to the Court

[1] Hertslet, *Treaties and Conventions between Great Britain and Foreign
Powers so far as they relate to Commerce and Navigation*, vol. xiv,
p. 1007.

[2] Hertslet, *op. cit.*, vol. xxi, p. 484.

of Arbitration, or to the Council, for examination and
report.

The International Council is to be framed, as in all
these schemes, with a peculiar regard for the so-called
eight Great Powers, each of whom is to appoint five
representatives, while the other States are to appoint
two each. There is elaborate provision for the subdivision of the Council into minor Councils:

(a) Of the eight Great Powers.

(b) Of the other Powers.

(c) Of the States of America.

(d) Of the States of Europe.

And the matter is so arranged that the eight Great
Powers, if they are unanimous, have a practical veto
upon any change.

The Court is to consist of fifteen Judges, one to be
nominated by each of the eight, the other seven to be
elected among the other States. (This gives the lesser
States somewhat less than Mr. Woolf proposes.) A power
of injunction *pendente lite* is to be given to the Court.
Justiciable matters, as defined in the scheme, are to go
to the Court; and the Court is to have a power of
deciding whether the matter is within its jurisdiction
or not.

It is contemplated that the Council will enter upon
a considerable amount of legislation, and that on matters
of secondary importance a three-fourths majority—provided that all the Great Powers are in the majority—
should be capable of making a law.

Then there are two Articles inserted by way of
suggestion, and doubtfully. They are headed, ' Provision
for Abrogation of Obsolete Treaties ' and ' Provision for
Cases in which International Law is vague, uncertain,
or incomplete '. These Articles are an elaboration of
Mr. Woolf's suggestion that in some cases, where a dispute

arises, first new law shall be made, and then a decision given upon the new law.

The first part of the Article (16 A) is harmless enough, but quite unnecessary. It contemplates cases where an earlier Treaty has not been expressly repealed, but has been substantially abrogated. It is quite unnecessary to have any provision for such cases. The sting is in the latter part. A State is to be able to make a claim to have it declared that a Treaty, to which it is a party, has become obsolete

'. . . by reason of one or other independent Sovereign State concerned in such Treaty or Agreement having ceased to exist as such, or by reason of such a change of circumstances that the very object and purpose for which all the parties made the Treaty or Agreement can no longer be attained.' [1]

In such a case, instead of the matter being submitted as a justiciable issue to the Court, it is to be brought before the Council, which may by a three-fourths majority, including all the Great Powers, decide that the Treaty is obsolete and ought to be abrogated ; and shall thereupon promptly deal with the question in dispute as a non-justiciable issue.

Under 16 B, a State may submit a claim that ' the International Law applicable to such issue is so vague or so uncertain or so incomplete as to render the strict application thereof to the issue in question impracticable or inequitable '. The Council is then, by the same majority, to have similar powers.

It is to be observed that, though the size of the majority may perhaps be a sufficient protection, almost any alteration of law for the benefit of some favoured State, and to the detriment of the State in possession, might be brought about under one or other of these Articles.

[1] *International Government*, Part III, p. 251. This is a form of statement of the well-known International position as to the application of the doctrine *rebus sic stantibus*.

The use of sanctions for enforcing a decision of the Court, including an interlocutory injunction, is worked out under twelve heads :

'(a) To lay an embargo on any or all ships belonging to the recalcitrant State ;

'(b) To prohibit any lending of capital or other moneys to the citizens . . . of the recalcitrant State, or to its national Government ;

'(c) To prohibit the issue or dealing in or quotation on the Stock Exchange or in the Press of any new loans . . . of the recalcitrant State, or of its national Government ;

'(d) To prohibit all postal, telegraphic, telephonic, and wireless communication with the recalcitrant State ;

'(e) To prohibit the payment of any debts due to the citizens . . . of the recalcitrant State, or to its national Government; and, if thought fit, to direct that payment of such debts shall be made only to one or other of the Constituent Governments . . .

'(f) To prohibit all imports, or certain specified imports . . .

'(g) To prohibit all exports, or certain specified exports . . .

'(h) To prohibit all passenger traffic (other than the exit of foreigners), . . . to or from the recalcitrant State ;

'(i) To prohibit the entrance into any port of the Constituent States of any of the ships registered as belonging to the recalcitrant State, except so far as may be necessary for any of them to seek safety, in which case such ship or ships shall be interned ;

'(j) To declare and enforce a decree of complete non-intercourse with the recalcitrant State . . .

'(k) To levy a special export duty on all goods destined for the recalcitrant State, . . .

'(l) To furnish a contingent of warships to maintain a combined blockade of one or more of the ports, or of the whole coast-line of the recalcitrant State' (op. cit., pp. 253, 254).

In the event of the State against which the decision goes engaging in war, and apparently also in the event of its entering into war before the matter has come before the Court or Council, the other signatory States are to make war upon it.

Part of this scheme of the Fabian Committee recalls
the paper constitutions which the Abbé Sieyès used from
time to time to produce during the French Revolution.

(e) *The Union of Democratic Control.*—The four cardinal
points in the policy of this Association are as follows :

'1. No province shall be transferred from one Government to
another without the consent by plebiscite, or otherwise, of the
population of such province.

'2. No Treaty, Arrangement, or Undertaking shall be entered
upon in the name of Great Britain without the sanction of
Parliament. Adequate machinery for ensuring democratic
control of foreign policy shall be created.

'3. The Foreign Policy of Great Britain shall not be aimed
at creating Alliances for the purpose of maintaining the Balance
of Power, but shall be directed to concerted action between the
Powers, and the setting up of an International Council whose
deliberations and decisions shall be public, with such machinery
for securing international agreement as shall be the guarantee
of an abiding peace.

'4. Great Britain shall propose as part of the Peace settlement
a plan for the drastic reduction, by consent, of the armaments of
all the belligerent Powers, and to facilitate that policy shall
attempt to secure the general nationalisation of the manufacture
of armaments, and the control of the export of armaments by
one country to another.'

And to these a fifth has lately been added :

'5. The European conflict shall not be continued by economic
war after the military operations have ceased. British policy
shall be directed towards promoting free commercial intercourse
between all nations and the preservation and extension of the
principle of the open door.'

The Union has published a number of pamphlets.
Some of the writers merely set forth the miseries and
mischiefs of war, which we all know. Others, writing
during the recent war, maintained that the enemy, if
properly approached, would come to reasonable terms ;

while others, indulged in half-veiled complaints of the government of their own country. All, however, unite in advocating their particular panacea, which they call Democratic Control of Foreign-Policy. Upon this last proposal short and, it is apprehended, sufficient observation has already been made.[1]

In several forms the writers favour a future League of Peace; and Mr. Lowes Dickinson, who has written a number of works developing the idea, and is a prominent member of the British League of Nations Society, has contributed one pamphlet to the publications of the Union, *Economic War after the War*. The Union has also published, in a pamphlet called *Towards an International Understanding*, some contributions from French and Dutch sources, the only one of value being by Dr. Noci Van Suchtelen, of Holland, who in general terms favours a European Confederation as the only solution for the future.

(*f*) *The ' Organisation Centrale pour une Paix durable'.*— The Executive Committee of this body contains members from the belligerents of both sides, and from neutrals. Its minimum programme is as follows :

' 1. No annexation or transfer of territory shall be made contrary to the interests and wishes of the population concerned. Where possible, their consent shall be obtained by plebiscite or otherwise. The States shall guarantee to the various nationalities included in their boundaries equality before the law,. religious liberty, and the free use of their native languages.

' 2. The States shall agree to introduce in their colonies, protectorates, and spheres of influence, liberty of commerce, or at least equal treatment for all nations.

' 3. The work of the Hague Conferences with a view to the peaceful organisation of the Society of Nations shall be developed. The Hague Conference shall be given a permanent organisation and meet at regular intervals. The States shall agree to submit

---

[1] See above, p. 27.

all their disputes to peaceful settlement. For this purpose there shall be created, in addition to the existent Hague Court of Arbitration, (a) a permanent Court of International Justice, (b) a permanent International Council of Investigation and Conciliation. The States shall bind themselves to take concerted action, diplomatic, economic, or military, in case any State should resort to military measures instead of submitting the dispute to judicial decision or to the mediation of the Council of Investigation and Conciliation.

'4. The States shall agree to reduce their armaments. In order to facilitate the reduction of naval armaments,·the right of capture shall be abolished and the freedom of the seas assured.

'5. Foreign policy shall be under the effective control of the parliaments of the respective nations. Secret treaties shall be void.'

It is somewhat strange that, advocating as it does in its third Article a permanent Court and a permanent Council, the Organisation should have issued among its 'Rapports' a contribution from M. Henri Lambert, a Belgian, saying that peace is not a thing to be organized, and that it seems to him that the great Supernational Council would have more need of peace than peace of it.[1]

The *Recueil de Rapports* issued by this Organisation began in 1916 and has reached four volumes, which contain Papers on the following subjects: the taking of plebiscites on proposed annexations; nationalities; freedom of trade; development of the Hague Conferences; International Court of Justice and Council of Conciliation; International Sanction; limitation of armaments; freedom of the seas; and parliamentary control of foreign policy.

Several of the writers[2] have already published their

[1] 'L'Organisation Centrale pour une Paix durable,' *Recueil de Rapports*, 1916, p. 145.

[2] Such as Mr. C. R. Buxton, Mr. Hobson, Mr. Aneurin Williams, and Mr. Thomas Raeburn White.

views in separate form. Their new Papers are not much more than repetitions of the old. Some come from Germany and Austria-Hungary, and some from neutral States.

There is also an official commentary on the Minimum Programme (undated); an *Exposé des Travaux de l'Organisation*, by Chr. L. Lange of Christiania, 1917; and a separate pamphlet, *Le Contrat social des Nations*, by Professor André de Maday (Neufchâtel, 1917). All the publications of the Organisation emanate from The Hague.

The most important document is the Draft Treaty prepared by the Dutch Commission, which is also to be found in an English translation in Woolf's *The Framework of a Lasting Peace*. This Draft is preceded by an ' Exposé des Motifs' (vol. i, pp. 240-93). Its plan is as follows. It takes the usual line of a Court and a Council of Conciliation, but as to the Court it differs from many of the other schemes ; and in respect of the composition of the Court it shows a tendency to return to the older theory of arbitration. So also as to the Council. The nations which énter into the Federation are to choose a certain number of Judges for the one body and Councillors for the other. The matter is to be heard—whether it be by the Court or by a Committee of the Council—by a body consisting of two nominees of each of the contending States with one President or Umpire. He is to be chosen by agreement between the parties, or nominated by the appropriate Presidential Bureau. It is with this latter body that the real power will lie. It consists of a President and two Vice-Presidents, chosen by a majority of votes from among the States forming the League, the eight Great Powers having each three votes, and all the others one. The Court is to sit on justiciable matters, defined in the ordinary way, with the addition that all matters which the States, as between themselves, have

by any special Treaty agreed to submit to arbitration
shall be called justiciable. If the States can agree upon
their submission to arbitration (*compromis*) the Court will
decide upon it. If they cannot agree upon the terms of
their submission, they may ask the Court to frame it,
when it will be called a *quasi-compromis*.

The Court can also act at the request of one party,
if it appear that the matter in question is included in
the list of those which by some special Treaty are to
be referred to arbitration. But even here its jurisdiction
is excluded if the other party denies that it is one of
those matters, unless indeed it has been made part
of the special Treaty that the Arbitral Tribunal shall
decide upon its own competence or jurisdiction. With
these exceptions the Draft Treaty returns to the old
view of the Hague Convention of no compulsory arbitration except in rare and special cases. But, say the
promoters, this defect is remedied by giving increased
competence to the Council. The Council can act in
the case of all disputes, either at the joint request of the
parties, or if, for any reason, the Court is incompetent.
So far good. But then, as the promoters with some
naïveté explain, little harm is done to the sovereignty
or independence of a State, because, though the Court
decides by a majority, the Committee of the Council
can only decide by a majority containing within it the
vote of one at least of the representatives of the State
against which the decision is given.

One matter is left to the whole Council by Article 107.
If its Committee cannot decide, by reason that neither
of the representatives of the State to be decided against
agrees with the decision ; or if neither party has appealed
to the Court or Council over some dispute which exists
between them ; or even if there is no dispute but
only reason to fear that a dispute will arise, the whole
Council may sit in full session, the Great Powers having

three votes each. But then it can only give officious advice (*avis d'office*).

This Draft Treaty is very elaborately worded, and there are, no doubt, some ingenious modes of avoiding difficulties. But it comes to very little; and its principal value is perhaps as showing that writers not of Anglo-American origin are more averse than others from interfering with the independence and sovereignty of various States.[1] The American writer, Mr. White, on the other hand, in his paper which appears in the same collection,[2] states that in his opinion it is the greatest objection to the Hague Convention, and to all the systems which arise from it, that the tribunals are composed of Judges named by the contending parties, who are practically certain to take the side of their own country, so that the real power of decision rests with one man, the Umpire or President.

It will be noticed that the Dutch scheme has no *moratorium*, and no clause binding the Treaty States to enforce obedience. There is, however, a clause (Art. 3) by which the several States bind themselves to respect and execute the decisions come to by Court or Council.

Mr. Aneurin Williams, who has a Paper in the same collection (vol. i, p. 233), would make it part of the Treaty that every State should obey, and that all other States should agree to compel it to obey, these decisions; but, as this might involve too great a derogation from independence and sovereignty, he would permit any State to withdraw from the Federation upon giving twelve months' notice.

[1] Compare Chief Justice Beichmann's pamphlet, which is referred to below (p. 49).

[2] Vol. i, p. 317.

3. *A Permanent International Tribunal*

Some useful criticisms upon the construction of a Permanent International Tribunal are to be found in an article by Chief Justice Beichmann, of Norway, in vol. xxi of *Scientia*.[1]   Dr. Beichmann was, and probably still is, one of the Norwegian representatives on the Hague Court. He thinks that a Permanent International Court of Justice will not be a very efficacious mode of preventing war.   He observes that wars are rarely provoked by justiciable disputes.   Political conflicts, he remarks, are those which really endanger peace ; and therefore he thinks that recourse to arbitration, the Arbitrators being selected from the members of the Hague Tribunal, has an advantage for two reasons: (1) that the Arbitrators appointed by each nation will act as Conciliators or Negotiators, and be in this way more useful than they would be as Judges ; (2) that the Tribunal ought to have the full confidence of the parties, and that each State would have confidence in its own Arbitrators, and (owing to the method of choosing the Umpire) in the Umpire as well.

His view is that the Great War will make it more difficult than it was to form a Confederation of the States of Europe, or to get any State to derogate from its sovereign rights in favour of a new central organization, executive or legislative ; that there will be so much rancour between the contending parties, and so much irritation among the neutral States at the way in which belligerents have used their powers, that they would never agree upon any International Tribunal. He further points out that, if there is to be a Tribunal competent to settle all sorts of disputes between States, every State will desire to be represented upon the Tribunal, as its

[1] A scientific Review published at Bologna, and also by Willams and Norgate of London.

decisions (at least, this appears to be his view) will not only bind the parties but form precedents of International Law.

In a volume of Essays called *The Ministry of Reconciliation*, edited by Mr. Hugh Martin, and published in March 1916, Dr. Evans Darby, former Secretary of the Peace Society, and the author of the most complete work on International Arbitration, has an Essay on 'The Political Machinery of International Peace'. In it he refers 'to the advantages of such confederations as the Swiss and German, and that of the United States'. He proceeds :

'Enough has been recorded to show that Federalism is no new or untried or impractical policy. It dominates half the world in all its continents. It is assumed, often unconsciously, by current discussions about international justice, international police, and the use of force for the maintenance of international relations. Without it these could not exist, for the very effort to establish them would involve some kind of Federation. This was abundantly illustrated in the last Peace Conference at The Hague by the failure, after strenuous efforts and after complete unanimity had generally been manifested, to establish a " Court of Arbitral Justice ", the only thing established being that the Powers represented were not prepared for any general Court of Control' (*op. cit.*, p. 74).

In the second volume of the Publications of the Grotius Society (1916), Dr. Darby has a Paper on 'The Enforcement of the Hague Conventions', read before the Society on November 28, 1916, in which he criticizes the proposals of the American League for the Enforcement of Peace, but returns to the idea of some form of Federation or Union, which is to have an International Police and International Administration. At the same time, consistently with his well-known views, he opposes the enforcement of any Treaty by war.[1]

----

[1] The Grotius Society has published other Papers on the subject,

He has again expressed himself at a meeting of the Peace Society as not being enthusiastic for a League of Nations for the enforcement of peace, on the grounds that peace cannot be enforced without war or the threat of war, and that the Federation of the World cannot be secured by an International Army, even if it is labelled International Police.[1] The Peace Society seems to hold the same, views.[1] The Dutch Committee, Chief Justice Beichmann, Dr. Darby, and perhaps the Peace Society, are upon the whole to be treated as adherents to the older system of arbitration.

A book entitled *Towards a Lasting Settlement* (undated, but published early in the war), edited by Mr. C. R. Buxton, has among its articles one on 'The Basis of Permanent Peace', by Mr. G. Lowes Dickinson, and one on 'The Organization of Peace', by Mr. H. N. Brailsford.

Mr. Dickinson has published several other pamphlets, *The War and the Way Out*, which has gone through a second edition (again undated, but written before the Revolution in Russia and the entry of the United States into the war); a pamphlet, *After the War*, published in 1915; another, *Economic War after the War*, for the Union of Democratic Control, published in August 1916; and his last and probably most complete work, *The Choice Before Us*, published in April 1917. He is a member of the League of Nations Society.

In *The War and the Way Out*, he contemplates a future Europe rearranged on 'a basis of nationality instead of on a basis of States', which he says 'would be a Europe ripe for a permanent league'. He proceeds :

'To secure the peace of Europe, the peoples of Europe must hand over their armaments, and the use of them for any

including one by Dr. Bisschop on 'The Advantage of International Leagues', vol. ii; read before the Society, November 14, 1916.

[1] *The Herald of Peace*, October 1917.

purpose except internal police, to an international authority. This authority must determine what force is required for Europe as a whole, acting as a whole in the still possible case of war against Powers not belonging to the league. It must apportion the quota of armaments between the different nations according to their wealth, population, resources, and geographical position. And it, and it alone, must carry on, and carry on in public, negotiations with Powers outside the League. All disputes that may arise between members of the League must be settled by judicial process. And none of the forces of the League must be available for purposes of aggression by any member against any other.

'With such a League of Europe constituted, the problem of reduction of armaments would be automatically solved. Whatever force a united Europe might suppose itself to require for possible defence would clearly be far less than the sum of the existing armaments of the separate States.'[1]

In the Preface to the second edition (p. 4), he says:

' I do not imagine a federation of Europe to be possible in an immediate future. What I do believe to be possible, as soon as the war is over, is a League of the Powers to keep the peace of Europe.'

In his pamphlet *After the War*, he writes:

' There was a time, when the whole civilized world of the West lay at peace under a single rule; when the idea of separate Sovereign States, always at war or in armed peace, would have seemed as monstrous and absurd as it now seems inevitable. And that great achievement of the Roman Empire left, when it sank, a sunset glow over the turmoil of the Middle Ages. Never would a medieval churchman or statesman have admitted that the independence of States was an ideal. It was an obstinate tendency, struggling into existence against all the preconceptions and beliefs of the time. " One Church, one Empire," was the ideal of Charlemagne, of Otho, of Barbarossa, of Hildebrand, of Thomas Aquinas, of Dante. The forces struggling against that ideal were the enemy to be defeated. They won. And thought, always parasitic on action, endorsed the victory. So that now

[1] *The War and the Way Out*, pp. 41, 42.

there is hardly a philosopher or historian who does not urge
that the sovereignty of independent States is the last word of
political fact and political wisdom.

'And no doubt, in some respects it has been an advance. In
so far as there are real nations, and these are coincident with
States, it is well that they should develop freely their specific
gifts and characters. The good future of the world is not with
uniformity, but with diversity. But it should be well understood that all the diversity required is compatible with political
union. The ideal of the future is federation; and to that ideal
all the significant facts of the present point. . . .

'The Powers, I propose, should found a League of Peace,
based on a Treaty, binding them to refer their disputes to
peaceable settlement before taking any military measures'
(*op. cit.*, pp. 20, 21, 26).

He proceeds to consider the sanction of the Treaty.
His view is that men are to rely on law, not on force.
But, after paying a tribute to the sincerity of those who
would act up to their principles, he feels driven to admit
that there must be the sanction of force. He says:

'It will be impossible, I believe, to win from public opinion
any support for the ideas I am putting forward, unless we are
prepared to add a sanction to our treaty. I propose, therefore,
that the Powers entering into the arrangement pledge themselves
to assist, if necessary, by their national forces, any member of
the League who should be attacked before the dispute provoking
the attack has been submitted to arbitration or conciliation.[1]

'Military force, however, is not the only weapon the Powers
might employ in such a case; economic pressure might sometimes be effective.'

And he proceeds to discuss suggestions for arbitration
and for a Council of Conciliation.

[1] 'It is in this case only that the Powers would be pledged to
employ force, if other means fail. As will be seen below, it is not
proposed that they should bind themselves to employ force to ensure
the performance of an award of the Court of Arbitration, or the
adoption of a recommendation of the Council of Conciliation' (*op.
cit.*, p. 27).

The Choice Before Us is his latest work, and the most elaborate. The first half of the book is a powerful exposition of the evils of war. Even in this there are passages which are already out of date, and there is a good deal of very controversial matter. But this does not detract from the value of the latter half of the book. He again puts forward the scheme of a League of Nations. He says:

'A European State, and *a fortiori* a World State, even in a form of the loosest federation that could be called a State, is not at present a serious political conception.

'But we are not therefore driven back at once upon international anarchy. The problem is to find the greatest measure of organization which the state of feeling and intelligence that will exist after the war will tolerate. I think it clear that they [*sic*] will not tolerate a World State nor yet a European State. What less than this might they tolerate?' (*op. cit.*, p. 172).

He proceeds to contemplate a League founded upon Treaty. As to the objection that Treaties will not be observed, he remarks:

'Grant the continued existence of independent States, and they can only organize by treaty. And the fulfilment of the treaty must depend, in the last resort, on their sense of honour or of interest, or of both. . . .

'But a treaty that is to guarantee justice and peace must be of a new kind. Its object is not to strengthen some States against others, but to substitute in some way and in some measure (presently to be discussed) peaceable settlement for war. And the first point to be made is, that it belongs to the nature of such a treaty that it should be open to all civilized nations desiring to come in. For to exclude any nation is to announce that between it and the contracting nations war, not peaceable settlement, is to be the rule. On the other hand, a nation refusing to come in would offer a presumption that it intends to continue the way of war. It would announce itself a potential enemy of the others, against which they must continue to guard themselves. And, should any State or States announce such a policy, the treaty would in effect constitute a defensive alliance against such a State or States' (p. 173).

He assumes that if the Great Powers come in, the smaller States will be willing to join, and proceeds :

'The practical question would then be, not who should be admitted, but who, if any, should be excluded. The only tests to apply here would be that of capacity for deliberative action and that of public honesty. The representatives of no State must be purchasable. What States might be legitimately excluded by such tests as these, it will be a difficult and invidious task to determine. It is superfluous and would indeed be pedantic to attempt it here. But it must be remarked that a League from which all small States, as such, should be excluded would be viewed by those States with great suspicion. For it might well look like a League for disposing unjustly of their interests. On the other hand, it is certain that in any League that might be formed the great States would predominate. The small States would have perforce to be content with the right to represent their views fairly and effectively' (p. 175).

The primary object of this League would be to keep peace. For this purpose he proposes that there should be an obligation on all the parties to 'refer disputes to peaceable settlement in the first instance, leaving open an ultimate resort to force'. During the interval of discussion with a view to peaceable settlement, he would forbid not only war but preparation for war. He feels the difficulty of defining 'preparation for war', and makes some suggestions. He holds that :

'There must not be, during this interval, a continuance of the act that is the cause of the dispute. This means that the Court or the Council, or both, must have the power of injunction. And, if a sanction is to be applied (a point to be discussed presently), there must be a sanction against breach of the injunction' (p. 177).

He assumes that any State would be reluctant to embark upon war in defiance of a decision of the International Authority, would be very unlikely to find allies, and would probably find the other parties to the Treaty intervening by force against it. He does not in terms deal with the case where the State, against which the International Authority had pronounced, simply paid no attention to the decision; but apparently he would contemplate with equanimity the other State embarking upon war to enforce the decision.

He follows the League, of which he is a member, in dividing disputes into 'justiciable' and 'non-justiciable' cases, and sending the one to an International Tribunal, and the other to a Council of Conciliation.

He devotes a chapter to 'Sanctions of the Treaty', but cannot apparently make up his mind whether a sanction can be put 'behind the decisions of the International Court of Justice'. He suggests that perhaps the sanction need not be that of armed force, and that it might be possible in some cases to apply an economic boycott. He does, however, accept the use of force by the other members of the League collectively against any member who goes to war before the *moratorium* has expired. He determines that, 'if the League is to have a reasonable chance of fulfilling its purpose,' there should be a clause in the Treaty limiting armaments.

In Chapter XII, which is entitled: 'International Regulations and Administration', Mr. Dickinson makes an advance beyond the scheme of the League of Nations Society. He wishes States to 'learn to legislate and administer in common'. He contemplates the enforcement of Free Trade tempered by provisions against 'trading methods generally recognized as unfair', provisions for enforcing the open door with only certain restrictions upon immigration; and, in fact, a Federation which would absorb much of the sovereignty of the Federated States.

Mr. J. A. Hobson is another writer upon the subject. He contributed a pamphlet to the publications of the Union of Democratic Control.[1] He has also written a book

---

[1] *A League of Nations*, No. 15 a. Published October 1915.

entitled *Towards International Government* (1915). Much
of it follows the general run of writers since the War in
the division of disputes, in the reference to Court or
Council as the case may be, and the desirability of a
Federation for these purposes. He is, however, frankly
critical of some of the proposals. For instance, he gives
up the problem of a general reduction of armaments as
hopeless (Chap. I). And he shows very forcibly the
difficulties which would attach to the proposed economic
boycott as a measure for enforcing compliance, and the
great probability that any such boycott would lead to
war (Chap. VII). He is strongly against Protection
(Chap. XI).

He dislikes all appointments of arbitrators *ad hoc*, and
indeed objects to arbitrations (as opposed to a Court)
as leading to compromises, and to the neglect of opportunities of laying down sound principles of International
Law.[1] He wants all orders carried out by force, even
those which may be made by a Council of Conciliation,
and attaches little weight to suggestions of those who,
like Dr. Darby and the Peace Society (cf. p. 51), would
rely ' upon conscience, the inner sense of justice, and on
public opinion' (Chaps. VI, XI).

His views tend strongly towards a super-State. He
thinks that International Government is the real cure ;
and he advocates an International Executive and a
Legislature which is to have power to act upon the
vote of a majority, notwithstanding the dissent of
the representatives of some States, and in which the
larger States are to have a preponderance of votes
(Chaps. IX, X).

Mr. Brailsford, as stated above (p. 51), wrote an article
on the ' Organization of Peace' in the collection entitled
Towards a Lasting Settlement. He also contributed

---

[1] See pp. 40, 61. The contrary view of Chief Justice Beichmann
has been mentioned, p. 49 above.

a pamphlet to the publications of the Union of Democratic Control, and he has since then written a book entitled *A League of Nations* (1917). This work is already out of date in respect of its references to the United States and to Russia. He is opposed to any trade discriminations against Germany after the peace, and he has a powerful argument in favour of Free Trade in the future (Chap. IX). Notwithstanding this argument, he admits the principle of State Control of Commerce, while he proposes, as some mitigation of the injuries which might thereby be done to certain nations, to give the aggrieved State a right to appeal to some International Commission on Commerce.

He would propose to begin his League of Peace with the Allies only (pp. 19, 81-4), an idea which many other writers have strongly deprecated as tending to form two rival camps. He is an advocate of force (pp. 194, 301), and is opposed to what he calls a ' static peace ' (pp. 75-9), holding that racial, economic, and colonial problems are incapable of a permanent solution.

In his final chapter he has some new suggestions, and is at the same time somewhat critical of various other writers who are nevertheless of his School. He suggests :

' 1. That every adherent of the League must agree to respect the cultural liberty of racial minorities;

' 2. That the obligations of allies to each other must, in case of conflict, yield to their obligation to the League;

' 3. That the extremer uses of sea-power shall be reserved for wars declared or sanctioned by the League ;[1]

' 4. That a general recognition of commercial freedom and commercial amity shall obtain within the League, which will by international commissions safeguard the "Open Door" for capital and trade, and ensure free access to raw materials in an open market ' (pp. 287, 288).

He agrees with the usual division into matters for

---

[1] This is an ingenious suggestion and worthy of consideration.

a Court and matters for a Council; but he would not have it that

'The States involved shall pledge themselves to accept the Council's recommendations, nor that the League itself shall be bound to enforce them. The essence of the obligation is simply that no member of the League will go to war until his case has been submitted to the Council of Conciliation, and for some short period after it has made its report' (p. 290).

He is not hopeful of the *moratorium* as a soother of the warlike temper, and he shows the great difficulty of enforcing it by reason of the impossibility of drawing the line where warlike preparations begin, and the advantage which any stay of preparations for war would give to a military State already prepared for aggression. Still, however, he considers,

'The fundamental obligation is that no member of the League shall go to war [or mobilize its army or fleet?] until it has submitted its case to arbitration or conciliation and allowed an interval [of six months?] to elapse after the Council or Tribunal has issued its recommendation or award' (p. 292).

And he thinks that

'The possibility of a war by the League against some defiant Power cannot be ignored, and ought not to be minimized. However the obligation to join in such a war may be worded, it would be cowardly to shirk the central fact that the League must contemplate the possibility of such common wars' (p. 293).

But, when he comes to consider how force shall be applied, his pages comprise difficulties rather than practical suggestions. He points out the vagueness of the proposals of the American League to Enforce Peace, and of the British League of Nations Society. He shows how difficult it would be for any Power which has been party to the Great War to co-operate, for many years to come, with one of its present enemies, or to coerce one of its present allies. He shows also how delicate would

be the position of small States, and how unlikely it would
be for remote States to interfere, while, if the League
was dominated by the Great Powers, it might ' come to
bear an unpleasant resemblance to the Holy Alliance '.
He concludes this part of his discussion as follows :

' The fact is that we are not yet sufficiently in possession of
the continental view to carry this discussion very far as yet.   It
must inevitably differ somewhat from the British and American
view.   The question whether the League is workable depends
very little upon paper treaties ' (p. 296).

Notwithstanding these cautions he proceeds to provide
a constitution of the League, avowedly following to a great
extent the work of the Fabian Society and Mr. Woolf.
He wants a Court and Council of Conciliation, an Executive, and a Legislature, in all of which the Great Powers
are to have larger rights of voting than the small ones ;
and his notion of an Executive is that it probably ought
to represent only the Great Powers (p. 302).

He would use sea-power as a weapon for States
carrying out the common interest, but would absolve
neutrals from compliance with the present laws of war
at sea (with certain exceptions), in cases where the war
was ' undertaken by the uncontrolled will of a single
State in pursuit of its own national interests, however
legitimate these may be ' (p. 206).

M. Auguste Schvan has written a book called *Les Bases
d'une Paix durable*.   The writer describes himself as a
Swede who was first in the Austrian army, then in that
of his own country with a training in a Prussian School
of Arms, and afterwards in the Swedish Diplomatic
Service, which he left in disgust to come to England.
He says that he offered his services to the English army
when war broke out, but was refused, and that he
subsequently went to the United States and carried out
a very effective anti-German propaganda.

The first part of his book is trenchantly critical of all previous proposals for securing a general peace in the future. The third chapter is called ' La Faillite du Pacifisme '. In this chapter he contends that an economic boycott would have had no effect to prevent the late War; and that the establishment of it as a future means of constraint would only mean that each State would render itself as self-sufficing and self-contained as possible. He also contends that the proposed Democratic Control, which is the panacea of some, would not tend towards peace, on the ground that democracies are ' as nationalist, as blindly patriotic, as imperialist, as full of prejudices and hypocrisy, as an aristocracy or an autocracy '.[1]

He is opposed to the idea of an International Parliament (which perhaps has hardly been seriously proposed); and, with regard to the somewhat attractive proposal that all private undertakings for the manufacture and supply of armaments and munitions should be suppressed as tending to make it a commercial interest of great capitalists to promote war, he makes some shrewd suggestions (pp. 67–9). He points out , that, in the event of a nation, which had not State arsenals of its own or only insufficient ones, becoming involved in war with a militarist enemy who had devoted his energies in time of peace to the perfecting of his naval and military armaments, the more peaceable and less prepared State would find itself at the mercy of the other. There would be no private commercial firms on which it could rely ; and it would be a breach of neutrality for any other State to supply it from a national arsenal.

He especially attacks the American League to Enforce Peace, which, he says, does not really differ from the old European Concert ; it would leave each member of the League bound to maintain its full military establishment,

---

[1] p. 70. The original is in French.

and just as likely to lose its head in a crisis as were several of the late belligerents.

His destructive criticisms certainly merit attention; but his constructive proposals, to which the greater portion of the book is devoted, are almost unintelligible. The main idea is that there should be a World Law and a World Court of Justice, and indeed a World State. What are now known as States are to be 'stripped of sovereignty and independence, and transformed into subdivisions of humanity' (p. 142).

His view apparently is that the present States should be reduced in area; that each entity to which it would be reasonable to grant Home Rule should become a separate subdivision of humanity; that in cases where rival nationalities are incurably intermixed the minority should be forcibly transplanted; that undeveloped countries should be administered internationally; that there should be a World Court sitting in fifty-five divisions, and composed of about 275 Judges—five for each division. Before this Court, States or Governments could not come, at any rate as plaintiffs. The plaintiffs would be individuals who would complain of injuries received from some subdivisional government. The navies and armies of the world would be reduced to a strength adequate for police purposes by land and sea.

When one asks how all this is to be effected, one gets little help. The chief effective provisions seem to be that no citizen is to swear allegiance to any State; that every man is to be a citizen of the world, subject to the administration and tribunals of the subdivision in which he happens to find himself from time to time; and that there should be universal and uncontrolled Free Trade without any Customs barriers.

Mr. Jacobs has written a very suggestive little book [1] which he has supplemented by a broadsheet, issued in

---

[1] *Neutrality versus Justice*, by A. J. Jacobs.

May 1918. His idea is that there should be no neutrals
and no neutrality, because every war should be construed
as a crime against mankind, and 'breach of the peace'
between nations be treated as breach of the peace in
domestic matters, and summarily restrained by the strong
hand. He would have as many States as possible enter
into a treaty to 'defend the territorial integrity of each,
no matter by whom or for what reason attacked'. He
starts with the following propositions or aphorisms :

'That the time-honoured policy of Neutrality towards Belligerents is incompatible with national safety or international
justice.
'That there is a safe and practical alternative policy based on
the opposite principle of Mutual Protection, requiring neither
arbitration nor disarmament agreements. . . .
'That the apparent impracticability of a general defensive
alliance, without the simultaneous acceptance of an international
tribunal, is a demonstrable fallacy.
'That a real system of International Law and the machinery
for its administration cannot be secured by any paper guarantees,
but must inevitably evolve from the situation created by an
international alliance for territorial defence.'

The prevailing idea of his book is that, if States be
prevented from fighting, they will arrange for some
method of settling their differences, and that some form
or forms of international tribunals will ultimately be
evolved. But he does not suggest that all forms of conflict should come to an end; he would permit of reprisals of
all sorts, provided they did not take the form of invasion
of territory by an armed force. In his supplementary
broadsheet he has endeavoured to provide against naval
or aerial attacks ; but these provisions do not seem to
cover warfare on the high seas. His proposals require
that the territorial limits of States should be previously
settled and accurately ascertained. The form which his
sanction would take would be that the other States of the

Confederacy should jointly declare war against the State which invaded the territory of another. The defect of his scheme in this respect is that the States are only to be required to act jointly, so that, if any one, or at any rate any powerful one, were to hang back, the whole scheme would apparently fall through.

Notwithstanding these defects, his general idea is well deserving of further elaboration. He differs from all the associations and writers to whom reference has previously been made, in that he makes no provision for international Courts or Councils, which, indeed, he regards as for the moment impossible to create, his view being that they will be evolved in process of time, as nations find that they are debarred from serious fighting and will have to discover some other mode of settling their differences.

As the Great War proceeded, the desirability of the formation of a league for preserving peace in future received more and more adhesions. Further declarations[1] in this sense have been made by Austrian and German statesmen. The Resolution of the Conference of the Socialist and Labour Parties of Allied Nations, February 14, 1915, to this effect was reaffirmed by the Inter-Allied Labour and Socialist Conference in London, held on February 20, 1918.[2]

To these should be added a declaration[3] by the *Comité d'Entente pour la Société des Nations,* February 1918; a letter[4] of *L'Union fédérative de la Libre Pensée de France* to President Wilson, March 1918; and a weighty letter by the Archbishop of Canterbury and others, which appeared in *The Times,* February 22, 1918.

[1] See above, p. 22.

[2] *The Times,* Feb. 25, 1918; *L'Humanité,* 23 and 24 Feb., 1918; *Holland News,* vol. ii, p. 387.

[3] *L'Humanité,* 25 Feb., 1918; *Holland News,* vol. ii, p. 441.

[4] *L'Humanité,* 6 March, 1918; *Holland News,* vol. ii, p. 442.

One of the latest contributions to the literature of
this subject is the inaugural address of Lord Robert
Cecil as Chancellor of the University of Birmingham,
delivered on November 12, 1918. In it he lays stress
on the importance of the League of Nations being open
to every nation which can be trusted by its fellows to
accept *ex animo* the principles and basis of such a society,
and suggests that possibly unwilling States should be
compelled to enter by economic or other pressure.

He pronounces against an international armed force,
but puts his trust in some international machinery which
would prevent war, at least until the dispute has been
submitted to and pronounced upon by an international
Tribunal or a conference of all the Powers of the League.

This obligation to refrain from war is to be enforced
by each of the signatories to the Treaty using its whole
force, economic as well as military, against any nation
that forces on war before a conference has been held.

V. SUGGESTIONS

In conclusion, a few practical remarks and suggestions
may be made.

The principle of the *moratorium* should be accepted, and
it should be obligatory to enforce it. Whether it should
take the form of merely forbidding recourse to arms, or
of forbidding warlike preparations, is a more difficult
question. On the whole, it appears better that it should
be limited to taking up arms, for two reasons: first, the
difficulty of deciding whether warlike preparations are
being taken, and the temptation thereby offered to any
State, whether wishing or not wishing to interfere, to take
that view of the facts which best coincides with its wishes
or interests; secondly, because, if one State is pacific,

F

and has kept its armaments on a low level, and the other State has acted on a contrary policy, it is very desirable that a State with a small armament should have the time to develop its armament, and bring it up, if possible, to the same level as the State better prepared for aggression. In fact, such a provision would tend towards the reduction of armaments.

There is (as some writers have pointed out) a correlative to the *moratorium*. Supposing that one State complains of a continuing injury, and is debarred from redressing it by force of arms during the hearing of the cause, should there be a power in the Tribunal which is to hear the cause, to stay the injury *pendente lite* by an interlocutory order or injunction? This idea commends itself to Anglo-American writers, to whom the legal process of 'injunction' is familiar.[1] It is doubtful whether it is so familiar to, or would be so easily understood by, other nations. Moreover, considering that the complainant will not find a Court sitting, and that there will be considerable delay before it can be constituted, considering also the further difficulty of its making, upon preliminary materials only, what will approach to a decision upon the merits of the case, it hardly seems that the process of injunction would be suitable.

Perhaps the best provision would be that the State suffering under a continuing injury might, at any time after presenting its complaint, require the other State to desist *pendente lite*, notify the International Executive that it had so required and been refused, and then claim, and, in an exceptional case, be accorded, the benefit of a relief from the *moratorium*.

A point which seems of great importance, and is a step beyond the Hague Conventions, though there is just a suggestion of it in that of 1907, is that the

[1] See above, p. 33.

Court—and the same principle applies to the Council—
should be one open to a party complaining. It should
not be merely an Arbitral Tribunal invoked by joint
consent, and therefore not acting until both parties
consent. In this respect the Dutch scheme, for instance,
and the views of all who have the old arbitration theory
before their mind, are defective and weak. It is essential
to any scheme for preserving peace by such means that
either party should be able to invoke the action of the
Court or Council, whether the other party likes it or not.

It is probably hopeless to bind the States to enforce
decrees or awards ; but the suggestion that all Treaties
of Alliance should be deemed void, if the State claiming
the benefit of such alliance is a State which has been
put in the wrong, may be of some value.

The Federation or League should agree to protect its
members against attacks by non-members. Schemes for
creating an International Legislature are, to say the
least, premature.

As to the limitation of armaments, no proposal for
it appears yet to have been put forward in a practical
form ; but it would be a step towards the prevention of
war if the nations of the world would agree to make
laws determining what is not permissible in war, either
as between belligerents, or as between a belligerent and
a neutral, and to enforce the observance of these laws
with all their power.

AUTHORITIES

ANCILLON, J. P. FRIEDRICH. *Tableau des Révolutions du Système politique de l'Europe.* 2 vols. Brussels, 1839.

ASHBEE, C. R. *The American League to Enforce Peace.* London, 1917.

BARCLAY, SIR THOMAS. *The Hague Court and Vital Interests.* Reprinted from the *Law Quarterly Review,* April 1905, London.

BEICHMANN, F. V. N. *The Construction of a Permanent International Tribunal.* Published in *Scientia,* vol. xxi. Bologna and London.

BISSCHOP, DR. W. R. *The Advantage of International Leagues.* Grotius Society Papers, vol. ii. London, 1916.

BRAILSFORD, H. N. *The Organisation of Peace.* Published in *Towards a Lasting Settlement,* edited by Charles Roden Buxton. London, 1915.

BRYCE, VISCOUNT, AND OTHERS. *Proposals for the Prevention of Future Wars.* London, 1917.

BUXTON, C. R. (Editor). *Towards a Lasting Settlement.* London, 1915.

CECIL, LORD ROBERT. Inaugural Address at Birmingham. *The Times,* Nov. 13, 1918.

DARBY, W. E. *International Tribunals.* Fourth Edition. London, 1904.

The Political Machinery of International Peace. Published in *The Ministry of Reconciliation,* edited by H. Martin. London, 1916.

The Enforcement of the Hague Conventions. Grotius Society Papers, vol. ii. London, 1916.

DICKINSON, G. LOWES. *The War and the Way Out.* London, 1915.

After the War. London, 1915.

The Basis of Permanent Peace. Published in *Towards a Lasting Settlement,* edited by C. R. Buxton. London, 1915.
The Choice Before Us. London, 1917.

FABIAN SOCIETY, THE. *A Project by a Fabian Committee for a Supernational Authority that will Prevent War.* Published in *The New Statesman,* July 1915, and in *International Government,* by L. S. Woolf. London, 1916.

GOLDSMITH, ROBERT. *A League to Enforce Peace.* New York, 1917.

Grotius Society. Papers, in 2 vols., London, 1916–17.

Herald, The, of Peace. London, October 1917.

HERTSLET, L. *Treaties and Conventions between Great Britain and Foreign Powers so far as they relate to Commerce and Navigation.* Three volumes. London, 1827.

HIGGINS, A. PEARCE. *The Hague Peace Conferences.* Cambridge, 1909.

HOBSON, J. A. *Towards International Government.* London, 1915.

Holland News, The. Review of the Nederlandsche Anti-Oorlog Raad. 2 vols. London, 1917, etc.

HOLT, HAMILTON. *Preparedness and Ultimate Reduction of Armaments.* Published in *An Enforced Peace,* by the American League to Enforce Peace. Washington, 1916.

JACOBS, A. J. *Neutrality versus Justice.* An Essay on International Relations. London, 1917.

KANT, I. *Perpetual Peace.* Translation and introduction by M. Campbell Smith, London, 1903.

LANGE, CHR. L. *Exposé des Travaux de l'Organisation [pour une Paix durable].* The Hague, 1917.

League to Enforce Peace, The American.
An Enforced Peace. Being the Proceedings of the First Annual National Assemblage of the League to Enforce Peace. Washington, 1916.
The League Bulletin. Published weekly. New York. In progress.
Independence Hall Conference held in the City of Philadelphia, Bunker Hill Day (June 17th), 1915, together with the speeches made at a public banquet in the Bellevue-Stratford Hotel on the preceding evening. New York.
(See also Short, W. H.)

League of Nations Society, The British.

The Project of a League of Nations. London, August 1917.

Treaty between the United Kingdom and the United States of America, with regard to the Establishment of a Peace Commission. Signed at Washington, September 15, 1914. L. N. S. Publication, No. 4. November 1916.

A League of Peace and How to Begin It. By Aneurin Williams, M.P. L. N. S. Publication, No. 8.

LOWELL, DR. A. L. *A League to Enforce Peace.* Boston, Mass., 1915.

MADAY, PROF. ANDRÉ DE. *Le Contrat social des Nations.* The Hague, 1917.

MARBURG, THEODORE. *The American League to Enforce Peace.* Published in *The Project of a League of Nations*, by the L. N. S. London, 1917.

A Reply to Critics. Published in *An Enforced Peace*, by the American League to Enforce Peace. Washington, 1916.

MARTIN, HUGH (Editor). *The Ministry of Reconciliation.* London, 1916.

MINOR, R. C. *A Republic of Nations.* New York, 1919.

MOLINARI, G. DE. *L'Abbé de Saint-Pierre.* Paris, 1857.

OPPENHEIM, L. *The League of Nations and its Problems.* Three Lectures. London, 1919.

Organisation Centrale pour une Paix durable. Recueil de Rapports. Four volumes. Published at The Hague, 1916, 1917.

PENN, WILLIAM. *Essay towards the Present and Future Peace of Europe by the Establishment of an European Dyet, Parliament, or Estates.* 1693-4. Reprinted, Gloucester, 1914.

PHILLIMORE, THE RT. HON. SIR WALTER, Bart. *Three Centuries of Treaties of Peace and their Teaching.* London, 1917.

SAINT-PIERRE, C. I. CASTEL DE. *Projet de traité pour rendre la Paix perpétuelle entre les Souverains Chrétiens.* Utrecht, 1717.

Abrégé du projet de Paix perpétuelle. Amsterdam, 1729.

(N.B. Neither of these publications has been directly studied by the author of this paper.)

SCHVAN, AUGUSTE. *Les Bases d'une Paix durable.* Paris, 1917.

Scientia. Vol. xxi. Bologna and London.

SHORT, W. H. *Program and Policies of the League to Enforce Peace.* New York, 1916.

Union of Democratic Control, The. Publications.

WAECHTER, Sir MAX. *After the War. The United States of Europe.* London, 1916. Privately printed.

WHITE, THOMAS RAEBURN. *The League Program.* Published in *An Enforced Peace,* by the American League to Enforce Peace. Washington, 1916.

WILLIAMS, ANEURIN. Papers in the publication of the League of Nations Society, and in the *Rapports* of the Organisation Centrale.

WOOLF, L. S. *International Government.* Published by the Fabian Society. London, 1916.

The Framework of a Lasting Peace. Edited by L. S. Woolf. London, 1917.

HANDBOOKS PREPARED UNDER THE DIRECTION OF THE HISTORICAL SECTION OF THE FOREIGN OFFICE.—No. 161

PRESIDENT WILSON'S POLICY

LONDON:

PUBLISHED BY H. M. STATIONERY OFFICE.

1920

TABLE OF CONTENTS

Wt. 9157/860. 1000. 6/20. O.U.P

PART 3. AFTER INTERVENTION.

April 1917—December 1918

TABLE OF CONTENTS

PAGE
APPENDIX

EXTRACTS FROM SPEECHES, &c.

PART 1. NEUTRAL PERIOD. AUGUST 1914—APRIL 1916

AUGUST 5, 1914. MESSAGE TO THE BELLIGERENTS

As official head of one of the Powers signatory to the
Hague Convention, I feel it to be my privilege and my
duty, under Article 3 of that Convention, to say to you in
a spirit of most earnest friendship that I should welcome
the opportunity to act in the interest of European peace,
either now or at any other time that might be thought
more suitable, as an occasion to serve you and all concerned
in a way that would afford me lasting cause for gratitude
and happiness.

AUGUST 18, 1914. APPEAL TO THE CITIZENS OF THE UNITED
STATES TO MAINTAIN NEUTRALITY

The people of the United States may be divided into
camps of hostile opinion, hot against each other, involved
in the war itself in impulse and opinion if not in action.

Such divisions among us would be fatal to our peace
of mind and might seriously stand in the way of the
proper performance of our duty as the one great nation
at peace, the one people holding itself ready to play a part
of impartial mediation and speak the counsels of peace
and accommodation, not as a partisan, but as a friend.

DECEMBER 8, 1914. SECOND ANNUAL ADDRESS TO
CONGRESS

We are the champions of peace and of concord. And
we should be very jealous of this distinction which we
have sought to earn. Just now we should be particularly
jealous of it, because it is our dearest present hope that

B

this character and reputation may presently, in God's providence, bring us an opportunity such as has seldom been vouchsafed any nation, the opportunity to counsel and obtain peace in the world and reconciliation and a healing settlement of many a matter that has cooled and interrupted the friendship of nations.

APRIL 20, 1915. SPEECH AT THE ASSOCIATED PRESS LUNCHEON, NEW YORK

Is it not likely that the nations of the world will some day turn to us for the cooler assessment of the elements engaged ? I am not now thinking so preposterous a thought as that we should sit in judgement upon them—no nation is fit to sit in judgement upon any other nation—but that we shall some day have to assist in reconstructing the processes of peace. . . .

We are the mediating nation of the world. I do not mean that we undertake not to mind our own business and to mediate where other people are quarrelling. I mean the word in a broader sense. We are compounded of the nations of the world ; we mediate their blood, we mediate their traditions, we mediate their sentiments, their tastes, their passions ; we are ourselves compounded of those things. We are, therefore, able to understand all nations ; we are able to understand them in the compound, not separately, as partisans, but unitedly as knowing and comprehending and embodying them all. It is in that sense that I mean that America is a mediating nation.

NOVEMBER 4, 1915. SPEECH AT THE MANHATTAN CLUB, NEW YORK

We shall, I confidently believe, never again take another foot of territory by conquest. We shall never in any circumstances seek to make an independent people subject to our dominion ; because we believe, we passionately believe, in the right of every people to choose their own allegiance and be free of masters altogether.

December 7, 1915. Third Annual Address to Congress

We have stood apart, studiously neutral. It was our manifest duty to do so. Not only did we have no part or interest in the policies which seem to have brought the conflict on ; it was necessary, if a universal catastrophe was to be avoided, that a limit should be set to the sweep of destructive war and that some part of the great family of nations should keep the processes of peace alive, if only to prevent collective economic ruin and the break-down throughout the world of the industries by which its populations are fed and sustained. It was manifestly the duty of the self-governed nations of this hemisphere to redress, if possible, the balance of economic loss and confusion in the other, if they could do nothing more. In the day of readjustment and recuperation we earnestly hope and believe that they can be of infinite service. . . .

I have spoken to you to-day, gentlemen, upon a single theme, the thorough preparation of the nation to care for its own security and to make sure of entire freedom to play the impartial rôle in this hemisphere and in the world which we all believe to have been providentially assigned to it. I have had in my mind no thought of any immediate or particular danger arising out of our relations with other nations. We are at peace with all the nations of the world, and there is reason to hope that no question in controversy between this and other Governments will lead to any serious breach of amicable relations, grave as some differences of attitude and policy have been and may yet turn out to be.

January 29, 1916. Speech at Cleveland, Ohio

In the meantime we, the people of the United States, are the one great disengaged Power, the one neutral Power, finding it exceedingly difficult to be neutral, because, like men everywhere else, we are human ; we have the deep passions of mankind in us ; we have sympathies that are as easily stirred as the sympathies of any other people ; we have interests which we see being drawn slowly into the maelstrom of this tremendous upheaval.

February 24, 1916. Letter to Senator Stone

Note.—This letter was addressed to the question of the expediency of American citizens exercising the right to travel upon British passenger steamers, in view of the German submarine policy.

For my own part, I cannot consent to any abridgement of the rights of American citizens in any respect. The honour and self-respect of the Nation is involved. We covet peace, and shall preserve it at any cost but the loss of honour. To forbid our people to exercise their rights for fear we might be called upon to vindicate them would be a deep humiliation indeed. It would be an implicit, all but an explicit, acquiescence in the violation of the rights of mankind everywhere and of whatever nation or allegiance.

PART 2. CRITICAL PERIOD. April 1916–April 1917

April 19, 1916. Address to Congress on German Submarine Policy

I have deemed it my duty, therefore, to say to the Imperial German Government that if it is still its purpose to prosecute relentless and indiscriminate warfare against vessels of commerce by the use of submarines, notwithstanding the now demonstrated impossibility of conducting that warfare in accordance with what the Government

of the United States must consider the sacred and indis-
putable rules of international law and the universally
recognized dictates of humanity, the Government of the
United States is at last forced to the conclusion that there
is but one course it can pursue ; and that unless the
Imperial German Government should now immediately
declare and effect an abandonment of its present methods
of warfare against passenger and freight-carrying vessels
this Government can have no choice but to sever diplomatic relations with the Government of the German
Empire altogether.

MAY 27, 1916. SPEECH TO AMERICAN LEAGUE TO ENFORCE
PEACE

Only when the great nations of the world have reached
some sort of agreement as to what they hold to be fundamental to their common interest, and as to some feasible
method of acting in concert when any nation or group
of nations seeks to disturb those fundamental things, can
we feel that civilization is at last in a way of justifying
its existence and claiming to be finally established. It
is clear that nations must in the future be governed by
the same high code of honour that we demand of individuals. . . .

The . principle of public right must henceforth take
precedence over the individual interests of particular
nations, and the nations of the world must in some way
band themselves together to see that that right prevails
as against any sort of selfish aggression ; henceforth
alliance must not be set up against alliance, understanding against understanding, but there must be a common
agreement for a common object, and at the heart of that
common object must lie the inviolable rights of peoples
and of mankind. . . .

We believe these fundamental things : First, that every
people has a right to choose the sovereignty under which

they shall live. Like other nations, we have ourselves no doubt once and again offended against that principle when for a little while controlled by selfish passion, as our franker historians have been honourable enough to admit ; but it has become more and more our rule of life and action. Second, that the small States of the world have a right to enjoy the same respect for their sovereignty and for their territorial integrity that great and powerful nations expect and insist upon. And, third, that the world has a right to be free from every disturbance of its peace that has its origin in aggression and disregard of the rights of peoples and nations. . . .

If it should ever be our privilege to suggest or initiate a movement for peace among the nations now at war, I am sure that the people of the United States would wish their Government to move along these lines : First, such a settlement with regard to their own immediate interests as the belligerents may agree upon. We have nothing material of any kind to ask for ourselves, and are quite aware that we are in no sense or degree parties to the present quarrel. Our interest is only in peace and its future guarantees. Second, an universal association of the nations to maintain the inviolate security of the high-way of the seas for the common and unhindered use of all the nations of the world, and to prevent any war begun either contrary to treaty covenants or without warning and full submission of the causes to the opinion of the world—a virtual guarantee of territorial integrity and political independence.

MAY 30, 1916. SPEECH ON MEMORIAL DAY, AT ARLINGTON

Some of the public prints have reminded me, as if I needed to be reminded, of what General Washington warned us against. He warned us against entangling alliances. I shall never myself consent to an entangling alliance, but I would gladly assent to a disentangling alliance—an alliance which would disentangle the peoples of the world from those combinations in which they seek their own separate and private interests and unite the people of the world to preserve the peace of the world upon a basis of common right and justice. There is liberty there, not limitation. There is freedom, not entanglement. There is the achievement of the highest things for which the United States has declared its principle.

June 13, 1916. Address to Graduating Class of United States Military Academy

I want to say a word to you young gentlemen about militarism. You are not militarists because you are military. Militarism does not consist in the existence of an army, not even in the existence of a very great army. Militarism is a spirit. It is a point of view. It is a system. It is a purpose. The purpose of militarism is to use armies for aggression.

September 2, 1916. Address on accepting Re-nomination

Look first at what it will be necessary that the nations of the world should do to make the days to come tolerable and fit to live and work in ; and then look at our part in what is to follow and our own duty of preparation. For we must be prepared both in resources and in policy.

There must be a just and settled peace, and we here in America must contribute the full force of our enthusiasm and of our authority as a nation to the organization of that peace upon world-wide foundations that cannot easily be shaken. No nation should be forced to take sides in any quarrel in which its own honour and integrity and the fortunes of its own people are not involved ; but no nation can any longer remain neutral as against any wilful disturbance of the peace of the world. The effects of war can no longer be confined to the areas of battle. No

nation stands wholly apart in interest when the life and
interests of all nations are thrown into confusion and peril.
If hopeful and generous enterprise is to be renewed, if
the healing and helpful arts of life are indeed to be revived
when peace comes again, a new atmosphere of justice
and friendship must be generated by means the world
has never tried before. The nations of the world must
unite in joint guarantees that whatever is done to disturb
the whole world's life must first be tested in the court of
the whole world's opinion before it is attempted.

December 18, 1916. Peace Note to Belligerents, in reply to German Overtures of Dec. 12

He (the President) takes the liberty of calling attention
to the fact that the objects which the statesmen of the
belligerents on both sides have in mind in this war are
virtually the same, as stated in general terms to their
own people and to the world. Each side desires to make
the rights and privileges of weak peoples and small States
as secure against aggression or denial in the future as the
rights and privileges of the great and powerful States now
at war. Each wishes itself to be made secure in the future,
along with all other nations and peoples, against the
recurrence of wars like this, and against aggression or
selfish interference of any kind. Each would be jealous
of the formation of any more rival leagues to preserve
an uncertain balance of power amidst multiplying sus-
picions; but each is ready to consider the formation of
a League of Nations to ensure peace and justice throughout
the world. Before that final step can be taken, however,
each deems it necessary first to settle the issues of the
present war upon terms which will certainly safeguard the
independence, the territorial integrity, and the political
and commercial freedom of the nations involved.

In the measures to be taken to secure the future peace
of the world the people and Government of the United

States are as vitally and as directly interested as the Governments now at war. Their interest, moreover, in the means to be adopted to relieve the smaller and weaker peoples of the world of the peril of wrong and violence is as quiek and ardent as that of any other people or Government. They stand ready, and even eager, to co-operate in the accomplishment of these ends, when the war is over, with every influence and resource at their command. But the war must first be concluded. The terms upon which it is to be concluded they are not at liberty to suggest; but the President does feel that it is his right and his duty to point out their intimate interest in its conclusion, lest it should presently be too late to accomplish the greater things which lie beyond its con-clusion, lest the situation of neutral nations, now exceed-ingly hard to endure, be rendered altogether intolerable, and lest, more than all, an injury be done to civilization itself which can never be atoned for or repaired.

The President therefore feels altogether justified in suggesting an immediate opportunity for a comparison of views as to the terms which must precede those ultimate arrangements for the peace of the world which all desire, and in which the neutral nations as well as those at war are ready to play their full responsible part.

JANUARY 22, 1917. ADDRESS TO THE SENATE OF THE UNITED STATES

The present war must first be ended; but we owe it to candour and to a just regard for the opinion of mankind to say that, so far as our participation in guarantees of future peace is concerned, it makes a great deal of difference in what way and upon what terms it is ended. The treaties and agreements which bring it to an end must embody terms which will create a peace that is worth guaranteeing and preserving, a peace that will win the approval of mankind, not merely a peace that will serve the several interests and immediate aims of the nations engaged. We shall have no voice in determining what those terms shall be, but we shall, I feel sure, have a voice in determining whether they shall be made lasting or not by the guarantees of a universal covenant; and our judgement upon what is fundamental and essential as a condition precedent to permanency should be spoken now, not afterwards when it may be too late. . . .

It will be absolutely necessary that a force be created as a guarantor of the permanency of the settlement so much greater than the force of any nation now engaged or any alliance hitherto formed or projected that no nation, no probable combination of nations, could face or withstand it. If the peace presently to be made is to endure, it must be a peace made secure by the organized major force of mankind. . . .

It must be a peace without victory. It is not pleasant to say this. I am seeking only to face realities and to face them without soft concealments. Victory would mean peace forced upon the loser, a victor's terms imposed upon the vanquished. It would be accepted in humiliation, under duress, at an intolerable sacrifice, and would leave a sting, a resentment, a bitter memory upon which terms of peace would rest, not permanently, but only as upon a quicksand. Only a peace between equals can last. Only a peace the very principle of which is equality and a common participation in a common benefit. The right state of mind, the right feeling between nations, is as necessary for a lasting peace as is the just settlement of vexed questions of territory or of racial and national allegiance.

The equality of nations upon which peace must be founded if it is to last must be an equality of rights; the guarantees exchanged must neither recognize nor imply a difference between big nations and small, between those that are powerful and those that are weak. Right must be based upon the common strength, not upon the indi-

vidual strength, of the nations upon whose concert peace
will depend. Equality of territory or of resources there
of course cannot be ; nor any other sort of equality not
gained in the ordinary peaceful and legitimate development
of the peoples themselves. . . .

No peace can last, or ought to last, which does not
recognize and accept the principle that Governments derive all their just powers from the consent of the governed,
and that no right anywhere exists to hand peoples about
from sovereignty to sovereignty as if they were property.
I take it for granted, for instance, if I may venture upon
a single example, that statesmen everywhere are agreed
that there should be a united, independent, and autonomous Poland, and that henceforth inviolable security of
life, of worship, and of industrial and social development
should be guaranteed to all peoples who have lived hitherto
under the power of Governments devoted to a faith and
purpose hostile to their own. . . .

So far as practicable, moreover, every great people now
struggling towards a full development of its resources and
of its powers should be assured a direct outlet to the
great highways of the sea. Where this cannot be done by
the cession of territory, it can no doubt be done by the
neutralization of direct rights of way under the general
guarantee which will assure the peace itself. With a right
comity of arrangement no nation need be shut away from
free access to the open paths of the world's commerce.

And the paths of the sea must alike in law and in fact
be free. The freedom of the seas is the *sine qua non* of
peace, equality, and co-operation. No doubt a somewhat
radical reconsideration of many of the rules of international practice hitherto thought to be established may
be necessary in order to make the seas indeed free and
common in practically all circumstances for the use of
mankind, but the motive for such changes is convincing
and compelling. There can be no trust or intimacy

between the peoples of the world without them. The free, constant, unthreatened intercourse of nations is an essential part of the process of peace and of development. It need not be difficult either to define or to secure the freedom of the seas if the Governments of the world sincerely desire to come to an agreement concerning it.

It is a problem closely connected with the limitation of naval armaments and the co-operation of the navies of the world in keeping the seas at once free and safe. And the question of limiting naval armaments opens the wider and perhaps more difficult question of the limitation of armies and of all programmes of military preparation. Difficult and delicate as these questions are, they must be faced with the utmost candour and decided in a spirit of real accommodation if peace is to come with healing in its wings, and come to stay. Peace cannot be had without concession and sacrifice. There can be no sense of safety and equality among the nations if great preponderating armaments are henceforth to continue here and there to be built up and maintained. The statesmen of the world must plan for peace, and nations must adjust and accommodate their policy to it as they have planned for war and made ready for pitiless contest and rivalry. The question of armaments, whether on land or sea, is the most immediately and intensely practical question connected with the future fortunes of nations and of mankind. . . .

I am proposing, as it were, that the nations should with one accord adopt the doctrine of President Monroe as the doctrine of the world : that no nation should seek to extend its polity over any other nation or people, but that every people should be left free to determine its own polity, its own way of development, unhindered, unthreatened, unafraid, the little along with the great and powerful.

I am proposing that all nations henceforth avoid entangling alliances which would draw them into competitions of power, catch them in a net of intrigue and selfish rivalry, and disturb their own affairs with influences intruded from without. There is no entangling alliance in a concert of power. When all unite to act in the same sense and with the same purpose, all act in the common interest and are free to live their own lives under a common protection.

I am proposing government by the consent of the governed ; that freedom of the seas which in international conference after conference representatives of the United States have urged with the eloquence of those who are the convinced disciples of liberty ; and that moderation of armaments which makes of armies and navies a power for order merely, not an instrument of aggression or of selfish violence.

February 3, 1917. Address to Congress announcing Severance of Diplomatic Relations with Germany

Note.—On January 31, the German Ambassador had presented a note proclaiming Germany's intention to sink all ships without exception, after February 1, in a zone placed round the Entente countries. After announcing the severance of diplomatic relations, the President added :

I refuse to believe that it is the intention of the German authorities to do in fact what they have warned us they will feel at liberty to do. I cannot bring myself to believe that they will indeed pay no regard to the ancient friendship between their people and our own or to the solemn obligations which have been exchanged between them, and destroy American ships and take the lives of American citizens in the wilful prosecution of the ruthless naval programme they have announced their intention to adopt. Only actual overt acts on their part can make me believe it even now.

If this inveterate confidence on my part in the sobriety and prudent foresight of their purpose should unhappily prove unfounded ; if American ships and American lives should in fact be sacrificed by their naval commanders in heedless contravention of the just and reasonable understandings of international law and the obvious dictates of humanity, I shall take the liberty of coming again before the Congress, to ask that authority be given me to use any means that may be necessary for the protection of our seamen and our people in the prosecution of their peaceful and legitimate errands on the high seas. I can do nothing less. I take it for granted that all neutral Governments will take the same course.

We do not desire any hostile conflict with the Imperial German Government. We are the sincere friends of the German people and earnestly desire to remain at peace with the Government which speaks for them. We shall not believe that they are hostile to us unless and until we are obliged to believe it ; and we purpose nothing more than the reasonable defence of the undoubted rights of our people. We wish to serve no selfish ends. We seek merely to stand true alike in thought and in action to the immemorial principles of our people which I sought to express in my address to the Senate only two weeks ago— seek merely to vindicate our right to liberty and justice and an unmolested life. These are the bases of peace, not war.

MARCH 5, 1917. SECOND INAUGURAL ADDRESS, WASHINGTON

These, therefore, are the things we shall stand for, whether in war or in peace :

That all nations are equally interested in the peace of the world and in the political stability of free peoples, and equally responsible for their maintenance ;

That the essential principle of peace is the actual equality of nations in all matters of right or privilege ;

That peace cannot securely or justly rest upon an armed balance of power ;

That Governments derive all their just powers from the consent of the governed and that no other powers should be supported by the common thought, purpose, or power of the family of nations.

That the seas should be equally free and safe for the use of all peoples, under rules set up by common agreement and consent, and that, so far as practicable, they should be accessible to all upon equal terms ;

That national armaments should be limited to the necessities of national order and domestic safety ;

That the community of interest and of power upon which peace must henceforth depend imposes upon each nation the duty of seeing to it that all influences proceeding from its own citizens meant to encourage or assist revolution in other states should be sternly and effectually suppressed and prevented.

APRIL 2, 1917. ADDRESS TO CONGRESS RECOMMENDING DECLARATION OF WAR

We have no quarrel with the German people. We have no feeling towards them but one of sympathy and friendship. It was not upon their impulse that their Government acted in entering this war. It was not with their previous knowledge or approval. . . .

A steadfast concert for peace can never be maintained except by a partnership of democratic nations. No autocratic Government could be trusted to keep faith within it or observe its covenants. It must be a league of honour, a partnership of opinion. Intrigue would eat its vitals away ; the plottings of inner circles who could plan what they would and render account to no one would be a corruption seated at its very heart. Only free peoples can hold their purpose and their honour steady to a common end and prefer the interests of mankind to any narrow interest of their own. . . .

We are now about to accept gage of battle with this

natural foe to liberty and shall, if necessary, spend the whole force of the nation to check and nullify its preten sions and its power. We are glad, now that we see the facts with no veil of false pretence about them, to fight thus for the ultimate peace of the world and for the libera- tion of its peoples, the German peoples included : for the rights of nations great and small and the privilege of men everywhere to choose their way of life and of obedience. The world must be made safe for democracy. Its peace must be planted upon the tested foundations of political liberty. We have no selfish ends to serve. We desire no conquest, no dominion. We seek no indemnities for ourselves, no material compensation for the sacrifices we shall freely make. We are but one of the champions of the rights of mankind. We shall be satisfied when those rights have been made as secure as the faith and the freedom of nations can make them.

PART 3.　AFTER INTERVENTION.[1]
APRIL 1917—DECEMBER 1918

APRIL 15, 1917.　ADDRESS TO HIS FELLOW-COUNTRYMEN CONCERNING THE WAR

There is not a single selfish element, so far as I can see, in the cause we are fighting for. We are fighting for what we believe and wish to be the rights of mankind and for the future peace and security of the world. To do this great thing worthily and successfully we must devote ourselves to the service without regard to profit or material advantage and with an energy and intelligence that will rise to the level of the enterprise itself. We must realize to the full how great the task is and how many things, how many kinds and elements of capacity and service and self-sacrifice, it involves.

[1] The United States Government declared war on Germany on April 6, 1917.

MAY 12, 1917. SPEECH AT THE DEDICATION OF THE RED
CROSS BUILDING, WASHINGTON

I say the heart of the country is in this war because
it would not have gone into it if its heart had not been
prepared for it. It would not have gone into it if it had
not first believed that here was an opportunity to express
the character of the United States.

We have gone in with no special grievance of our own,
because we have always said that we were the friends and
servants of mankind. We look for no profit. We look for
no advantage. We will accept no advantage out of this war.

We go because we believe that the very principles
upon which the American Republic was founded are now
at stake and must be vindicated.

JUNE 9, 1917. COMMUNICATION TO PROVISIONAL
GOVERNMENT OF RUSSIA

In view of the approaching visit of the American
delegation to Russia to express the deep friendship of the
American people for the people of Russia and to discuss
the best and most practical means of co-operation between
the two peoples in carrying the present struggle for the
freedom of all peoples to a successful consummation, it
seems opportune and appropriate that I should state again,
in the light of this new partnership, the objects the United
States has had in mind in entering the war. Those objects
have been very much beclouded during the past few weeks
by mistaken and misleading statements, and the issues at
stake are too momentous, too tremendous, too significant,
for the whole human race to permit any misinterpreta-
tions or misunderstandings, however slight, to remain
uncorrected for a moment.

The war has begun to go against Germany, and in their
desperate desire to escape the inevitable ultimate defeat,
those who are in authority in Germany are using every

possible instrumentality, are making use even of the influence of groups and parties among their own subjects to whom they have never been just or fair, or even tolerant, to promote a propaganda on both sides of the sea which will preserve for them their influence at home and their power abroad, to the undoing of the very men they are using.

The position of America in this war is so clearly avowed that no man can be excused for mistaking it. She seeks no material profit or aggrandizement of any kind. She is fighting for no advantage or selfish object of her own, but for the liberation of peoples everywhere from the aggressions of autocratic force.

The ruling classes in Germany have begun of late to profess a like liberality and justice of purpose, but only to preserve the power they have set up in Germany and the selfish advantages which they have wrongly gained for themselves and their private projects of power all the way from Berlin to Baghdad and beyond. Government after Government has by their influence, without open conquest of its territory, been linked together in a net of intrigue directed against nothing less than the peace and liberty of the world. The meshes of that intrigue must be broken, but cannot be broken unless wrongs already done are undone ; and adequate measures must be taken to prevent it from ever again being rewoven or repaired.

Of course, the Imperial German Government and those whom it is using for their own undoing are seeking to obtain pledges that the war will end in the restoration of the *status quo ante*. It was the *status quo ante* out of which this iniquitous war issued forth, the power of the Imperial German Government within the Empire and its widespread domination and influence outside of that Empire. That status must be altered in such fashion as to prevent any such hideous thing from ever happening again.

We are fighting for the liberty, the self-government, and

the undictated development of all peoples, and every feature of the settlement that concludes this war must be conceived and executed for that purpose. Wrongs must first be righted and then adequate safeguards must be created to prevent their being committed again. We ought not to consider remedies merely because they have a pleasing and sonorous sound. Practical questions can be settled only by practical means. Phrases will not accomplish the result. Effective readjustments will, and whatever readjustments are necessary must, be made.

But they must follow a principle; and that principle is plain. No people must be forced under sovereignty under which it does not wish to live. No territory must change hands except for the purpose of securing those who inhabit it a fair chance of life and liberty. No indemnities must be insisted on except those that constitute payment for manifest wrongs done. No readjustments of power must be made except such as will tend to secure the future peace of the world and the future welfare and happiness of its peoples.

And then the free peoples of the world must draw together in some common covenant, some genuine and practical co-operation that will in effect combine their force to secure peace and justice in the dealings of nations with one another. The brotherhood of mankind must no longer be a fair but empty phrase: it must be given a structure of force and reality. The nations must realize their common life and effect a workable partnership to secure that life against the aggressions of autocratic and self-pleasing power.

JUNE 14, 1917. ADDRESS ON FLAG DAY, WASHINGTON

It is plain enough how we were forced into the war. The extraordinary insults and aggressions of the Imperial German Government left us no self-respecting choice but to take up arms in defence of our rights as a free people and of our honour as a sovereign Government. The

military masters of Germany denied us the right to be
neutral. They filled our unsuspecting communities with
vicious spies and conspirators and sought to corrupt the
opinion of our people in their own behalf. When they
found that they could not do that, their agents diligently
spread sedition amongst us and sought to draw our own
citizens from their allegiance,—and some of those agents
were men connected with the official Embassy of the
German Government itself here in our own capital. They
sought by violence to destroy our industries and arrest our
commerce. They tried to incite Mexico to take up arms
against us and to draw Japan into a hostile alliance with
her,—and that, not by indirection, but by direct suggestion
from the Foreign Office in Berlin. They impudently denied
us the use of the high seas and repeatedly executed their
threat that they would send to their death any of our
people who ventured to approach the coasts of Europe.
And many of our own people were corrupted. Men began
to look upon their own neighbours with suspicion and to
wonder in their hot resentment and surprise whether there
was any community in which hostile intrigue did not lurk.
What great nation in such circumstances would not have
taken up arms? Much as we had desired peace, it was
denied us, and not of our own choice. This flag under
which we serve would have been dishonoured had we with-
held our hand.

But that is only part of the story. We know now as
clearly as we knew before we were ourselves engaged that
we are not the enemies of the German people and that
they are not our enemies. They did not originate or desire
this hideous war or wish that we should be drawn into it ;
and we are vaguely conscious that we are fighting their
cause, as they will some day see it, as well as our own.
They are themselves in the grip of the same sinister power
that has now at last stretched its ugly talons out and
drawn blood from us. The whole world is at war because

the whole world is in the grip of that power and is trying out the great battle which shall determine whether it is to be brought under its mastery or fling itself free.

The war was begun by the military masters of Germany, who proved to be also the masters of Austria-Hungary. These men have never regarded nations as peoples, men, women, and children of like blood and frame as themselves, for whom Governments existed and in whom Governments had their life. They have regarded them merely as service-able organizations which they could by force or intrigue bend or corrupt to their own purpose. They have regarded the smaller States, in particular, and the peoples who could be overwhelmed by force, as their natural tools and in-struments of domination. Their purpose has long been avowed. The statesmen of other nations, to whom that purpose was incredible, paid little attention; regarded what German professors expounded in their classrooms and German writers set forth to the world as the goal of German policy as rather the dream of minds detached from practical affairs, as preposterous private conceptions of German destiny, than as the actual plans of responsible rulers; but the rulers of Germany themselves knew all the while what concrete plans, what well-advanced intrigues lay back of what the professors and the writers were saying, and were glad to go forward unmolested, filling the thrones of Balkan states with German princes, putting German officers at the service of Turkey to drill her armies and make interest with her Government, developing plans of sedition and rebellion in India and Egypt, setting their fires in Persia. The demands made by Austria upon Serbia were a mere single step in a plan which compassed Europe and Asia, from Berlin to Baghdad. They hoped those demands might arouse Europe, but they meant to press them whether they did or not, for they thought themselves ready for the final issue of arms.

Their plan was to throw a broad belt of German military

power and political control across the very centre of
Europe and beyond the Mediterranean into the heart of
Asia ; and Austria-Hungary was to be as much their tool
and pawn as Serbia or Bulgaria or Turkey or the ponderous
states of the East.   Austria-Hungary, indeed, was to become part of the central German Empire, absorbed and
dominated by the same forces and influences that had originally cemented the German states themselves.   The
dream had its heart at Berlin. It could have had a heart
nowhere else ! It rejected the idea of solidarity of race
entirely. The choice of peoples played no part in it at all.
It contemplated binding together racial and political units
which could be kept together only by force,—Czechs,
Magyars, Croats, Serbs, Rumanians, Turks, Armenians,
—the proud states of Bohemia and Hungary, the stout
little commonwealths of the Balkans, the indomitable
Turks, the subtle peoples of the East. These peoples did
not wish to be united. They ardently desired to direct
their own affairs, would be satisfied only by undisputed
independence. They could be kept quiet only by the
presence or the constant threat of armed men. They would
live under a common power only by sheer compulsion and
await the day of revolution. But the German military
statesmen had reckoned with all that and were ready to
deal with it in their own way.

And they have actually carried the greater part of that
amazing plan into execution ! Look how things stand.
Austria is at their mercy. It has acted, not upon its own
initiative or upon the choice of its own people, but at
Berlin's dictation ever since the war began. Its people
now desire peace, but cannot have it until leave is granted
from Berlin. The so-called Central Powers are in fact
but a single Power. Serbia is at its mercy, should its hands
be but for a moment freed. Bulgaria has consented to its
will, and Rumania is overrun. The Turkish armies, which
Germans trained, are serving Germany, certainly not them-

selves, and the guns of German warships lying in the harbour at Constantinople remind Turkish statesmen every day that they have no choice but to take their orders from Berlin. From Hamburg to the Persian Gulf the net is spread.

Is it not easy to understand the eagerness for peace that has been manifested from Berlin ever since the snare was set and sprung ?   Peace, peace, peace has been the talk of her Foreign Office for now a year and more ; not peace upon her own initiative, but upon the initiative of the nations over which she now deems herself to hold the advantage.   A little of the talk has been public, but most of it has been private.   Through all sorts of channels it has come to me, and in all sorts of guises, but never with the terms disclosed which the German Government would be willing to accept.   That Government has other valuable pawns in its hands besides those I have mentioned.   It still holds a valuable part of France, though with slowly relaxing grasp, and practically the whole of Belgium.   Its armies press close upon Russia and overrun Poland at their will.   It cannot go farther ; it dare not go back.   It wishes to close its bargain before it is too late and it has little left to offer for the pound of flesh it will demand.

The military masters under whom Germany is bleeding see very clearly to what point Fate has brought them. If they fall back or are forced back an inch, their power both abroad and at home will fall to pieces like a house of cards.   It is their power at home they are thinking about now more than their power abroad.   It is that power which is trembling under their very feet ; and deep fear has entered their hearts.   They have but one chance to perpetuate their military power or even their controlling political influence.   If they can secure peace now with the immense advantages still in their hands which they have up to this point apparently gained, they will have justified themselves before the German people : they will have gained by force what they promised to gain by it : an

immense expansion of German power, an immense enlarge-
ment of German industrial and commercial opportunities.
Their prestige will be secure, and with their prestige their
political power. If they fail, their people will thrust them
aside; a Government accountable to the people themselves
will be set up in Germany as it has been in England, in the
United States, in France, and in all the great countries of
the modern time except Germany. If they succeed they
are safe, and Germany and the world are undone; if they
fail, Germany is saved and the world will be at peace. If
they succeed, America will fall within the menace. We and
all the rest of the world must remain armed, as they will
remain, and must make ready for the next step in their
aggression; if they fail, the world may unite for peace and
Germany may be of the union.

Do you not now understand the new intrigue, the intrigue
for peace, and why the masters of Germany do not hesitate
to use any agency that promises to effect their purpose, the
deceit of the nations? Their present particular aim is to
deceive all those who throughout the world stand for the
rights of peoples and the self-government of nations; for
they see what immense strength the forces of justice and
of liberalism are gathering out of this war. They are em-
ploying liberals in their enterprise. They are using men,
in Germany and without, as their spokesmen whom they
have hitherto despised and oppressed, using them for their
own destruction—Socialists, the leaders of labour, the
thinkers they have hitherto sought to silence. Let them
once succeed and these men, now their tools, will be ground
to powder beneath the weight of the great military empire
they will have set up; the revolutionists in Russia will be
cut off from all succour or co-operation in western Europe
and a counter-revolution fostered and supported; Germany herself will lose her chance of freedom; and all
Europe will arm for the next, the final struggle.

The sinister intrigue is being no less actively conducted

in this country than in Russia and in every country in
Europe to which the agents and dupes of the Imperial
German Government can get access. That Government
has many spokesmen here, in places high and low. They
have learned discretion. They keep within the law. It is
opinion they utter now, not sedition. They proclaim the
liberal purposes of their masters; declare this a foreign
war which can touch America with no danger to either
her lands or her institutions ; set England at the centre of
the stage and talk of her ambition to assert economic
dominion throughout the world ; appeal to our ancient
tradition of isolation in the politics of the nations ; and
seek to undermine the Government with false professions
of loyalty to its principles.

But they will make no headway. The false betray
themselves always in every accent. It is only friends and
partisans of the German Government whom we have
already identified who utter these thinly disguised dis-
loyalties. The facts are patent to all the world, and nowhere are they more plainly seen than in the United States,
where we are accustomed to deal with facts and not with
sophistries ; and the great fact that stands out above all
the rest is that this is a Peoples' War, a war for freedom
and justice and self-government amongst all the nations of
the world, a war to make the world safe for the peoples
who live upon it and have made it their own, the German
people themselves included ; and that with us rests the
choice to break through all these hypocrisies and patent
cheats and masks of brute force and help set the world free,
or else stand aside and let it be dominated a long age
through by sheer weight of arms and the arbitrary
choices of self-constituted masters, by the nation which
can maintain the biggest armies and the most irresistible
armaments—a power to which the world has afforded no
parallel and in the face of which political freedom must
wither and perish.

For us there is but one choice. We have made it. Woe
be to the man or group of men that seeks to stand in our
way in this day of high resolution when every principle we
hold dearest is to be vindicated and made secure for the
salvation of the nations. We are ready to plead at the bar
of history, and our flag shall wear a new lustre. Once more
we shall make good with our lives and fortunes the great
faith to which we were born, and a new glory shall shine in
the face of our people.

August 27, 1917. Reply to the Pope's Appeal for Peace dated August 1

Secretary of State Lansing to His Holiness Benedictus XV, Pope:

In acknowledgement of the communication of Your
Holiness to the belligerent peoples, dated August 1, 1917,
the President of the United States requests me to transmit
the following reply :

' Every heart that has not been blinded and hardened
by this terrible war must be touched by this moving
appeal of His Holiness the Pope, must feel the dignity
and force of the humane and generous motives which
prompted it, and must fervently wish that we might
take the path of peace he so persuasively points out. But
it would be folly to take it if it does not in fact lead to
the goal he proposes. Our response must be based upon
the stern facts and upon nothing else. It is not a mere
cessation of arms he desires ; it is a stable and enduring
peace. This agony must not be gone through with again,
and it must be a matter of very sober judgement what will
ensure us against it.

' His Holiness in substance proposes that we return
to the *status quo ante bellum,* and that then there be a
general condonation, disarmament, and a concert of
nations based upon an acceptance of the principle of
arbitration ; that by a similar concert freedom of the
seas be established ; and that the territorial claims of

France and Italy, the perplexing problems of the Balkan
States, and the restitution of Poland be left to such con-
ciliatory adjustments as may be possible in the new
temper of such a peace, due regard being paid to the
aspirations of the peoples whose political fortunes and
affiliations will be involved.

' It is manifest that no part of this programme can be
successfully carried out unless the restitution of the *status
quo ante* furnishes a firm and satisfactory basis for it.
The object of this war is to deliver the free peoples of the
world from the menace and the actual power of a vast
military establishment controlled by an irresponsible
Government which, having secretly planned to dominate
the world, proceeded to carry the plan out without regard
either to the sacred obligations of treaty or the long-estab-
lished practices and long-cherished principles of international action and honour; which chose its own time
for the war; delivered its blow fiercely and suddenly;
stopped at no barrier either of law or of mercy; swept
a whole continent within the tide of blood—not the blood
of soldiers only, but the blood of innocent women and
children also and of the helpless poor; and now stands
baulked but not defeated, the enemy of four-fifths of the
world. This power is not the German people. It is the
ruthless master of the German people. It is no business
of ours how that great people came under its control or
submitted with temporary zest to the domination of its
purpose; but it is our business to see to it that the history
of the rest of the world is no longer left to its handling.

' To deal with such a power by way of peace upon the
plan proposed by His Holiness the Pope would, so far as
we can see, involve a recuperation of its strength and a
renewal of its policy; would make it necessary to create
a permanent hostile combination of nations against the
German people, who are its instruments; and would
result in abandoning the new-born Russia to the intrigue,

the manifold subtle interference, and the certain counter-revolution which would be attempted by all the malign influences to which the German Government has of late accustomed the world. Can peace be based upon a restitution of its power or upon any word of honour it could pledge in a treaty of settlement and accommodation ?

' Responsible statesmen must now everywhere see, if they never saw before, that no peace can rest securely upon political or economic restrictions meant to benefit some nations and cripple or embarrass others, upon vindictive action of any sort, or any kind of revenge or deliberate injury. The American people have suffered intolerable wrongs at the hands of the Imperial German Government, but they desire no reprisal upon the German people, who have themselves suffered all things in this war, which they did not choose. They believe that peace should rest upon the rights of peoples, not the rights of Governments—the rights of peoples great or small, weak or powerful—their equal right to freedom and security and self-government and to a participation upon fair terms in the economic opportunities of the world, the German people of course included if they will accept equality and not seek domination.

' The test, therefore, of every plan of peace is this : Is it based upon the faith of all the peoples involved, or merely upon the word of an ambitious and intriguing Government on the one hand and of a group of free peoples on the other ? This is a test which goes to the root of the matter ; and it is the test which must be applied.

' The purposes of the United States in this war are known to the whole world, to every people to whom the truth has been permitted to come. They do not need to be stated again. We seek no material advantage of any kind. We believe that the intolerable wrongs done in this war by the furious and brutal power of the Imperial German Government ought to be repaired, but not at

the expense of the sovereignty of any people—rather
a vindication of the sovereignty both of those that are
weak and of those that are strong.   Punitive damages,
the dismemberment of empires, the establishment of selfish
and exclusive economic leagues, we deem inexpedient and
in the end worse than futile, no proper basis for a peace
of any kind, least of all for an enduring peace.   That must
be based upon justice and fairness and the common rights
of mankind.

' We cannot take the word of the present rulers of
Germany as a guarantee of anything that is to endure,
unless explicitly supported by such conclusive evidence
of the will and purpose of the German people themselves
as the other peoples of the world would be justified in
accepting.   Without such guarantees treaties of settlement,
agreements for disarmament, covenants to set up arbitration in the place of force, territorial adjustments, recon-
stitutions of small nations, if made with the German
Government, no man, no nation could now depend on.
We must await some new evidence of the purposes of the
great peoples of the Central Powers.   God grant it may
be given soon and in a way to restore the confidence of
all peoples everywhere in the faith of nations and the
possibility of a covenanted peace.'

NOVEMBER 12, 1917.   SPEECH TO THE AMERICAN FEDERA-
TION OF LABOUR CONVENTION, BUFFALO

I think that in order to realize just what this moment
of counsel is it is very desirable that we should remind
ourselves just how this war came about and just what it
is for.   You can explain most wars very simply, but the
explanation of this is not so simple.   Its roots run deep
into all the obscure soils of history, and in my view this
is the last decisive issue between the old principle of power
and the new principle of freedom.

The war was started by Germany. Her authorities deny that they started it, but I am willing to let the statement I have just made await the verdict of history. And the thing that needs to be explained is why Germany started the war. Remember what the position of Germany in the world was—as enviable a position as any nation has ever occupied. The whole world stood in admiration of her wonderful intellectual and material achievements. All the intellectual men of the world went to school to her. As a university man I have been surrounded by men trained in Germany, men who had resorted to Germany because nowhere else could they get such thorough and searching training, particularly in the principles of science and the principles that underlie modern material achievement. Her men of science had made her industries perhaps the most competent industries of the world, and the label ' Made in Germany ' was a guarantee of good workmanship and of sound material. She had access to all the markets of the world, and every other nation who traded in those markets feared Germany because of her effective and almost irresistible competition. She had a ' place in the sun '.

Why was she not satisfied ? What more did she want ? There was nothing in the world of peace that she did not already have and have in abundance. We boast of the extraordinary pace of American advancement. We show with pride the statistics of the increase of our industries and of the population of our cities. Well, those statistics did not match the recent statistics of Germany. Her old cities took on youth and grew faster than any American cities ever grew. Her old industries opened their eyes and saw a new world and went out for its conquest. And yet the authorities of Germany were not satisfied. You have one part of the answer to the question why she was not satisfied in her methods of competition. There is no important industry in Germany upon which the Government has not laid its hands, to direct it and, when necessity arose, control it; and you have only to ask any man whom you meet who is familiar with the conditions that prevailed before the war in the matter of national competition to find out the methods of competition which the German manufacturers and exporters used under the patronage and support of the Government of Germany. You will find that they were the same sort of competition that we have tried to prevent by law within our own borders. If they could not sell their goods cheaper than we could sell ours at a profit to themselves they could get a subsidy from the Government which made it possible to sell them cheaper anyhow, and the conditions of competition were thus controlled in large measure by the German Government itself.

But that did not satisfy the German Government. All the while there was lying behind its thought and in its dreams of the future a political control which would enable it in the long run to dominate the labour and the industry of the world. They were not content with success by superior achievement; they wanted success by authority. I suppose very few of you have thought much about the Berlin to Baghdad Railway. The Berlin–Baghdad Railway was constructed in order to run the threat of force down the flank of the industrial undertakings of half a dozen other countries; so that, when German competition came in, it would not be resisted too far, because there was always the possibility of getting German armies into the heart of that country quicker than any other armies could be got there.

Look at the map of Europe now! Germany is thrusting upon us again and again the discussion of peace talks—about what? Talks about Belgium; talks about northern France; talks about Alsace-Lorraine. Well, those are deeply interesting subjects to us and to them, but they are not the heart of the matter. Take the map and look at it. Germany has absolute control of Austria-Hungary, practical control of the Balkan States, control of Turkey, control of Asia Minor. I saw a map in which the whole thing was printed in appropriate black the other day, and the black stretched all the way from Hamburg to Baghdad— the bulk of German power inserted into the heart of the world. If she can keep that, she has kept all that her dreams contemplated when the war began. If she can keep that, her power can disturb the world as long as she keeps it, always provided, for I feel bound to put this proviso in— always provided the present influences that control the German Government continue to control it. I believe that the spirit of freedom can get into the hearts of Germans and find as fine a welcome there as it can find in any other hearts, but the spirit of freedom does not suit the plans of the Pan-Germans. Power cannot be used with concentrated force against free peoples if it is used by free people.

You know how many intimations come to us from one of the Central Powers that it is more anxious for peace than the chief Central Power, and you know that it means that the people in that Central Power know that if the war ends as it stands they will in effect themselves be vassals of Germany, notwithstanding that their populations are compounded of all the peoples of that part of the world, and notwithstanding the fact that they do not wish in their pride and proper spirit of nationality to be so absorbed and dominated. Germany is determined that the political power of the world shall belong to her. There have been such ambitions before. They have been in part realized, but never before have those ambitions been based upon so exact and precise and scientific a plan of domination.

May I not say that it is amazing to me that any group of persons should be so ill-informed as to suppose, as some groups in Russia apparently suppose, that any reforms

planned in the interest of the people can live in the presence
of a Germany powerful enough to undermine or overthrow
them by intrigue or force ? Any body of free men that
compounds with the present German Government is com-
pounding for its own destruction. But that is not the
whole of the story. Any man in America or anywhere
else that supposes that the free industry and enterprise of
the world can continue if the Pan-German plan is achieved
and German power fastened upon the world is as fatuous
as the dreamers in Russia. What I am opposed to is not
the feeling of the pacifists, but their stupidity. My heart
is with them, but my mind has a contempt for them.
I want peace, but I know how to get it, and they do not.

You will notice that I sent a friend of mine, Col. House,
to Europe, who is as great a lover of peace as any man in
the world ; but I didn't send him on a peace mission yet.
I sent him to take part in a conference as to how the war
was to be won, and he knows, as I know, that that is the
way to get peace, if you want it for more than a few
minutes.

All of this is a preface to the conference that I have
referred to with regard to what we are going to do. If
we are true friends of freedom, our own or anybody else's,
we will see that the power of this country and the pro-
ductivity of this country is raised to its absolute maximum,
and that absolutely nobody is allowed to stand in the way
of it. When I say that nobody is allowed to stand in the
way I do not mean that they shall be prevented by the
power of Government but by the power of the American
spirit. Our duty, if we are to do this great thing and show
America to be what we believe her to be—the greatest
hope and energy of the world—is to stand together night
and day until the job is finished.

NOVEMBER 17, 1917. TELEGRAM TO THE KING OF THE
BELGIANS

HIS MAJESTY ALBERT,
    King of the Belgians, Havre.

I take pleasure in extending to Your Majesty greetings
of friendship and goodwill on this your fête day.

For the people of the United States, I take this occasion
to renew expressions of deep sympathy for the sufferings
which Belgium has endured under the wilful, cruel, and
barbaric force of a disappointed Prussian autocracy.

The people of the United States were never more in
earnest than in their determination to prosecute to a
successful conclusion this war against that Power and to
secure, for the future, obedience to the laws of nations and
respect for the rights of humanity.

DECEMBER 4, 1917. ADDRESS TO CONGRESS

GENTLEMEN OF THE CONGRESS:

Eight months have elapsed since I last had the honour
of addressing you. They have been months crowded with
events of immense and grave significance for us. I shall
not undertake to retail or even to summarize those events.
The practical particulars of the part we have played in them
will be laid before you in the reports of the Executive Departments. I shall discuss only our present outlook upon
these vast affairs, our present duties, and the immediate
means of accomplishing the objects we shall hold always
in view.

I shall not go back to debate the causes of the war. The
intolerable wrongs done and planned against us by the
sinister masters of Germany have long since become too
grossly obvious and odious to every true American to need
to be rehearsed. But I shall ask you to consider again and
with a very grave scrutiny our objectives and the measures

by which we mean to attain them ; for the purpose of discussion here in this place is action, and our action must move straight towards definite ends. Our object is, of course, to win the war ; and we shall not slacken or suffer ourselves to be diverted until it is won. But it is worth while asking and answering the question, When shall we consider the war won ?

From one point of view it is not necessary to broach this fundamental matter. I do not doubt that the American people know what the war is about and what sort of an outcome they will regard as a realization of their purpose in it. As a nation we are united in spirit and intention. I pay little heed to those who tell me otherwise. I hear the voices of dissent—who does not ? I hear the criticism and the clamour of the noisily thought-less and troublesome. I also see men here and there fling themselves in impotent disloyalty against the calm, in-domitable power of the nation. I hear men debate peace who understand neither its nature nor the way in which we may attain it with uplifted eyes and unbroken spirits. But I know that none of these speaks for the nation. They do not touch the heart of anything. They may safely be left to strut their uneasy hour and be forgotten.

But from another point of view I believe that it is necessary to say plainly what we here at the seat of action consider the war to be for and what part we mean to play in the settlement of its searching issues. We are the spokesmen of the American people, and they have a right to know whether their purpose is ours. They desire peace by the overcoming of evil, by the defeat once for all of the sinister forces that interrupt peace and render it impossible, and they wish to know how closely our thought runs with theirs and what action we propose. They are impatient with those who desire peace by any sort of compromise—deeply and indignantly impatient—but they will be equally impatient with us if we do not make it plain to them what

our objectives are and what we are planning for in seeking
to make conquest of peace by arms.

I believe that I speak for them when I say two things :
First, that this intolerable Thing of which the masters of
Germany have shown us the ugly face, this menace of combined intrigue and force which we now see so clearly as the
German power, a Thing without conscience or honour or
capacity for covenanted peace, must be crushed and, if
it be not utterly brought to an end, at least shut out from
the friendly intercourse of the nations ; and, second, that
when this Thing and its power are indeed defeated and the
time comes that we can discuss peace—when the German
people have spokesmen whose word we can believe and
when those spokesmen are ready in the name of their
people to accept the common judgement of the nations as
to what shall henceforth be the bases of law and of covenant
for the life of the world—we shall be willing and glad to
pay the full price for peace, and pay it ungrudgingly. We
know what that price will be. It will be full, impartial
justice—justice done at every point and to every nation
that the final settlement must affect, our enemies as well
as our friends.

You catch, with me, the voices of humanity that are in
the air. They grow daily more audible, more articulate,
more persuasive, and they come from the hearts of men
everywhere. They insist that the war shall not end in
vindictive action of any kind ; that no nation or people
shall be robbed or punished because the irresponsible
rulers of a single country have themselves done deep and
abominable wrong. It is this thought that has been expressed in the formula ' No annexations, no contributions,
no punitive indemnities '. Just because this crude formula
expresses the instinctive judgement as to right of plain men
everywhere it has been made diligent use of by the masters
of German intrigue to lead the people of Russia astray,
and the people of every other country their agents could

reach, in order that a premature peace might be brought
about before autocracy has been taught its final and convincing lesson, and the people of the world put in control
of their own destinies.

But the fact that a wrong use has been made of a just
idea is no reason why a right use should not be made of it.
It ought to be brought under the patronage of its real
friends. Let it be said again that autocracy must first be
shown the utter futility of its claims to power or leadership
in the modern world. It is impossible to apply any standard
of justice so long as such forces are unchecked and unde-
feated as the present masters of Germany command. Not
until that has been done can Right be set up as arbiter and
peace-maker among the nations. But when that has been
done—as, God willing, it assuredly will be—we shall at
last be free to do an unprecedented thing, and this is the
time to avow our purpose to do it. We shall be free to base
peace on generosity and justice, to the exclusion of all
selfish claims to advantage even on the part of the
victors.

Let there be no misunderstanding. Our present and
immediate task is to win the war, and nothing shall turn
us aside from it until it is accomplished. Every power
and resource we possess, whether of men, of money, or of
materials, is being devoted, and will continue to be devoted,
to that purpose until it is achieved. Those who desire to
bring peace about before that purpose is achieved I counsel
to carry their advice elsewhere. We will not entertain it.
We shall regard the war as won only when the German
people say to us, through properly accredited representatives, that they are ready to agree to a settlement based
upon justice and the reparation of the wrongs their rulers
have done. They have done a wrong to Belgium which
must be repaired. They have established a power over
other lands and peoples than their own—over the great
Empire of Austria-Hungary, over hitherto free Balkan

states, over Turkey, and within Asia—which must be relinquished.

Germany's success by skill, by industry, by knowledge, by enterprise we did not grudge or oppose, but admired, rather. She had built up for herself a real empire of trade and influence, secured by the peace of the world. We were content to abide the rivalries of manufacture, science, and commerce that were involved for us in her success and stand or fall as we had or did not have the brains and the initiative to surpass her. But at the moment when she had conspicuously won her triumphs of peace she threw them away, to establish in their stead what the world will no longer permit to be established, military and political domination by arms, by which to oust where she could not excel the rivals she most feared and hated. The peace we make must deliver the once fair lands and happy peoples of Belgium and northern France from the Prussian conquest and the Prussian menace, but it must also deliver the peoples of Austria-Hungary, the peoples of the Balkans, and the peoples of Turkey, alike in Europe and in Asia, from the impudent and alien dominion of the Prussian military and commercial autocracy.

We owe it, however, to ourselves to say that we do not wish in any way to impair or to rearrange the Austro-Hungarian Empire. It is no affair of ours what they do with their own life, either industrially or politically. We do not purpose or desire to dictate to them in any way. We only desire to see that their affairs are left in their own hands, in all matters, great or small. We shall hope to secure for the peoples of the Balkan peninsula and for the people of the Turkish Empire the right and opportunity to make their own lives safe, their own fortunes secure against oppression or injustice and from the dictation of foreign courts or parties.

And our attitude and purpose with regard to Germany herself are of a like kind. We intend no wrong against the

German Empire, no interference with her internal affairs. We should deem either the one or the other absolutely unjustifiable, absolutely contrary to the principles we have professed to live by and to hold most sacred throughout our life as a nation.

The people of Germany are being told by the men whom they now permit to deceive them and to act as their masters that they are fighting for the very life and existence of their Empire, a war of desperate self-defence against deliberate aggression. Nothing could be more grossly or wantonly false, and we must seek by the utmost openness and candour as to our real aims to convince them of its falseness. We are in fact fighting for their emancipation from fear, along with our own—from the fear as well as from the fact of unjust attack by neighbours or rivals or schemers after world empire. No one is threatening the existence or the independence or the peaceful enterprise of the German Empire.

The worst that can happen to the detriment of the German people is this, that if they should still, after the war is over, continue to be obliged to live under ambitious and intriguing masters interested to disturb the peace of the world, men or classes of men whom the other peoples of the world could not trust, it might be impossible to admit them to the partnership of nations which must henceforth guarantee the world's peace. That partnership must be a partnership of peoples, not a mere partnership of Governments. It might be impossible, also, in such untoward circumstances, to admit Germany to the free economic intercourse which must inevitably spring out of the other partnerships of a real peace. But there would be no aggression in that ; and such a situation, inevitable because of distrust, would in the very nature of things sooner or later cure itself, by processes which would assuredly set in.

The wrongs, the very deep wrongs, committed in this war will have to be righted. That of course. But they cannot and must not be righted by the commission of similar wrongs against Germany and her allies. The world will not permit the commission of similar wrongs as a means of reparation and settlement. Statesmen must by this time have learned that the opinion of the world is everywhere wide awake and fully comprehends the issues involved. No representative of any self-governed nation will dare disregard it by attempting any such covenants of selfishness and compromise as were entered into at the Congress of Vienna. The thought of the plain people here and everywhere throughout the world, the people who enjoy no privilege and have very simple and unsophisticated standards of right and wrong, is the air all Governments must henceforth breathe if they would live. It is in the full disclosing light of that thought that all policies must be conceived and executed in this midday hour of the world's life. German rulers have been able to upset the peace of the world only because the German people were not suffered under their tutelage to share the comradeship of the other peoples of the world either in thought or in purpose. They were allowed to have no opinion of their own which might be set up as a rule of conduct for those who exercised authority over them. But the congress that concludes this war will feel the full strength of the tides that run now in the hearts and consciences of free men everywhere. Its conclusion will run with those tides.

All these things have been true from the very beginning of this stupendous war ; and I cannot help thinking that if they had been made plain at the very outset the sympathy and enthusiasm of the Russian people might have been once for all enlisted on the side of the Allies, suspicion and distrust swept away, and a real and lasting union of purpose effected. Had they believed these things at the very moment of their revolution and had they been confirmed in that belief since, the sad reverses which have recently marked the progress of their affairs towards an

ordered and stable government of free men might have
been avoided. The Russian people have been poisoned by
the very same falsehoods that have kept the German people
in the dark, and the poison has been administered by the
very same hands. The only possible antidote is the truth.
It cannot be uttered too plainly or too often.

From every point of view, therefore, it has seemed to
be my duty to speak these declarations of purpose, to add
these specific interpretations to what I took the liberty of
saying to the Senate in January. Our entrance into the
war has not altered our attitude towards the settlement
that must come when it is over. When I said in January
that the nations of the world were entitled not only to
free pathways upon the sea but also to assured and unmolested access to those pathways I was thinking, and
I am thinking now, not of the smaller and weaker nations
alone, which need our countenance and support, but also
of the great and powerful nations, and of our present
enemies as well as our present associates in the war. I was
thinking, and am thinking now, of Austria herself, among
the rest, as well as of Serbia and of Poland. Justice and
equality of rights can be had only at a great price. We
are seeking permanent, not temporary, foundations for the
peace of the world and must seek them candidly and fear-
lessly. As always, the right will prove to be the expedient.

What shall we do, then, to push this great war of freedom
and justice to its righteous conclusion ? We must clear
away with a thorough hand all impediments to success, and
we must make every adjustment of law that will facilitate
the full and free use of our whole capacity and force as
a fighting unit.

One very embarrassing obstacle that stands in our way
is that we are at war with Germany but not with her allies.
I therefore very earnestly recommend that the Congress
immediately declare the United States in a state of war
with Austria-Hungary. Does it seem strange to you that

this should be the conclusion of the argument I have just
addressed to you ? It is not. It is in fact the inevitable
logic of what I have said. Austria-Hungary is for the time
being not her own mistress but simply the vassal of the
German Government. We must face the facts as they are
and act upon them without sentiment in this stern business.
The Government of Austria-Hungary is not acting upon
its own initiative or in response to the wishes and feelings
of its own peoples, but as the instrument of another nation.
We must meet its force with our own and regard the
Central Powers as but one. The war can be successfully
conducted in no other way. The same logic would lead
also to a declaration of war against Turkey and Bulgaria.
They also are the tools of Germany. But they are mere
tools and do not yet stand in the direct path of our
necessary action. We shall go wherever the necessities of
this war carry us, but it seems to me that we should go
only where immediate and practical considerations lead us
and not heed any others. . . .

We know that for us this is a war of high principle,
debased by no selfish ambition of conquest or spoliation ;
because we know, and all the world knows, that we have
been forced into it to save the very institutions we live
under from corruption and destruction. The purposes of
the Central Powers strike straight at the very heart of
everything we believe in ; their methods of warfare out-
rage every principle of humanity and of knightly honour ;
their intrigue has corrupted the very thought and spirit of
many of our people ; their sinister and secret diplomacy
has sought to take our very territory away from us and
disrupt the Union of the States. Our safety would be at
an end, our honour for ever sullied and brought into contempt, were we to permit their triumph. They are striking
at the very existence of democracy and liberty.

It is because it is for us a war of high, disinterested
purpose, in which all the free peoples of the world are

banded together for the vindication of right, a war for the preservation of our nation and of all that it has held dear of principle and of purpose, that we feel ourselves doubly constrained to propose for its outcome only that which is righteous and of irreproachable intention, for our foes as well as for our friends. The cause being just and holy, the settlement must be of like motive and quality. For this we can fight, but for nothing less noble or less worthy of our traditions. For this cause we enter the war and for this cause will we battle until the last gun is fired.

I have spoken plainly because this seems to me the time when it is most necessary to speak plainly, in order that all the world may know that even in the heat and ardour of the struggle and when our whole thought is of carrying the war through to its end we have not forgotten any ideal or principle for which the name of America has been held in honour among the nations and for which it has been our glory to contend in the great generations that went before us. A supreme moment of history has come. The eyes of the people have been opened and they see. The hand of God is laid upon the nations. He will show them favour, I devoutly believe, only if they rise to the clear heights of His own justice and mercy.

JANUARY 8, 1918. ADDRESS TO CONGRESS ON CONDITIONS
OF PEACE (THE FOURTEEN POINTS)

GENTLEMEN OF THE CONGRESS :

Once more, as repeatedly before, the spokesmen of the Central Empires have indicated their desire to discuss the objects of the war and the possible bases of a general peace. Parleys have been in progress at Brest-Litovsk between Russian representatives and representatives of the Central Powers, to which the attention of all the belligerents has been invited for the purpose of ascertaining whether it may be possible to extend these parleys into a general conference with regard to terms of peace and settlement. The Russian representatives presented not only a perfectly definite statement of the principles upon which they would be willing to conclude peace, but also an equally definite programme of the concrete application of those principles. The representatives of the Central Powers, on their part, presented an outline of settlement which, if much less definite, seemed susceptible of liberal interpretation until their specific programme of practical terms was added. That programme proposed no concessions at all either to the sovereignty of Russia or to the preferences of the populations with whose fortunes it dealt, but meant, in a word, that the Central Empires were to keep every foot of territory their armed forces had occupied—every province, every city, every point of vantage—as a permanent addition to their territories and their power. It is a reasonable conjecture that the general principles of settlement which they at first suggested originated with the more liberal statesmen of Germany and Austria, the men who have begun to feel the force of their own peoples' thought and purpose, while the concrete terms of actual settlement came from the military leaders who have no thought but to keep what they have got. The negotiations have been broken off. The Russian representatives were sincere and in earnest. They cannot entertain such proposals of conquest and domination.

The whole incident is full of significance. It is also full of perplexity. With whom are the Russian representatives dealing? For whom are the representatives of the Central Empires speaking? Are they speaking for the majorities of their respective parliaments or for the minority parties, that military and imperialistic minority which has so far dominated their whole policy and controlled the affairs of Turkey and of the Balkan states which have felt obliged to become their associates

in this war ?   The Russian representatives have insisted,
very justly, very wisely, and in the true spirit of modern
democracy, that the conferences they have been holding
with Teutonic and Turkish statesmen should be held
within open, not closed, doors, and all the world has been
audience, as was desired.   To whom have we been listening, then ?   To those who speak the spirit and intention of
the Resolutions of the German Reichstag of the nineteenth
of July last, the spirit and intention of the liberal leaders
and parties of Germany, or to those who resist and defy
that spirit and intention and insist upon conquest and
subjugation ?   Or are we listening, in fact, to both, un-
reconciled and in open and hopeless contradiction ?   These
are very serious and pregnant questions.   Upon the answer
to them depends the peace of the world.

But, whatever the results of the parleys at Brest-
Litovsk, whatever the confusions of counsel and of purpose
in the utterances of the spokesmen of the Central Empires,
they have again attempted to acquaint the world with
their objects in the war and have again challenged their
adversaries to say what their objects are and what sort
of settlement they would deem just and satisfactory.
There is no good reason why that challenge should not be
responded to, and responded to with the utmost candour.
We did not wait for it.   Not once, but again and again,
we have laid our whole thought and purpose before the
world, not in general terms only, but each time with
sufficient definition to make it clear what sort of definitive
terms of settlement must necessarily spring out of them.
Within the last week Mr. Lloyd George has spoken with
admirable candour and in admirable spirit for the people
and Government of Great Britain.   There is no confusion
of counsel among the adversaries of the Central Powers,
no uncertainty of principle, no vagueness of detail.   The
only secrecy of counsel, the only lack of fearless frankness,
the only failure to make definite statement of the objects

of the war, lies with Germany and her Allies. The issues of life and death hang upon these definitions. No statesman who has the least conception of his responsibility ought for a moment to permit himself to continue this tragical and appalling outpouring of blood and treasure unless he is sure beyond a peradventure that the objects of the vital sacrifice are part and parcel of the very life of Society and that the people for whom he speaks think them right and imperative as he does.

There is, moreover, a voice calling for these definitions of principle and of purpose which is, it seems to me, more thrilling and more compelling than any of the many moving voices with which the troubled air of the world is filled. It is the voice of the Russian people. They are prostrate and all but helpless, it would seem, before the grim power of Germany, which has hitherto known no relenting and no pity. Their power, apparently, is shattered. And yet their soul is not subservient. They will not yield either in principle or in action. Their conception of what is right, of what it is humane and honourable for them to accept, has been stated with a frankness, a largeness of view, a generosity of spirit, and a universal human sympathy which must challenge the admiration of every friend of mankind; and they have refused to compound their ideals or desert others that they themselves may be safe. They call to us to say what it is that we desire, in what, if in anything, our purpose and our spirit differ from theirs; and I believe that the people of the United States would wish me to respond, with utter simplicity and frankness. Whether their present leaders believe it or not, it is our heartfelt desire and hope that some way may be opened whereby we may be privileged to assist the people of Russia to attain their utmost hope of liberty and ordered peace.

It will be our wish and purpose that the processes of peace, when they are begun, shall be absolutely open and that they shall involve and permit henceforth no secret understandings of any kind. The day of conquest and aggrandizement is gone by ; so is also the day of secret covenants entered into in the interest of particular Governments and likely at some unlooked-for moment to upset the peace of the world. It is this happy fact, now clear to the view of every public man whose thoughts do not still linger in an age that is dead and gone, which makes it possible for every nation whose purposes are consistent with justice and the peace of the world to avow now or at any other time the objects it has in view.

We entered this war because violations of right had occurred which touched us to the quick and made the life of our own people impossible unless they were corrected and the world secured once for all against their recurrence. What we demand in this war, therefore, is nothing peculiar to ourselves. It is that the world be made fit and safe to live in ; and particularly that it be made safe for every peace-loving nation which, like our own, wishes to live its own life, determine its own institutions, be assured of justice and fair dealing by the other peoples of the world as against force and selfish aggression. All the peoples of the world are in effect partners in this interest, and for our own part we see very clearly that unless justice be done to others it will not be done to us. The programme of the world's peace, therefore, is our programme ; and that programme, the only possible programme, as we see it, is this :

I. Open covenants of peace, openly arrived at, after which there shall be no private international understandings of any kind, but diplomacy shall proceed always frankly and in the public view.

II. Absolute freedom of navigation upon the seas, outside territorial waters, alike in peace and in war, except as the seas may be closed in whole or in part by international action for the enforcement of international covenants.

III. The removal, so far as possible, of all economic barriers and the establishment of an equality of trade conditions among all the nations consenting to the peace and associating themselves for its maintenance.

IV. Adequate guarantees given and taken that national armaments will be reduced to the lowest point consistent with domestic safety.

V. A free, open-minded, and absolutely impartial adjustment of all colonial claims, based upon a strict observance of the principle that in determining all such questions of sovereignty the interests of the populations concerned must have equal weight with the equitable claims of the government whose title is to be determined.

VI. The evacuation of all Russian territory and such a settlement of all questions affecting Russia as will secure the best and freest co-operation of the other nations of the world in obtaining for her an unhampered and unembarrassed opportunity for the independent determination of her own political development and national policy and assure her of a sincere welcome into the society of free nations under institutions of her own choosing; and, more than a welcome, assistance also of every kind that she may need and may herself desire. The treatment accorded Russia by her sister nations in the months to come will be the acid test of their goodwill, of their comprehension of her needs as distinguished from their own interests, and of their intelligent and unselfish sympathy.

VII. Belgium, the whole world will agree, must be evacuated and restored, without any attempt to limit the sovereignty which she enjoys in common with all other free nations. No other single act will serve as this will serve to restore confidence among the nations in the laws which they have themselves set and determined for the government of their relations with one another. Without this healing act the whole structure and validity of international law is for ever impaired.

VIII. All French territory should be freed and the invaded portions restored, and the wrong done to France by Prussia in 1871 in the matter of Alsace-Lorraine, which has unsettled the peace of the world for nearly fifty years, should be righted, in order that peace may once more be made secure in the interest of all.

IX. A readjustment of the frontiers of Italy should be effected along clearly recognizable lines of nationality.

X. The peoples of Austria-Hungary, whose place among the nations we wish to see safeguarded and assured, should be accorded the freest opportunity of autonomous development.

XI. Rumania, Serbia, and Montenegro should be evacuated; occupied territories restored; Serbia accorded free and secure access to the sea; and the relations of the several Balkan states to one another determined by friendly counsel along historically established lines of allegiance and nationality; and international guarantees of the political and economic independence and territorial integrity of the several Balkan states should be entered into.

XII. The Turkish portions of the present Ottoman Empire should be assured a secure sovereignty, but the other nationalities which are now under Turkish rule should be assured an undoubted security of life and an absolutely unmolested opportunity of autonomous development, and the Dardanelles should be permanently opened as a free passage to the ships and commerce of all nations under international guarantees.

XIII. An independent Polish state should be erected which should include the territories inhabited by indisputably Polish populations, which should be assured a free and secure access to the sea, and whose political and economic independence and territorial integrity should be guaranteed by international covenant.

XIV. A general association of nations must be formed under specific covenants for the purpose of affording

E

mutual guarantees of political independence and territorial integrity to great and small states alike.

In regard to these essential rectifications of wrong and assertions of right we feel ourselves to be intimate partners of all the Governments and peoples associated together against the Imperialists. We cannot be separated in interest or divided in purpose. We stand together until the end.

For such arrangements and covenants we are willing to fight and to continue to fight until they are achieved; but only because we wish the right to prevail and desire a just and stable peace such as can be secured only by removing the chief provocations to war, which this programme does remove. We have no jealousy of German greatness, and there is nothing in this programme that impairs it. We grudge her no achievement or distinction of learning or of pacific enterprise such as have made her record very bright and very enviable. We do not wish to injure her or to block in any way her legitimate influence or power. We do not wish to fight her either with arms or with hostile arrangements of trade if she is willing to associate herself with us and the other peace-loving nations of the world in covenants of justice and law and fair dealing. We wish her only to accept a place of equality among the peoples of the world—the new world in which we now live—instead of a place of mastery.

Neither do we presume to suggest to her any alteration or modification of her institutions. But it is necessary, we must frankly say, and necessary as a preliminary to any intelligent dealings with her on our part, that we should know whom her spokesmen speak for when they speak to us, whether for the Reichstag majority or for the military party and the men whose creed is imperial domination.

We have spoken now, surely, in terms too concrete to admit of any further doubt or question. An evident principle runs through the whole programme I have out-lined. It is the principle of justice to all peoples and nationalities, and their right to live on equal terms of liberty and safety with one another, whether they be strong or weak. Unless this principle be made its founda-tion no part of the structure of international justice can stand. The people of the United States could act upon no other principle ; and to the vindication of this principle they are ready to devote their lives, their honour, and everything that they possess. The moral climax of this the culminating and final war for human liberty has come, and they are ready to put their own strength, their own highest purpose, their own integrity and devotion to the test.

FEBRUARY 11, 1918. ADDRESS TO CONGRESS (FOUR PRINCI-PLES) IN REPLY TO THE STATEMENTS OF THE GERMAN CHANCELLOR AND AUSTRO-HUNGARIAN FOREIGN MINISTER. (See Appendix 1)

GENTLEMEN OF THE CONGRESS :

On the eighth of January I had the honour of addressing you on the objects of the war as our people conceive them. The Prime Minister of Great Britain had spoken in similar terms on the fifth of January. To these addresses the German Chancellor replied on the twenty-fourth and Count Czernin, for Austria, on the same day. It is gratifying to have our desire so promptly realized that all exchanges of view on this great matter should be made in the hearing of all the world.

Count Czernin's reply, which is directed chiefly to my own address of the eighth of January, is uttered in a very friendly tone. He finds in my statement a sufficiently encouraging approach to the views of his own Government to justify him in believing that it furnishes a basis for a more detailed discussion of purposes by the two Govern-

ments. He is represented to have intimated that the views
he was expressing had been communicated to me beforehand and that I was aware of them at the time he was
uttering them : but in this I am sure he was misunderstood.
I had received no intimation of what he intended to say.
There was, of course, no reason why he should communicate
privately with me. I am quite content to be one of his
public audience.

Count von Hertling's reply is, I must say, very vague
and very confusing. It is full of equivocal phrases and
leads it is not clear where. But it is certainly in a very
different tone from that of Count Czernin, and apparently
of an opposite purpose. It confirms, I am sorry to say,
rather than removes, the unfortunate impression made by
what we had learned of the conferences at Brest-Litovsk.
His discussion and acceptance of our general principles
lead him to no practical conclusions. He refuses to apply
them to the substantive items which must constitute the
body of any final settlement. He is jealous of international
action and of international counsel. He accepts, he says,
the principle of public diplomacy, but he appears to insist
that it be confined, at any rate in this case, to generalities,
and that the several particular questions of territory
and sovereignty, the several questions upon whose settlement must depend the acceptance of peace by the twenty-
three states now engaged in the war, must be discussed
and settled, not in general council, but severally by the
nations most immediately concerned by interest or neigh-
bourhood. He agrees that the seas should be free, but
looks askance at any limitation to that freedom by international action in the interest of the common order. He
would without reserve be glad to see economic barriers
removed between nation and nation, for that could in
no way impede the ambitions of the military party with
whom he seems constrained to keep on terms. Neither
does he raise objection to a limitation of armaments.

That matter will be settled of itself, he thinks, by the economic conditions which must follow the war. But the German colonies, he demands, must be returned without debate. He will discuss with no one but the representatives of Russia what disposition shall be made of the peoples and the lands of the Baltic provinces ; with no one but the Government of France the ' conditions ' under which French territory shall be evacuated ; and only with Austria what shall be done with Poland. In the determination of all questions affecting the Balkan states he defers, as I understand him, to Austria and Turkey ; and with regard to the agreements to be entered into concerning the non-Turkish peoples of the present Ottoman Empire, to the Turkish authorities themselves. After a settlement all round, effected in this fashion, by individual barter and concession, he would have no objection, if I correctly interpret his statement, to a league of nations which would undertake to hold the new balance of power steady against external disturbance.

It must be evident to every one who understands what this war has wrought in the opinion and temper of the world that no general peace, no peace worth the infinite sacrifices of these years of tragical suffering, can possibly be arrived at in any such fashion. The method the German Chancellor proposes is the method of the Congress of Vienna. We cannot and will not return to that. What is at stake now is the peace of the world. What we are striving for is a new international order based upon broad and universal principles of right and justice—no mere peace of shreds and patches. Is it possible that Count von Hertling does not see that, does not grasp it, is in fact living in his thought in a world dead and gone ? Has he utterly forgotten the Reichstag Resolutions of the nineteenth of July, or does he deliberately ignore them ? They spoke of the conditions of a general peace, not of national aggrandizement or of arrangements between state and state. The peace of the world depends upon the just settlement of each of the several problems to which I adverted in my recent address to the Congress. I, of course, do not mean that the peace of the world depends upon the acceptance of any particular set of suggestions as to the way in which those problems are to be dealt with. I mean only that those problems each and all affect the whole world; that unless they are dealt with in a spirit of unselfish and unbiased justice, with a view to the wishes, the natural connexions, the racial aspirations, the security, and the peace of mind of the peoples involved, no permanent peace will have been attained. They cannot be discussed separately or in corners. None of them constitutes a private or separate interest from which the opinion of the world may be shut out. Whatever affects the peace affects mankind, and nothing settled by military force, if settled wrong, is settled at all. It will presently have to be reopened.

Is Count von Hertling not aware that he is speaking in the court of mankind, that all the awakened nations of the world now sit in judgement on what every public man, of whatever nation, may say on the issues of a conflict which has spread to every region of the world? The Reichstag Resolutions of July themselves frankly accepted the decisions of that court. There shall be no annexations, no contributions, no punitive damages. Peoples are not to be handed about from one sovereignty to another by an international conference or an understanding between rivals and antagonists. National aspirations must be respected; peoples may now be dominated and governed only by their own consent. ' Self-determination ' is not a mere phrase. It is an imperative principle of action, which statesmen will henceforth ignore at their peril. We cannot have general peace for the asking, or by the mere arrangements of a peace conference. It cannot be pieced together out of individual understandings between powerful states. All the parties to this war must join in the settlement of every issue anywhere involved in it; because what we are seeking is a peace that we can all unite to guarantee and maintain, and every item of it must be submitted to the common judgement whether it be right and fair, an act of justice rather than a bargain between sovereigns.

The United States has no desire to interfere in European affairs or to act as arbiter in European territorial disputes. She would disdain to take advantage of any internal weakness or disorder to impose her own will upon another people. She is quite ready to be shown that the settlements she has suggested are not the best or the most enduring. They are only her own provisional sketch of principles and of the way in which they should be applied. But she entered this war because she was made a partner, whether she would or not, in the sufferings and indignities inflicted by the military masters of Germany, against the peace and security of mankind; and the conditions of peace will touch her as nearly as they will touch any other nation to which is entrusted a leading part in the maintenance of civilization. She cannot see her way to peace until the causes of this war are removed, its renewal rendered as nearly as may be impossible.

This war had its roots in the disregard of the rights of small nations and of nationalities which lacked the union and the force to make good their claim to determine their own allegiances and their own forms of political life. Covenants must now be entered into which will render such things impossible for the future; and those covenants must be backed by the united force of all the nations that love justice and are willing to maintain it at any cost. If territorial settlements and the political relations of great populations which have not the organized power to resist are to be determined by the contracts of the powerful Governments which consider themselves most directly affected, as Count von Hertling proposes, why may not economic questions also ? It has come about in the altered world in which we now find ourselves that justice and the rights of peoples affect the whole field of international dealing as much as access to raw materials and fair and equal conditions of trade. Count von Hertling wants the essential bases of commercial and industrial life to be safeguarded by common agreement and guarantee, but he cannot expect that to be conceded him if the other matters to be determined by the articles of peace are not handled in the same way as items in the final accounting. He cannot ask the benefit of common agreement in the one field without according it in the other. I take it for granted that he sees that separate and selfish compacts with regard to trade and the essential materials of manufacture would afford no foundation for peace. Neither, he may rest assured, will separate and selfish compacts with regard to provinces and peoples.

Count Czernin seems to see the fundamental elements of peace with clear eyes and does not seek to obscure them. He sees that an independent Poland, made up of all the indisputably Polish peoples who lie contiguous to one another, is a matter of European concern and must of course be conceded ; that Belgium must be evacuated and restored, no matter what sacrifices and concessions that may involve ; and that national aspirations must be satisfied, even within his own Empire, in the common interest of Europe and mankind. If he is silent about questions which touch the interest and purpose of his allies more nearly than they touch those of Austria only, it must of course be because he feels constrained, I suppose, to defer to Germany and Turkey in the circumstances. Seeing and conceding, as he does, the essential principles involved and the necessity of candidly applying them, he naturally feels that Austria can respond to the purpose of peace as expressed by the United States with less

embarrassment than could Germany. He would probably
have gone much farther had it not been for the embarrass-
ments of Austria's alliances and of her dependence upon
Germany.

After all, the test of whether it is possible for either
Government to go any further in this comparison of views
is simple and obvious. The principles to be applied are
these :

First, that each part of the final settlement must be
based upon the essential justice of that particular case
and upon such adjustments as are most likely to bring
a peace that will be permanent ;

Second, that peoples and provinces are not to be bartered
about from sovereignty to sovereignty as if they were
mere chattels and pawns in a game, even the great game,
now for ever discredited, of the balance of power ; but that

Third, every territorial settlement involved in this war
must be made in the interest and for the benefit of the
populations concerned, and not as a part of any mere
adjustment or compromise of claims amongst rival states ;
and

Fourth, that all well-defined national aspirations shall
be accorded the utmost satisfaction that can be accorded
them without introducing new or perpetuating old elements of discord and antagonism that would be likely in
time to break the peace of Europe and consequently of
the world.

A general peace erected upon such foundations can be
discussed. Until such a peace can be secured we have
no choice but to go on. So far as we can judge, these
principles that we regard as fundamental are already
everywhere accepted as imperative except among the
spokesmen of the military and annexationist party in
Germany. If they have anywhere else been rejected, the
objectors have not been sufficiently numerous or influential
to make their voices audible. The tragical circumstance

is that this one party in Germany is apparently willing and able to send millions of men to their death to prevent what all the world now sees to be just.

I should not be a true spokesman of the people of the United States if I did not say once more that we entered this war upon no small occasion, and that we can never turn back from a course chosen upon principle. Our resources are in part mobilized now, and we shall not pause until they are mobilized in their entirety. Our armies are rapidly going to the fighting front, and will go more and more rapidly. Our whole strength will be put into this war of emancipation—emancipation from the threat and attempted mastery of selfish groups of autocratic rulers—whatever the difficulties and present partial delays. We are indomitable in our power of independent action and can in no circumstances consent to live in a world governed by intrigue and force. We believe that our own desire for new international order under which reason and justice and the common interests of mankind shall prevail is the desire of enlightened men everywhere. Without that new order the world will be without peace and human life will lack tolerable conditions of existence and development. Having set our hand to the task of achieving it, we shall not turn back.

I hope that it is not necessary for me to add that no word of what I have said is intended as a threat. That is not the temper of our people. I have spoken thus only that the whole world may know the true spirit of America—that men everywhere may know that our passion for justice and for self-government is no mere passion of words but a passion which, once set in action, must be satisfied. The power of the United States is a menace to no nation or people. It will never be used in aggression or for the aggrandizement of any selfish interest of our own. It springs out of freedom and is for the service of freedom.

April 6, 1918. Speech at the Opening of the Third
        Liberty Loan Campaign, Baltimore

Fellow-citizens :

This is the anniversary of our acceptance of Germany's
challenge to fight for our right to live and be free, and for
the sacred rights of free men everywhere. The Nation is
awake. There is no need to call to it. We know what
the war must cost, our utmost sacrifice, the lives of our
fittest men and, if need be, all that we possess. The loan
we are met to discuss is one of the least parts of what we
are called upon to give and to do, though in itself imperative. The people of the whole country are alive to the
necessity of it, and are ready to lend to the utmost, even
where it involves a sharp skimping and daily sacrifice to
lend out of meagre earnings. They will look with repro-
bation and contempt upon those who can and will not,
upon those who demand a higher rate of interest, upon
those who think of it as a mere commercial transaction.
I have not come, therefore, to urge the loan. I have come
only to give you, if I can, a more vivid conception of what
it is for.

The reason for this great war, the reason why it had
to come, the need to fight it through, and the issues that
hang upon its outcome, are more clearly disclosed now
than ever before. It is easy to see just what this particular
loan means because the cause we are fighting for stands
more sharply revealed than at any previous crisis of the
momentous struggle. The man who knows least can now
see plainly how the cause of Justice stands and what the
imperishable thing is he is asked to invest in. Men in
America may be more sure than they ever were before
that the cause is their own, and that, if it should be lost,
their own great nation's place and mission in the world
would be lost with it.

I call you to witness, my fellow-countrymen, that at

no stage of this terrible business have I judged the purposes of Germany intemperately. I should be ashamed in the presence of affairs so grave, so fraught with the destinies of mankind throughout all the world, to speak with truculence, to use the weak language of hatred or vindictive purpose. We must judge as we would be judged. I have sought to learn the objects Germany has in this war from the mouths of her own spokesmen, and to deal as frankly with them as I wished them to deal with me. I have laid bare our own ideals, our own purposes, without reserve or doubtful phrase, and have asked them to say as plainly what it is that they seek.

We have ourselves proposed no injustice, no aggression. We are ready, whenever the final reckoning is made, to be just to the German people, deal fairly with the German power, as with all others. There can be no difference between peoples in the final judgement, if it is indeed to be a righteous judgement. To propose anything but justice, even-handed and dispassionate justice, to Germany at any time, whatever the outcome of the war, would be to renounce and dishonour our own cause. For we ask nothing that we are not willing to accord.

It has been with this thought that I have sought to learn from those who spoke for Germany whether it was justice or dominion and the execution of their own will upon the other nations of the world that the German leaders were seeking. They have answered, answered in unmistakable terms. They have avowed that it was not justice but dominion and the unhindered execution of their own will.

The avowal has not come from Germany's statesmen. It has come from her military leaders, who are her real rulers. Her statesmen have said that they wished peace, and were ready to discuss its terms whenever their opponents were willing to sit down at the conference table with them. Her present Chancellor has said—in indefinite

and uncertain terms, indeed, and in phrases that often
seem to deny their own meaning, but with as much
plainness as he thought prudent—that he believed that
peace should be based upon the principles which we had
declared would be our own in the final settlement. At
Brest-Litovsk her civilian delegates spoke in similar
terms ; professed their desire to conclude a fair peace
and accord to the peoples with whose fortunes they were
dealing the right to choose their own allegiances. But
action accompanied and followed the profession. Their
military masters, the men who act for Germany and
exhibit her purpose in execution, proclaimed a very
different conclusion. We cannot mistake what they have
done—in Russia, in Finland, in the Ukraine, in Rumania.
The real test of their justice and fair play has come. From
this we may judge the rest. They are enjoying in Russia
a cheap triumph in which no brave or gallant nation can
long take pride. A great people, helpless by their own
act, lies for the time at their mercy. Their fair professions
are forgotten. They nowhere set up justice, but everywhere impose their power and exploit everything for their
own use and aggrandizement ; and the peoples of conquered
provinces are invited to be free under their dominion !

Are we not justified in believing that they would do
the same things at their western front if they were not
there face to face with armies whom even their countless
divisions cannot overcome ? If, when they have felt
their check to be final, they should propose favourable and
equitable terms with regard to Belgium and France and
Italy, could they blame us if we concluded that they did
so only to assure themselves of a free hand in Russia and
the East ?

Their purpose is undoubtedly to make all the Slavic
peoples, all the free and ambitious nations of the Baltic
peninsula, all the lands that Turkey has dominated and
misruled, subject to their will and ambition and build

upon that dominion an empire of force upon which they fancy that they can then erect an empire of gain and commercial supremacy—an empire as hostile to the Americas as to the Europe which it will overawe—an empire which will ultimately master Persia, India, and the peoples of the Far East. In such a programme our ideals, the ideals of justice and humanity and liberty, the principle of the free self-determination of nations upon which all the modern world insists, can play no part. They are rejected for the ideals of power, for the principle that the strong must rule the weak, that trade must follow the flag, whether those to whom it is taken welcome it or not, that the peoples of the world are to be made subject to the patronage and overlordship of those who have the power to enforce it.

That programme once carried out, America and all who care or dare to stand with her must arm and prepare themselves to contest the mastery of the World, a mastery in which the rights of common men, the rights of women and of all who are weak, must for the time being be trodden under foot and disregarded, and the old, age-long struggle for freedom and right begin again at its beginning. Everything that America has lived for and loved and grown great to vindicate and bring to a glorious realization will have fallen in utter ruin and the gates of mercy once more pitilessly shut upon mankind !

The thing is preposterous and impossible ; and yet is not that what the whole course and action of the German armies has meant wherever they have moved ? I do not wish, even in this moment of utter disillusionment, to judge harshly or unrighteously. I judge only what the German arms have accomplished with unpitying thoroughness throughout every fair region they have touched.

What, then, are we to do ? For myself, I am ready, ready still, ready even now, to discuss a fair and just and honest peace at any time that it is sincerely purposed

—a peace in which the strong and the weak shall fare alike. But the answer, when I proposed such a peace, came from the German commanders in Russia, and I cannot mistake the meaning of the answer.

I accept the challenge. I know that you accept it. All the world shall know that you accept it. It shall appear in the utter sacrifice and self-forgetfulness with which we shall give all that we love and all that we have to redeem the world and make it fit for free men like ourselves to live in. This now is the meaning of all that we do. Let everything that we say, my fellow-countrymen, everything that we henceforth plan and accomplish, ring true to this response till the majesty and might of our concerted power shall fill the thought and utterly defeat the force of those who flout and misprize what we honour and hold dear. Germany has once more said that force, and force alone, shall decide whether Justice and Peace shall reign in the affairs of men, whether Right as America conceives it or Dominion as she conceives it shall determine the destinies of mankind. There is, therefore, but one response possible from us : Force, Force to the utmost, Force without stint or limit, the righteous and triumphant Force which shall make Right the law of the world, and cast every selfish dominion down in the dust.

May 18, 1918. Speech at the New York Opera House

There are two duties with which we are face to face. The first duty is to win the war. And the second duty is that which goes hand in hand with it; it is to win it greatly and worthily, showing not only the real quality of our power, but the real quality of our purpose and of ourselves. Of course the duty that we must keep in the foreground until it is accomplished is to win the war. I have heard gentlemen recently say that we must get five million men ready. Why limit it to five million ? I have asked the Congress of the United States to name no limit, because Congress intends, I am sure, as we all intend, that every ship that can carry men or supplies shall go laden upon every voyage, with every man and every supply she can carry.

And we are not to be diverted from the grim purpose of winning the war by any insincere approaches upon the subject of peace. I can say with a clear conscience that I have tested those intimations and have found them insincere. I now recognize them for what they are, an opportunity to have a free hand, particularly in the East, to carry out the purposes of conquest and exploitation. Every proposal with regard to accommodation in the West involves a reservation with regard to the East.

Now, so far as I am concerned, I intend to stand by Russia as well as France. The helpless and friendless are the very ones that need friends and succour, and if any man in Germany thinks we are going to sacrifice anybody for our own sake I tell them now they are mistaken, for the glory of this war, my fellow-citizens, so far as we are concerned, is that it is, perhaps for the first time in history, an unselfish war; I could not be proud to fight for a selfish purpose, but I can be proud to fight for mankind. If they wish for peace, let them come forward through accredited representatives and lay their terms on the table. We have laid ours, and they know what they are.

Have you formed a picture in your imagination of what this war is doing for us and for the world? In my own mind I am convinced that not a hundred years of peace could have knitted this nation together as this single year of war has knitted it together, and, better even than that, if possible, it is knitting the world together. Look at the picture. In the centre of the scene four nations engaged against the world, and at every point of vantage showing that they are seeking selfish aggrandizement; and against them twenty-three Governments representing the greater part of the population of the world, drawn together into

society that govern the individual citizens of all modern
States, and in their relations with one another to the
end that all promises and covenants may be sacredly
observed, no private plots or conspiracies hatched, no
selfish injuries wrought with impunity, and a mutual
trust established upon the handsome foundation of a
mutual respect for right.

Fourth, the establishment of an organization of peace
which shall make it certain that the combined power of
free nations will check every invasion of right, and serve
to make peace and justice the more secure by affording
a definite tribunal of opinion to which all must submit, and
by which every international readjustment that cannot
be amicably agreed upon by the peoples directly concerned shall be sanctioned.

These great objects can be put into a single sentence:
*What we seek is the reign of law based upon the consent of
the governed, and sustained by the organized opinion of
mankind.* These great ends cannot be achieved by debating
and seeking to reconcile and accommodate what statesmen
may wish, with their projects for balances of power and of
national opportunity. They can be realized only by the
determination of what the thinking peoples of the world
desire, with their longing hope for justice and for social
freedom and opportunity.

I can fancy that the air of this place carries the accents
of such principles with a peculiar kindness. Here were
started forces which the great nation against which they
were primarily directed at first regarded as a revolt against
its rightful authority, but which it has long since seen to
have been a step in the liberation of its own people as well
as of the people of the United States. And I stand here
now to speak—speak proudly and with confident hope—
of the spread of this revolt, this liberation, to the great
stage of the world itself.

The blinded rulers of Prussia have aroused forces they

knew little of, forces which, once roused, can never be crushed to earth again, for they have at their heart an inspiration and a purpose which are deathless, and of the very stuff of triumph.

SEPTEMBER 27, 1918. SPEECH AT THE OPENING OF THE FOURTH LIBERTY LOAN CAMPAIGN, NEW YORK (THE FIVE CONDITIONS)

... The war has lasted more than four years, and the whole world has been drawn into it. The common will of mankind has been substituted for the particular purposes of individual States. Individual statesmen may have started the conflict, but neither.they nor their opponents can stop it as they please. It has become a peoples' war, and peoples of all sorts and races, of every degree of power and variety of fortune, are involved in its sweeping processes of change and settlement.

We came into it when its character had become fully defined, and it was plain that no nation could stand apart or be indifferent to its outcome. Its challenge drove to the heart of everything we cared for and lived for. The voice of the war had become clear and gripped our hearts. Our brothers from many lands, as well as our own murdered dead under the sea, were calling to us; and we responded fiercely and of courage. The air was clear about us. We saw things in their full convincing proportions as they were; and we have seen them with steady eyes and unchanging comprehension ever since. We accepted the issues of the war as facts, not as any group of men either here or elsewhere had defined them, and we can accept no outcome which does not squarely meet and settle them.

The issues are these :

Shall the military power of any nation, or group of nations, be suffered to determine the fortunes of peoples over whom they have no right to rule except the right of force ?

Shall strong nations be free to wrong weak nations and make them subject to their purposes and interest ?

Shall peoples be ruled and dominated, even in their own internal affairs, by arbitrary and irresponsible force, or by their own will and choice ?

Shall there be a common standard of right and privilege for all peoples and nations, or shall the strong do as they will, and the weak suffer without redress ?

Shall the assertion of right be haphazard and by casual alliance, or shall there be a common concert to oblige the observance of common rights ?

No man, no group of men, chose these to be the issues of the struggle. They are issues of it ; and they must be settled—by no arrangement or compromise or adjustment of interests, but definitely and once for all, and with a full and unequivocal acceptance of the principle that the interest of the weakest is as sacred as the interest of the strongest. This is what we mean when we speak of a permanent peace, if we speak sincerely, intelligently, and with a real knowledge and comprehension of the matter we deal with.

We all agree that there can be no peace obtained by any kind of bargain or compromise with the Governments of the Central Empires, because we have dealt with them already and have seen them deal with other Governments that were parties to this struggle, at Brest-Litovsk and Bucarest. They have convinced us that they are without honour, and do not intend justice. They observe no covenants, accept no principle but force and their own interest. We cannot come to terms ' with them. They have made it impossible. The German people must by this time be fully aware that we cannot accept the word of those who forced this war upon us. We do not think the same thoughts or speak the same language of agreement.

It is of capital importance that we should also be explicitly agreed that no peace shall be obtained by any kind of compromise or abatement of the principles we have avowed as the principles for which we are fighting. There should exist no doubt about that. I am, therefore, going to take the liberty of speaking with the utmost frankness about the tactical implications that are involved in it.

If it be, in deed and in truth, the common object of the Governments associated against Germany and of the nations whom they govern, as I believe it to be, to achieve by the coming settlements a secure and lasting peace, it will be necessary that all who sit down at the peace table shall come ready and willing to pay the price, the only price, that will procure it; and ready and willing also to create in some virile fashion the only instrumentality by which it can be made certain that the agreements of the peace will be honoured and fulfilled. That price is impartial justice in every item of the settlement, no matter whose interest is crossed; and of not only impartial justice, but also the satisfaction of the several peoples whose fortunes are dealt with. That indispensable instrumentality is a League of Nations formed under covenants that will be inefficacious without such an instrumentality by which the peace of the world can be guaranteed. Peace will rest in part upon the word of outlaws, and only upon that word. For Germany will have to redeem her character, not by what happens at the peace table but by what follows.

And as I see it, the constitution of that League of Nations and the clear definition of its objects must be a part, in a sense the most essential part, of the peace settlement itself. It cannot be formed now. If formed now it would be merely a new alliance confined to the nations associated against a common enemy. It is not likely that it could be formed after the settlement. It is necessary to guarantee the peace; and the peace cannot be guaranteed as an afterthought. The reason, to speak in plain terms again, why it must be guaranteed is that there will be parties to the peace whose promises have

proved untrustworthy, and means must be found in connexion with the peace settlement itself to remove that
source of insecurity. It would be folly to leave the
guarantee to the subsequent voluntary action of the
Governments we have seen destroy Russia and deceive
Rumania.

But these general terms do not disclose the whole
matter. Some details are needed to make them sound
less like a thesis and more like a practical programme.
These, then, are some of the particulars, and I state them
with the greater confidence because I can state them
authoritatively as representing this Government's interpretation of its own duty with regard to peace :

First, the impartial justice meted out must involve no
discrimination between those to whom we wish to be just
and those to whom we do not wish to be just. It must be
a justice that plays no favourites and knows no standards
but the equal rights of the several peoples concerned.

Second, no special or separate interest of any single
nation or any group of nations can be made the basis
of any part of the settlement which is not consistent
with the common interest of all.

Third, there can be no leagues or alliances or special
covenants and understandings within the general and
common family of the League of Nations.

Fourth, and more specifically, there can be no special,
selfish economic combinations within the League, and
no employment of any form of economic boycott or
exclusion, except as the power of economic penalty,
by exclusion from the markets of the world, may be
vested in the League of Nations itself as a means of
discipline and control.

Fifth, all international agreements and treaties of
every kind must be made known in their entirety to
the rest of the world.

Special alliances and economic rivalries and hostilities

have been the prolific source in the modern world of the plans and passions that produce war. It would be an insincere as well as an insecure peace that did not exclude them in definite and binding terms.

The confidence with which I venture to speak for our people in these matters does not spring from our traditions merely, and the well-known principles of international action which we have always professed and followed. In the same sentence in which I say that the United States will enter into no special arrangements or understandings with particular nations let me say also that the United States is prepared to assume its full share of responsibility for the maintenance of the common covenants and understandings upon which peace must henceforth rest.

We still read Washington's immortal warning against 'entangling alliances' with full comprehension and an answering purpose. But only special and limited alliances entangle; and we recognize and accept the duty of a new day in which we are permitted to hope for a general alliance, which will avoid entanglements and clear the air of the world for common understandings and the maintenance of common rights.

I have made this analysis of the international situation, which the war has created, not, of course, because I doubted whether the leaders of the great nations and peoples with whom we are associated were of the same mind and entertained a like purpose, but because the air every now and again gets darkened by mists and groundless doubting and mischievous perversions of counsel, and it is necessary once and again to sweep all the irresponsible talk about peace intrigue and weakening *moral* and doubtful purpose on the part of those in authority utterly, and if need be unceremoniously, aside, and say things in the plainest words that can be found, even when it is only to say over again what has been said before, quite as plainly, if in less varnished terms.

As I have said, neither I, nor any other man in Governmental authority, created or gave form to the issues of this war. I have simply responded to them with such vision as I could command. But I have responded gladly, and with a resolution that has grown warm and more confident as the issues have grown clearer and clearer. It is now plain that they are issues which no man can pervert unless it be wilfully. I am bound to fight for them, and fight for them as time and circumstances have revealed them to me as to all the world. Our enthusiasm for them grows more and more irresistible as they stand out in more and more vivid and unmistakable outline.

And the forces that fight for them draw into closer and closer array, organize their millions into more and more unconquerable might, as they become more and more distinct to the thought and purpose of the peoples engaged. It is the peculiarity of this great war that, while statesmen have seemed to cast about for definitions of their purpose and have sometimes seemed to shift their ground and their point of view, the thought of the mass of men, whom statesmen are supposed to instruct and lead, has grown more and more unclouded, more and more certain of what it is that they are fighting for. National purposes have fallen more and more into the background ; and the common purpose of enlightened mankind has taken their place. The counsels of plain men have become on all hands more simple and straightforward and more unified than the counsels of sophisticated men of affairs, who still retain the impression that they are playing a game of power and playing for high stakes. That is why I have said that this is a peoples' war, not a statesmen's. Statesmen must follow the clarified common thought or be broken.

I take that to be the significance of the fact that assemblies and associations of many kinds made up of plain workaday people have demanded, almost every time that they came together, and are still demanding, that the leaders of their Governments declare to them plainly what it is, exactly what it is, that they are seeking in this war, and what they think the items of their final settlement should be. They are not yet satisfied with what they have been told. They still seem to fear that they are getting what they ask for only in statesmen's terms—only in the terms of territorial arrangements and discussions of power, and not in terms of broad-visioned justice and mercy and peace and the satisfaction of these deep-seated longings of oppressed and distracted men and women and enslaved peoples that seem to them the only things worth fighting a war for that engulfs the world. Perhaps statesmen have not always recognized this changed aspect of the whole world of policy and action. Perhaps they have not always spoken in direct reply to the question asked because they did not know how searching these questions were and what sort of answers they demanded.

But I, for one, am glad to attempt the answer again and again, in the hope that I may make it clearer and clearer that my one thought is to satisfy those who struggle in the ranks and are, perhaps above all others, entitled to a reply whose meaning no one can have any excuse for misunderstanding, if he understands the language in which it is spoken, or can get some one to translate it correctly into his own. And I believe that the leaders of the Governments with which we are associated will speak, as they have occasion, as plainly as I have tried to speak.

I hope that they will feel free to say whether they think that I am in any degree mistaken in my interpretation of the issues involved or in my purpose with regard to the means by which a satisfactory settlement of these issues may be obtained. Unity of purpose and of counsel are as imperatively necessary in this war as was unity of command in the battlefield ; and with perfect unity of purpose and counsel will come assurance of complete victory. It can be had in no other way.

' Peace drives ' can be effectively neutralized and silenced only by showing that every victory of the nations associated against Germany brings the nations nearer the sort of peace which will bring security and reassurance to all peoples, and make the recurrence of another such struggle of pitiless force and bloodshed for ever impossible, and that nothing else can. Germany is constantly intimating the ' terms ' she will accept, and always finds that the world does not want terms of peace ; it wishes the final triumph of justice and fair dealing.

OCTOBER 8, 1918. REPLY[1] TO GERMAN PEACE NOTE OF
OCTOBER 4. (See Appendix 2)

I have the honour to acknowledge, on behalf of the President, your Note of October 6, enclosing a communication from the German Government to the President ; and I am instructed by the President to request you to make the following communication to the Imperial German Chancellor :

Before making a reply to the request of the Imperial German Government, and in order that the reply shall be as candid and straightforward as the momentous interests involved require, the President of the United States deems it necessary to assure himself of the exact meaning of the Note of the Imperial Chancellor. Does the Imperial Chancellor mean that the Imperial German Government accepts the terms laid down by the President in his address to the Congress of the United States on January 8 last and in subsequent addresses, and that its object in entering into discussions would be only to agree upon the practical details of their application ? The President feels bound to say, with regard to the suggestion of an armistice, that he would

[1] This reply was addressed to the Swiss Minister at Washington.

not feel at liberty to propose a cessation of arms to the Governments with which the Government of the United States is associated against the Central Powers so long as the armies of those Powers are upon their soil. The good faith of any discussion would manifestly depend upon the consent of the Central Powers immediately to withdraw their forces everywhere from invaded territory.

The President also feels that he is justified in asking whether the Imperial Chancellor is speaking merely for the constituted authorities of the Empire who have so far conducted the war. He deems the answer to these questions vital from every point of view.

ROBERT LANSING.

October 8, 1918.

OCTOBER 14, 1918. REPLY[1] TO GERMAN COMMUNICATION OF OCTOBER 12. (See Appendix 3)

In reply to the communication of the German Government dated the twelfth instant which you handed me to-day I have the honour to request you to transmit the following answer :

The unqualified acceptance by the present German Government and by a large majority of the German Reichstag of the terms laid down by the President of the United States of America in his addresses to the Congress of the United States on January 8, 1918, and in his subsequent addresses justifies the President in making a frank and direct statement of his decision in regard to the communications of the German Government of the 8th[2] and 12th of October, 1918.

It must be clearly understood that the process of evacuation and the conditions of an armistice are matters which must be left to the judgement and advice of the military

---

[1] This reply was addressed to the Swiss Minister at Washington.

[2] Thus in original reply : the real date being the 4th, handed to the President on the 6th.

advisers of the Government of the United States and the Allied Governments, and the President feels it his duty to say that no arrangement can be accepted by the Government of the United States which does not provide absolutely satisfactory safeguards and guarantees of the maintenance of the present military supremacy of the Armies of the United States and of the Allies in the field. He feels confident that he can safely assume that this will also be the judgement and decision of the Allied Governments.

The President feels that it is also his duty to add that neither the Government of the United States nor, he is quite sure, the Governments with which the Government of the United States is associated as a belligerent, will consent to consider an armistice so long as the armed forces of Germany continue the illegal and inhumane practices which they persist in. At the very time the German Government approaches the Government of the United States with proposals of peace its submarines are engaged in sinking passenger ships at sea, and not the ships alone, but the very boats in which their passengers and crews seek to make their way to safety; and in their present enforced withdrawal from Flanders and France the German armies are pursuing a course of wanton destruction which has always been regarded as in direct violation of the rules and practices of civilized warfare. Cities and villages, if not destroyed, are being stripped not only of all they contain, but often of their very inhabitants. The nations associated against Germany cannot be expected to agree to a cessation of arms while acts of inhumanity, spoliation, and desolation are being continued which they justly look upon with horror and with burning hearts.

It is necessary also, in order that there may be no possibility of misunderstanding, that the President should very solemnly call the attention of the Government of Germany to the language and plain intent of one of the terms of peace which the German Government has now accepted. It is contained in the address of the President delivered at Mount Vernon on July 4 last. It is as follows :

' The destruction of every arbitrary power anywhere that can separately, secretly, and of its single choice disturb the peace of the world ; or, if it cannot be presently destroyed, at least its reduction to virtual impotency.'

The power which has hitherto controlled the German nation is of the sort here described. It is within the choice of the German nation to alter it. The President's words just quoted naturally constitute a condition precedent to peace, if peace is to come by the action of the German people themselves.

The President feels bound to say that the whole process of peace will, in his judgement, depend upon the definiteness and satisfactory character of the guarantees which can be given in this fundamental matter. It is indispensable that the Governments associated against Germany should know beyond a peradventure with whom they are dealing.

October 14, 1918.   ROBERT LANSING.

OCTOBER 23, 1918. REPLY [1] TO GERMAN COMMUNICATION OF OCTOBER 20. (See Appendix 4)

I have the honour to acknowledge the receipt of your Note of the 22nd, transmitting a communication, under date of the 20th, from the German Government, and to advise you that the President has instructed me to reply thereto as follows :

Having received the solemn and explicit assurance of the German Government that it unreservedly accepts the terms of peace laid down in his address to Congress of the United States on the 8th January, 1918, and the principles of settlement enunciated in his subsequent addresses, parti-

[1] This reply was addressed to the Swiss Minister in Washington.

cularly the address of the 27th September, and that it desires to discuss the details of their application ; and that this wish and purpose emanate, not from those who have hitherto dictated German policy and conducted the present war on Germany's behalf, but from Ministers who speak for the majority of the Reichstag and for an overwhelming majority of the German people ; and having received also the explicit promise of the present German Government that the humane rules of civilized warfare will be observed both on land and sea by the German armed forces, the President of the United States feels that he cannot decline to take up with the Governments with which the Government of the United States is associated the question of an armistice.

He deems it is his duty to say again, however, that the only armistice he would feel justified in submitting for consideration would be one which should leave the United States and the Powers associated with her in a position to enforce any arrangements that may be entered into, and to make a renewal of hostilities on the part of Germany impossible. The President has therefore transmitted his correspondence with the present German authorities to the Governments with which the Government of the United States is associated as a belligerent, with the suggestion that, if those Governments are disposed to effect peace upon the terms and principles indicated, their military advisers and the military advisers of the United States be asked to submit to the Governments associated against Germany the necessary terms of such an armistice as will fully protect the interests of the peoples involved and ensure to the Associated Governments the unrestricted power to safeguard and enforce the details of the peace to which the German Government has agreed, provided they deem such an armistice possible from the military point of view. Should such terms of armistice be suggested, their acceptance by Germany will afford the best concrete evidence of her unequivocal acceptance of the terms and principles of peace from which the whole action proceeds.

The President would deem himself lacking in candour did he not point out in the frankest possible terms the reason why extraordinary safeguards must be demanded. Significant and important as the constitutional changes seem to be which are spoken of by the German Foreign Secretary in his Note of the 20th October, it does not appear that the principle of a Government responsible to the German people has yet been fully worked out, or that any guarantees either exist or are in contemplation that the alterations of principle and of practice now partially agreed upon will be permanent.

Moreover, it does not appear that the heart of the present difficulty has been reached. It may be that future wars have been brought under the control of the German people, but the present war has not been, and it is with the present war that we are dealing. It is evident that the German people have no means of commanding the acquiescence of the military authorities of the Empire in the popular will, that the power of the King of Prussia to control the policy of the Empire is unimpaired, that the determining initiative still remains with those who have hitherto been the masters of Germany.

Feeling that the whole peace of the world depends now on plain speaking and straightforward action, the President deems it his duty to say, without any attempt to soften what may seem harsh words, that the nations of the world do not and cannot trust the word of those who have hitherto been the masters of German policy, and to point out once more that, in concluding peace and attempting to undo the infinite injuries and injustices of this war, the Government of the United States cannot deal with any but veritable representatives of the German people, who have been assured of a genuine constitutional standing as the real rulers of Germany.

If it must deal with the military masters and the monarchical autocrats of Germany now, or if it is likely to have to deal with them later in regard to the international obligations of the German Empire, it must demand, not peace negotiations, but surrender. Nothing can be gained by leaving this essential thing unsaid.

ROBERT LANSING.

October 23, 1918.

DECEMBER 2, 1918. ANNUAL ADDRESS TO CONGRESS

The year that has elapsed since I last stood before you to fulfil my constitutional duty to give to Congress from time to time information on the state of the Union has been so crowded with great events, great processes, and great results that I cannot hope to give you an adequate picture of its transactions or of the far-reaching changes which have been brought about in the life of our nation and of the world. You have yourselves witnessed these things as I have. It is too soon to assess them, and we who stand in the midst of them and are part of them are less qualified than men of another generation will be to say what they mean or even what they have been. But some great outstanding facts are unmistakable, and constitute, in a sense, part of the public business with which it is our duty to deal. To state them is to set the stage for the legislative and executive action which must grow out of them, and which we have yet to shape and determine. A year ago we had sent 145,918 men overseas. Since then we have sent 1,950,513, an average of 162,542 each month, the number, in fact, rising in May last to 245,951, in June to 278,760, in July to 307,182, and continuing to reach similar figures in August and September—in August 289,570 and in September 257,438. No such movement of troops ever took place before across 3,000 miles of sea, followed by adequate equipment and supplies, and carried safely through extraordinary dangers which were alike strange

and infinitely difficult to guard against. In all this movement only 758 men were lost by enemy attack, 630 of
whom were upon a single English transport which was sunk
near the Orkney Islands.

I need not tell you what lay at the back of this great
movement of men and material. It is not invidious to say
that at the back of it lay a supporting organization of the
industries of the country and of all of its productive acti-
vities more complete, more thorough in the method and
effective in result, more spirited and unanimous in purpose
and effort than any other great belligerent had been able
to effect. We profited greatly by the experience of the
nations which had already been engaged for nearly three
years in exigent and exacting business, their every resource
and every executive proficiency taxed to the utmost. We
were their pupils. But we learned quickly, and acted with
a promptness and readiness of co-operation that justify our
great pride that we were able to serve the world with un-
paralleled energy and quick accomplishment.

But it is not the physical scale and executive efficiency
of preparation, supply, equipment, and dispatch that I
would dwell upon, but the mettle and quality of the officers
and men we sent over, and of the sailors who kept the seas
and the spirit of the nation that stood behind them. No
soldiers or sailors ever proved themselves more quickly
ready for the test of battle or acquitted themselves with
more splendid courage and achievement when put to the
test. Those of us who played some part in directing the
great processes by which the war was pushed irresistibly
forward to final triumph may now forget all that, and
delight our thoughts with the story of what our men did.
Their officers understood the grim and exacting task they
had undertaken, and performed it with an audacity and
efficiency and an unhesitating courage that touch the story
of convoy and battle with imperishable distinction at every
turn, whether the enterprise were great or small, from their

great chiefs, Pershing and Sims, down to the youngest
lieutenant ; and their men were worthy of them, such
men as hardly need be commanded and go to their
terrible adventure blithely and with the quick intelligence
of those who know just what it is they would accomplish.
I am proud to be a fellow-countryman of men of such stuff
and valour.

. . . .

And now we are sure of the great triumph for which every
sacrifice was made. It has come in its completeness, and,
with the pride and inspiration of these days of achievement
quick within us, we turn to the tasks of peace again—peace
secure against the violence of irresponsible monarchs and
ambitious military coteries—and made ready for a new
order, for new foundations of justice and fair dealing. We
are about to give order and organization to this peace, not
only for ourselves, but for the other peoples of the world as
well, as far as they will suffer us to serve them. It is international justice we seek, not domestic safety merely. Our
thoughts have dwelt of late upon Europe, upon Asia, upon
the Near and Far East, very little upon the acts of peace
and accommodation that wait to be performed at our own
doors.

. . . .

So far as our domestic affairs are concerned, the problem
of our return to peace is a problem of economic and industrial readjustment. That problem is less serious for us than
it may turn out to be for nations which have suffered the
disarrangements and losses of war longer than we. Our
people, moreover, do not wait to be coached and led. They
know their own business, are quick and resourceful at
every readjustment, definite in purpose, and self-reliant in
action. Any leading strings we might seek to put them in
would speedily become hopelessly tangled, because they
would pay no attention to them and go their own way.

. . . .

I have spoken of the control which must yet for a while —perhaps for a long while—be exercised over shipping, because of the priority of service to which our forces oversea are entitled, and which should also be accorded to the shipments which are to save the recently liberated peoples from starvation and many devastated regions from permanent ruin. May I not say a special word about the needs of Belgium and northern France ? No sums of money paid by way of indemnity will serve of themselves to save them from hopeless disadvantage for years to come. Something more must be done than merely find the money. If they had the money and raw materials in abundance to-morrow they could not resume their place in the industry of the world to-morrow—the very important place they held before the flag of war swept across them. Many of their factories are razed to the ground. Much of their machinery is destroyed, or has been taken away. Their people are scattered, and many of their best workmen are dead. Their markets will be taken by others if they are not in some special way assisted to rebuild their factories and replace their lost instruments of manufacture. They should not be left to the vicissitudes of the sharp competition for materials and for industrial facilities which is now to set in. I hope, therefore, that Congress will not be unwilling, if it should become necessary to grant to some such agency as the War Trade Board the right to establish priorities of export and supply for the benefit of these people whom we have been so happy to assist in saving from the German terror, and whom we must not now thoughtlessly leave to shift for themselves in a pitiless competitive market.

. . . .

I take it for granted that the Congress will carry out the naval programme which was undertaken before we entered the war. The Secretary of the Navy has submitted to your Committees for authorization that part of the programme which covers the building plans of the next three years. These plans have been prepared along the lines and in accordance with the policy which the Congress established, not under the exceptional conditions of the war but with the intention of adhering to a definite method of development for the Navy. Earnestly I recommend the uninterrupted pursuit of this policy. It would clearly be unwise for us to attempt to adjust our programme to a future world-policy as yet undetermined.

.   .   .   .

I welcome this occasion to announce to Congress my purpose to join in Paris the representatives of the Governments with which we have been associated in the war against the Central Empires for the purpose of discussing with them the main features of the Treaty of Peace. I realize the great inconveniences that will attend my leaving the country, particularly at this time, but the conclusion that it was my paramount duty to go has been forced upon me by considerations which I hope will seem as conclusive to you as they have seemed to me. The Allied Governments have accepted the basis of peace which I outlined to Congress on January 8 last, as the Central Empires also have, and they very reasonably desire my personal counsel in their interpretation and application, and it is highly desirable I should give it in order that the sincere desire of our Government to contribute without selfish purpose of any kind to the settlements that will be of common benefit to all nations concerned may be made fully manifest.

The peace settlements which are now to be agreed upon are of transcendent importance both to us and to the rest of the world, and I know of no business or interest which should take precedence over them. The gallant men of our armed forces on land and sea have consciously fought for ideals which they knew to be the ideals of their country ; I have sought to express these ideals ; they have been accepted by statesmen as the substance of their own thoughts and purpose as the associated Governments have accepted them ; I owe it to them to see to it so far as in me lies that no false or mistaken interpretation is put upon them and no possible effort omitted to realize them. It is now my duty to play my full part in making good what they offered their lives and blood to obtain. I can think of no call to service which could transcend this. I shall be in close touch with you and with affairs on this side of the water and you will know all that I do.

APPENDIX

1. EXTRACTS FROM SPEECHES OF COUNT HERTLING AND COUNT CZERNIN, JANUARY 24, 1918

(a) COUNT HERTLING

. . . And now, gentlemen, I come to President Wilson. Here also I admit that the tone has changed. It appears that the unanimous rejection at the time of the attempt of Mr. Wilson, in the reply to the Papal Note, to sow discord between the German Government and the German nation has done its work. It was possibly this unanimous rejection which led Mr. Wilson on to the right road, and perhaps a beginning has been made because now there is, at least, no longer any question of the suppression of the German nation by an autocratic Government, and the former attacks against the House of Hohenzollern are not repeated. I will not go into the distorted representations of German policy which are even yet to be found in Mr. Wilson's message, but I will discuss in detail the points which Mr. Wilson brings forward. There are no less than fourteen points in which he formulates his peace programme, and I beg you to have patience if I bring forward these fourteen points for discussion, as briefly as possible.

I.—*No secret international agreements.*

History records that we were the first to be able to declare ourselves in agreement with the most extensive publicity of diplomatic agreements. I remind you of the fact that our defensive alliance with Austria-Hungary has been known to all the world since the year 1889, whilst the offensive agreements of our enemies have had to be disclosed during the course of this war, chiefly by the publication of the Russian secret documents. The full publicity also given to the negotiations at Brest-Litovsk proves that we were in a position to consent readily to this proposal, and to declare the publication of negotiations as a general political principle.

II.—*The freedom of the seas.*

Complete freedom of navigation on the seas in war and peace is also put forward by Germany as one of the first and most important demands for the future. Here, therefore, there is no difference of opinion whatever. The restriction mentioned by Mr. Wilson towards the end is incomprehensible and seems superfluous. It should therefore be suppressed. It would, however, be important in a high degree for the future freedom of the seas if claims to strongly fortified naval bases on important international shipping routes, such as England maintains at Gibraltar, Malta, Aden, Hong-kong, on the Falkland Islands, and at many other points, were renounced.

III.—*The abandonment of all economic restrictions which hinder commerce in an unnecessary manner.*

With this we wholly agree. We also condemn an economic war which would inevitably bring with it causes for future warlike complications.

IV.—*The limitation of armaments.*

As has already been declared by us on previous occasions, the subject of the limitation of armaments is a matter quite suitable for discussion. The financial situation of all the European States after the war should further its satisfactory solution in a most effective manner.

It will be seen that as to the first four points of the programme agreement could be reached without difficulty.

V.—*The amicable arrangement of all colonial claims.*

The practical carrying out of the principle laid down by Mr. Wilson will, in this world of realities, meet with some difficulties. In any case I believe that, for the time being, it may be left to the greatest colonial Empire—England—to determine as to how she will come to terms with her ally regarding this proposal. We shall have to talk about this point of the programme at the time of the reconstruction of the colonial possessions of the world, which has also been demanded unconditionally by us.

VI.—*The evacuation of Russian territory.*

The Entente States having refused to join in the negotiations within the period agreed upon by Russia and the Four Allied

Powers, I must decline, in the name of the latter, any subsequent interference. The question here involved is one which alone concerns Russia and the Four Allied Powers. I cherish the hope that, under the conditions of the recognition of the right of self-determination for the nations within the western boundaries of the former Russian Empire, it will be possible to be on good relations with these nations, as well as with the rest of Russia, for whom we urgently wish a return of guarantees which will secure a peaceful order of things and the welfare of the country.

VII.—*The Belgian question.*

As far as the Belgian question is concerned, it has been declared repeatedly by my predecessors in office that at no time during the war has the forcible annexation of Belgium by the German Empire formed a point in the programme of German politics. The Belgian question belongs to a complexity of questions, the details of which will have to be regulated during the peace negotiations. As long as our enemies do not unreservedly adopt the attitude that the integrity of the territory of the Allies offers the only possible foundation for peace negotiations, I must adhere to the standpoint which, up to the present, has always been taken, and must decline any discussion of the Belgian question until the general discussion takes place.

VIII.—*The liberation of French territory.*

The occupied parts of France are a valuable pawn in our hands. Here also forcible annexation forms no part of the official German policy. The conditions and mode of the evacuation, which must take into consideration the vital interests of Germany, must be agreed between Germany and France. I can only once again expressly emphasize that there can never be any question of the separation of the Imperial Provinces. We will never permit ourselves to be robbed of Alsace-Lorraine by our enemies under the pretext of any fine phrases—of Alsace-Lorraine, which, in the meantime, has become more and more closely allied internally with German life, which is developing more and more economically in a highly satisfactory manner, and where more than 87 per cent. of the people speak the German mother tongue.

IX, X, and XI.—*The Italian frontiers, the question of nationalities of the Danube Monarchy, and the Balkan States.*

As regards the questions dealt with by President Wilson under these clauses, they embrace questions of paramount importance to the political interests of our ally, Austria-Hungary. Where German interests are concerned, we will guard them to the utmost, but the reply to President Wilson's proposals in connexion with these points I would prefer to leave in the first instance to the Foreign Minister of the Austro-Hungarian Monarchy. A close connexion with the allied Danube Monarchy is the vital point of our policy to-day and must be a guiding line for the future. The faithful comradeship in arms, which has proved itself so brilliantly during the war, must continue to have its effect also in peace, and we on our part will bring everything to bear in order to bring about for Austria-Hungary a peace which takes into account her justified claims.

XII.—*Turkey.*

Also in connexion with the point which concerns our brave and powerful ally Turkey, I would like in no way to forestall the attitude of Turkish statesmen. The integrity of Turkey and the security of her capital, which is closely connected with the questions of the Straits, are important and vital interests also of the German Empire. Our ally can in this respect always rely on our most explicit assistance.

XIII.—*Poland.*

It was not the Entente—who found nothing but meaningless words for Poland and before the war never mediated on her behalf with Russia—but the German Empire and Austria-Hungary who freed Poland from the Tsaristic *régime* which was oppressing her national individuality. Therefore, it must be left to Germany and Austria-Hungary and Poland to come to an agreement about the future organization of that country. We are, as has been proved by the negotiations and declarations of the last year, well under way with the task.

XIV.—*The League of Nations.*

In regard to this point I am sympathetic, as is shown by my previous political activity towards any thought which for the future excludes all possibility and probability of wars and tends

to promote a peaceful and harmonious co-operation between
the nations. If the conception of the 'League of Nations'
mentioned by President Wilson demonstrates, under further
development and after trial, that it really was conceived in
a spirit of complete justice to all, and with complete freedom
from prejudice, the Imperial Government will be gladly prepared—after all the other questions in suspense have been
settled—to investigate the principles of such a national union.

(b) COUNT CZERNIN

... When peace has been concluded with Russia, it will not be
possible, in my opinion, to prevent for long the conclusion of
a general peace, in spite of the efforts of Entente statesmen.
Although I am under no delusion, and know that the fruit of
peace cannot be matured in twenty-four hours, I am nevertheless convinced that it is now maturing, and that the question
whether or not an honourable general peace can be secured is
merely a question of resistance. President Wilson's peace offer
confirms me in this opinion.

Naturally, an offer of this kind cannot be regarded as a matter
acceptable in every detail, for that would obviously render any
negotiations superfluous. I think there is no harm in stating
that I regard the recent proposals of President Wilson as an
appreciable approach to the Austro-Hungarian point of view,
and that to some of them Austria-Hungary could joyfully give
her approval, but I must first lay down this principle—that in
so far as these propositions concern her Allies, whether in the
case of Germany's possession of Belgium or in the case of
Turkey, Austria-Hungary, faithful to her engagements to fight
to the end in defence of her Allies, will defend the possessions
of her war Allies as she would her own. That is the standpoint
of the four Allies, in regard to which there is perfect reciprocity.

I have no objection to the suppression of secret diplomacy,
although I doubt whether this method is in every case the most
practical and rapid way to arrive at a result. The public discussion of diplomatic treaties might, for example, in the case
of an economic agreement, make impossible the conclusion of
such an agreement, which is nothing but a commercial transaction, and might increase the friction between the two States.
It is the same in the case of political agreements.

If by the suppression of secret diplomacy it is meant that there should no longer be any secret treaties, I have no objection to make to the realization of this idea, although I do not know how one can execute and control this realization ; but these are supplementary details which could be discussed.

As to the second point, the liberty of the seas, President Wilson has responded to the views of all, and I absolutely and entirely support this paragraph.

Article III of President Wilson's declaration, which pronounces in a formal manner against a future economic war, is so just and reasonable, and its application has so often been urged by us, that we have nothing to add to it.

Article IV, which demands general disarmament, expresses in a particularly clear and just manner the necessity of bringing the rivalry in armaments to the limit already indicated in the President's profession of faith, and therefore I greet with gratitude any voice which makes itself heard in the sense of my previous statements.

We have already shown by acts that we desire to establish good neighbourly relations with Russia. [Article VI.]

On the subject of Italy, Serbia, Montenegro, and Rumania [Articles IX and XI], I repeat what I have already said to the Hungarian Delegation : ' I refuse to place a premium on the military adventures of our enemies. I refuse to make our enemies, who obstinately persist in wishing to wage war until final victory, one-sided concessions by which the Monarchy would permanently suffer and which would give them the infinite advantage of being able to drag on the war, relatively without risk. . . .'

We are also supporters of the creation of an independent Polish State [Article XIII], which should include all the territories the populations of which are indisputably Polish. On this point, also, we believe we should quickly come to an understanding with President Wilson.

Finally, in his idea of a League of Peoples [Article XIV], the President would very probably meet with no opposition in the Monarchy.

We are, therefore, in agreement in the main. Our views are identical not only in the broad principles regarding the new organization of the world after the war, but also in several concrete questions ; and the differences which still exist do not appear to me to be so great that a conversation regarding them would not lead to enlightenment and a *rapprochement*. This situation, which doubtless arises from the fact that Austria-Hungary, on the one side, and the United States, on the other, are composed of States whose interests are least at variance with one another, tempts one to ask if an exchange of ideas could not be the point of departure for a personal conversation between all the States which have not yet joined in the peace negotiations ?

2. GERMAN PEACE NOTE, OCTOBER 4, 1918

The German Government requests the President of the United States of America to take in hand the restoration of peace, acquaint all belligerents with this request, and invite them to send plenipotentiaries for the purpose of opening negotiations. The German Government accepts the pro-gramme set forth by the President of the United States in his message to Congress of January 8, 1918, and in his later pronouncements, especially his speech of September 27, as a basis for peace negotiations. With a view to avoiding further bloodshed, the German Government requests the immediate conclusion of an armistice on land and water and in the air.

MAX, PRINCE OF BADEN,
Imperial Chancellor.

3. GERMAN REPLY TO AMERICAN NOTE OF OCTOBER 8, 1918

In reply to the questions of the President of the United States of America, the German Government hereby declares :

The German Government has accepted the terms laid down by President Wilson in his Address of January 8 and in his subsequent Addresses on the foundation of a per-manent peace of justice. Consequently, its object in enter-ing into discussions would be only to agree upon practical details of the application of these terms.

The German Government believes that the Governments of the Powers associated with the Government of the United States also adopt the position taken by President Wilson in his Address.

The German Government, in accordance with the Austro-Hungarian Government, for the purpose of bringing about an armistice, declares itself ready to comply with the propositions of the President in regard to evacuation. The German Government suggests that the President may occasion the meeting of a mixed Commission for making the necessary arrangements concerning the evacuation.

The present German Government, which has undertaken the responsibility for this step towards peace, has been formed by conferences and in agreement with the great majority of the Reichstag. The Chancellor, supported in all of his actions by the will of this majority, speaks in the name of the German Government and of the German People.

(Signed) SOLF,

State Secretary of Foreign Office.

BERLIN, *October* 12, 1918.

4. GERMAN REPLY TO AMERICAN NOTE OF OCTOBER 14, 1918

In complying with the proposal to evacuate occupied territories the German Government started from the standpoint that the procedure in this evacuation and the conditions of armistice are to be left to the judgement of military advisers, and that the present relative strength on the fronts must be made the basis of arrangements that will safeguard and guarantee it. The German Government leaves it to the President to create an opportunity to settle the details. It trusts that the President of the United States will approve no demand that would be irreconcilable with the honour of the German people and with paving the way to a peace of justice.

The German Government protests against the charge of illegal and inhuman practices that is made against the German land and sea forces, and thereby against the German People. Destructions (*Zerstörungen*) will always be necessary to cover a retreat, and are in so far permitted under international law. The German troops have the strictest instructions to respect private property and to care for the population according to their ability. Where, notwithstanding this, excesses occur, the guilty are punished.

The German Government also denies that in sinking ships the German Navy has purposely destroyed lifeboats with their